RESTORATIVE GARDENS

RESTORATIVE GARDENS

The Healing Landscape

Nancy Gerlach-Spriggs

Richard Enoch Kaufman

Sam Bass Warner, Jr.

YALE UNIVERSITY PRESS
NEW HAVEN AND LONDON

Designed by Lisa C. Tremaine
Set in Centaur type by Amy Storm
Printed in Hong Kong through World Print

Gerlach-Spriggs, Nancy, 1950–
    Restorative gardens: The healing landscape / Nancy Gerlach-
Spriggs, Richard Enoch Kaufman, and Sam Bass Warner, Jr.
        p.   cm.
    Includes bibliographical reference (p.   ) and index.
    ISBN 0-300-07238-4
    1. Health facilities—Landscape architecture—United States—Case
studies. 2. Gardens—Therapeutic use—United States—Case studies.
I. Kaufman, Richard Enoch, 1945–. II. Warner, Sam Bass, 1928–.
III. Title.
RA967.7.G47   1998
155.9'1—dc21   97-53190
                                                            CIP

A catalogue record for this book is available from the British Library.

The paper in this book meets the guidelines for permanence and durability of the Committee on Production Guidelines for Book Longevity of the Council on Library Resources.

10 9 8 7 6 5 4 3 2 1

Contents

Acknowledgments

A book that draws on such wide-ranging material and interests cannot be completed without the assistance and cooperation of many generous and knowledgeable people. Chapter 2 merits a special acknowledgment, for it draws together formerly separate literatures: the history of medicine, the history of hospitals, and the history of gardens. I (Sam Bass Warner, Jr.) could not have accomplished such a marriage without the generous help of many scholars and librarians. My thanks go to Clifford Backman, Joseph Boskin, and Stephanie Carroll of Boston University; Alice DeLana of Miss Porter's School, Connecticut; Mark Francis of the University of California, Davis; Faye Marie Getz of the University of Wisconsin; Dorothy Gillerman of Cambridge, Massachusetts; Kathryn L. Gleason of the University of Pennsylvania; Grace Goldin of Swarthmore, Pennsylvania; Louis S. Greenbaum of Amherst, Massachusetts; Oscar Handlin of Harvard University; Vince Healy of San Francisco; Peregrine Horden, All Souls' College, Oxford University; William Jordy of Brown University; Karen Kettlety of Northeast Harbor, Maine; Ted Lentz of St. Paul, Minnesota; Charles A. Lewis of the Morton Arboretum, Illinois; Elisabeth Mac-Dougall and Annie Thatcher of Dumbarton Oaks, Washington, D.C.; Terry Hill and Leo Marx of MIT; Jacoba von Gimborn of the Massachusetts Horticultural Society; Guenter B. Riise of the University of California, San Francisco; Charles Rosenberg and Anne Whiston Spirn of the University of Pennsylvania; Dora Weiner of the School of Medicine, University of California, Los Angeles; and Richard Wolff and Dela Zitkus of the Countway Library, Harvard Medical School.

We are indebted to the staff and community members who took time to explain the workings of their institutions to us: Nancy K. Chambers and Sophia K. Chiotelis of the Howard A. Rusk Institute of Rehabilitation Medicine; Sister Cecilia Mary, Sister Genevieve Regina, and Sister Elisabeth Anne of the Little Sisters of the Poor, and Mary Fallon of the Queen of Peace Residence; Nina P. Wickman, Porter Storey, Marion Wilson, Herbert Pickworth, Graham Luhn, Charles Estes, Stephanie Cambio, Katherine Miller, and Susan Nelms of the Hospice at the Texas Medical Center; Gary L. Gottlieb, Edward C. Leonard, Jr., Lyn Boocock-Taylor, Mona Gold, Dale R. Nemec, Judith Kelius, Jennifer McClure, and Elizabeth Foley of Friends Hospital; John S. Rutt, Dave Fitch, Paul Jaeger, Don Oakland, Dave Zastrow, Judy Landowski, Kathy Drengler, Darlene Huffcutt, Sister Francine Kosednar, Ann Juliot, Kathy Drengler, Kitty Switlick, and Linda Grilley of Wausau Hospital, Betty Foster, Leroy Rusch, Tom and Elsie Miller, Tom Mack, Edward Drott, Sue Landretti, William McCormick, Betty McEachron, Jean Morehead, and Bev Smith of the Wausau community, and Martin H. Cohen of Armonk, N.Y., architect of the Wausau Hospital; and Jay Hudson, Karen Sonnergren, Mark Ambers, John Affinito, Kurt Krieg, John Monteforte, Karol Orr, Joy Colangelo, Chris Hall, Marie Stewart-Helms, Cynthia Peck, and Robin Beckman-Jones of the Community Hospital of the Monterey Peninsula.

As always, the advice and assistance of librarians proved invaluable: Walter T. Punch, formerly librarian of the Massachusetts Horticultural Society; Ted Goodman of the Avery Library, Columbia University; Margaret DePopolo and Michael Lenninger of the

Rotch Library, Massachusetts Institute of Technology; Richard Wolff and Dela Zitkus of the Countway Library, Harvard Medical School; Annie Thatcher of the Library at Dumbarton Oaks, Washington, D.C.; Victor H. Bausch of the Monterey Public Library; Jan Malcheski of the Boston Athenaeum; Angelyn Singer of Yale University Alumni Records; and Mary Jane Hettinga, of the library of the Marathon County Historical Museum, Wausau, Wisconsin.

We wish also to thank our photographic team: Felice Frankel of MIT, who organized the far-flung effort; Chris Faust of St. Paul, Minn.; Karen Balogh of Brooklyn, N.Y.; Jane Lidz of San Francisco, Calif.; Scott Campbell of Pacific Grove, Calif.; David Sladky of Merrill, Wisc.; Dave Stock of Dallas, Tex.; and Richard Payne of Houston, Tex. Vince Healy helped locate photos and photographers, and Debby L. Carter of New York City assisted with their selection.

For help with the acquisition and reproduction of historic photographs, we would like to acknowledge the Office of Public Affairs of New York University Medical Center; Tara Wenger of the Houston Public Library; Bryan Butcher of the San Jacinto Museum, LaPorte, Tex.; Mary Jane Hettinga of the Marathon County Historical Museum, Wausau, Wisc.; Paul Jaeger of Wausau Hospital; Mary Fallon of Queen of Peace; Robin Beckman-Jones of the Community Hospital of the Monterey Peninsula; Jennifer McClure of Friends Hospital; and Steve Agard of Hyperion Studios, Madison, Wisc.

Materials for the production of garden plans were provided by Gloria Desjardins of New York University Medical Center; Mark Ambers of the Community Hospital of the Monterey Peninsula; Herbert Pickworth of Houston, Texas; and Paul Jaeger of Wausau Hospital.

David Kamp of New York City drew the garden plans and supported the project intellectually and spiritually.

Linda Massey, enduring much confusion in the processing of the manuscript, has been our ardent reader and staunch typist.

Several people have given us thoughtful readings, and we thank them for their suggestions and corrections: Jonathan, Jill, and Jessica Kaufman, Suzanne Speaker, and Tamar Wallace.

Our thanks to Geraldine Weinstein-Breunig, who has been consulting with us for more than a decade and whose insights and suggestions have been invaluable.

Our special thanks go to landscape designer Vince Healy of San Francisco. It was Vince who led us to this subject a decade ago. He has helped unfailingly with references, phone numbers, photographs, confidence, and encouragement.

Close to home we have depended on the unwavering support of Susan Kaufman, David Spriggs, and Judith Martin.

Introduction

Restorative or healing gardens for the sick have been part of the landscape of healing since medieval times. Such gardens have been parts of hospitals, hospices, rehabilitation centers, and more recently nursing homes for the infirm and elderly. In the late twentieth century, the AIDS epidemic and other new viruses of frightening virulence, the economic debates about managed care, and the exorbitant costs of high-tech medicine are the compelling issues of the day. Why at this moment of dramatic medical turbulence would a historian, a landscape architect, and a physician choose to examine the history and role of restorative gardens?

Perhaps it is precisely because we have reached a transition in medical care that the wisdom of our connection with nature must be re-examined. The innovations of scientific medicine have rendered many previously lethal diseases innocuous or merely a nuisance. At the extremes of suffering, however, medical care remains an inadequate means of remedy and consolation. In such extremity a second medical mode often comes into play. Even in the age of "hard science," medicine maintains and values the long tradition of artistry in healing. Whether that artistry derives from the soothing tones of a compassionate physician or nurse, or some felt beneficence of groups that share and commiserate on their common disorders, something of the ineffable has always been associated with healing and recovery.

At the present medical moment health professionals, for very practical reasons, have tended to avoid the mystery associated with healing. Foremost is the fact that the battle to make medical care scientifically based has been hard won, and still just barely so; it is

a battle that continues. Second, the tests, techniques, and medications of contemporary medicine are more easily defined and, quite simply, the quantifiable is easier to budget for. At the same time the public seems to be turning increasingly to alternative medicine and the blandishments of the "natural" and the mysterious. It may well be that because the purveyors of scientific medicine and hospital care have less and less time to indulge in the supposed frills of patient care, the general public demands a less mechanistic and more humane approach. We will suggest, in fact, that the restorative garden may be a bridge between the humane and the molecular. The history of restorative gardens, their continual reappearance at centers of medical and aesthetic innovation in moments of medical uncertainty, suggests that some biological force insists on the importance of healing gardens in the medical armamentarium. An emerging body of medical and psychological literature supports this view.

Given these trends in medicine and public inclination, how do we define a restorative garden? Perhaps we should begin by stating what it is not. We are not speaking of farms where, once upon a more pastoral time, patients used to "work" to get better. Nor are we referring to a particular place for horticultural therapy, for that is a separate active discipline, which may call on the restorative garden but which is not an essential part of, and in most cases does not exist in the context of, the healing landscape.

A restorative garden is a less precise event. It is, to put it simply, an environment beyond the building. This environment may be a vast, exquisitely planned arboretum such as that at Friends Hospital in Philadelphia, or it may be merely a view out a patient's window that has been subtly planned for the patient's aesthetic pleasure and contact with nature. Whatever the precise design, a restorative garden is a healing landscape. It can sometimes be soothing in its sensitivity or stimulating in its exuberance, but at either extreme it is intended to engage the viewer in an act of invigoration. A restorative garden is intended by its planners to evoke rhythms that energize the body, inform the spirit, and ultimately enhance the recuperative powers inherent in an infirm body or mind. Where recovery is not possible, intimate contact with the cycle and flow of nature may yet calm the spirit.

As we have looked at six contemporary restorative gardens and searched for common threads, we have seen extraordinary contrasts. In California at the Community Hospital of the Monterey Peninsula views of the Pacific coastline are the distant vistas that frame and lend background to the more intimate gardens that immediately surround the hospital. In New York City at the Rusk Institute small, cool, elegant spaces carved out of barely discernible concrete canyons provide an equally lovely setting for serene repose. At the same institution, the Enid Haupt Greenhouse with its hints of light and exotic plant life acts as an interior garden that introduces a connection to nature even within vast urban corridors.

Friends Hospital in Philadelphia has a hundred-acre meandering arboretum filled with specimen trees and vast banks of mature azaleas. The Little Sisters' Queen of Peace Residence offers the opposite: a tiny rondelle serving to hint at a more lavish rose garden. The grounds of the Wausau Hospital in Wisconsin are on a larger scale, though restrained in appearance and scope, a perfect example of Midwestern understatement. The Hospice at the Texas Medical Center features a fine suburban formal garden facing a new communal residence.

There seems to be no precise formula. As the six case studies of this book suggest, a restorative garden that engages the senses transcends all boundaries and preconceptions of size, style, complexity of horticul-tural material, and historical roots. The effects of a successful restorative garden are felt throughout the institution. As one nurse insightfully put it, "When the hospital was first built, not everyone was sure environment was important. Now we all know."

Hospital planners have, in fact, begun to address these issues, and as the nature of hospital services shifts so too do the architecture and environs. Virtually every new hospital building has a large atrium with fountains, pools, plants, and seating. Hospital entrances and public spaces now follow the model of contemporary hotel lobbies. By presenting an accommodating and familiar aspect, these public spaces are intended to humanize the introduction to an often terrifying modern institution.

The nature of the hospital lobby has changed because the role of the hospital and the nature of its patients have changed. Until recently, hospitals were often places for leisurely recovery from moderately severe illnesses. No longer. Economic pressures, the advent of highly proficient home care, and changes in medical technology have limited hospital inpatient populations to the exceedingly ill or those requiring highly technical acute care. The success of a hospital, its economic well-being, is no longer measured solely by how many beds are full, but, in addition, by the brevity of the average patient stay. Patients no longer come to *reside* in hospitals for days or weeks. Given that the thrust of present-day patient care is to keep people out of the hospital, those who must be hospitalized are often too ill to recognize, let alone appreciate, any environmental niceties. At the same time, however, the hospital has become a center for visitors. Patients and their families come for highly specialized, very brief treatments: one-day surgery, radiation therapy, chemotherapy, blood transfusions, and renal dialysis. Each of these procedures may take minutes to hours, but nearly always less than a full work day. The hospital is now much more a provider of services than of healing environments. In contemporary medicine treatment is to take place in a hospital; healing often occurs elsewhere.

It may be thought that this is as it should be. Even physician-writer Oliver Sacks, describing his own recovery from a psychologically dislocating but not life-threatening injury, finds the garden of most value when he leaves the hospital and goes to an inpatient rehabilitation center.

This was a great joy—to be out in the air—for I had not been outside in almost a month. A pure and intense joy, a blessing, to feel the sun on my face, and the wind in my hair, to hear birds, to see, touch and fondle the living plants. Some essential connection and communion with nature was re-established after the horrible isolation and alienation I had known. Some part of me came alive, when I was taken to the garden, which had been starved, and died, perhaps without my knowing it.

What he experiences at that moment of reinvigoration is in many ways the impetus for this book. Sacks continues:

I suddenly felt what I have often felt intensely before, but never thought to apply to my own time in hospital: that one needs open-air hospitals with gardens, set in country and woods . . . a hospital like a home, not a fortress or institution, a hospital like a home—perhaps like a village.[1]

Being a patient is disorienting and terrifying. Even for physician-patients, who might know better from their familiarity with patients, patienthood is utterly dislocating. The distortion of perception, sapping of the identity, and loss of connectedness to the external world are overwhelming. As in Sacks's case, recovery comes slowly in hospital settings. Perhaps having gardens and views—and all they imply—during the earliest phases of hospitalization, and throughout the entire recovery, might well reduce this loss of connection and enhance healing and recovery. We maintain that the data support this supposition.

If, however, the economic and social exigencies of the time are changing the nature and role of hospitals and places of healing, does the notion of a hospital garden have value? Increasingly, inpatients stay on only if they are extremely sick—and less able to appreciate any environment. Outpatients, corre- spondingly, are healthier, or at least more functional, and seem to have little need of nurturing, sustaining environments. The nature of patienthood has shifted, as has its locale. Medical care is now administered not only in hospitals but at specialty centers of various sorts. We now have medical hotels, "surgicenters," convalescent or nursing homes for the healthy and infirm elderly, and, for care of the rapidly dying, hospices. We see in each of these medical formats a place for the restorative garden.

We have in fact looked at six gardens, situated in different parts of the country, that represent varying medical models. In Wausau, Wisconsin, and in Monterey, California, we studied two traditional general hospitals. In Philadelphia we looked at a classic psychiatric hospital undergoing dramatic changes in its role and method of operation. In New York, at the Rusk Institute, we looked at its several gardens and greenhouses, each with differing agendas. In Queens Village, New York, we examined the modest gardens of an exemplary nursing home, and in Houston a hospice offering meticulously loving care to the dying.

Each setting has different roots, a different role, and a somewhat different mission. Each, however, is in the service of patient care and each values its gardens. As we search for the common elements that have brought all these medical institutions, with their disparate geographies, origins, and models of care, to cherish their gardens, we ask a series of questions. How have restorative gardens come to be created in these very diverse settings? Why in these particular places and in relatively few others? At the same time, why are we suddenly seeing a flourishing renewal of interest in healing landscapes? What impulses keep these gardens alive? What makes a good or successful restorative garden—are there guidelines? And finally, if restorative gardens have value and confer value on their institutions, how do we encourage their promulgation and preserve their tradition?

Among the first themes to emerge was that in each of our gardens a guiding idea or person provided the impulse for the garden's creation. The Emersonian notion that "an institution is the lengthened shadow of one man" finds its confirmation in the presence of restorative gardens. Restorative gardens originated in the context of monasteries and other religious places of healing. Whether man or woman or specific religious ideal, a founding spirit that held the idea of a garden dear fostered each of the six sites we focus on. In Philadelphia it was the Quaker ideal of the "Moral Treatment." At the Queen of Peace Residence of the Little Sisters of the Poor it is the mendicant tradition of French Catholicism. At Monterey the aesthetic of a single man (perhaps knowingly based on Feng Shui principles) pervades every aspect of a hospital whose gardens and interiors exist in unusual harmony. At the Rusk Institute the founding spirit of Howard Rusk created the place and the possibility for its urban gardens. At the hospice in Houston two women—the founder, and the chief fund-raiser and aesthetic prime mover—made the place their mission. Last, at Wausau, the closest of our case studies to a classic general hospital, the Midwestern social history and milieu engendered the ideal of the garden as a critical part of the healing effort.

As we wend our way through these six gardens, another theme emerges clearly. Where gardens appear as an integral part of the institution, a deeply felt—and usually perceived—set of values is at work. Even though the desire to care for patients lies at the heart of all medical facilities, the impulse seems heightened and refined at those where there are gardens. Institutions with restorative gardens, we found, cherish an emphasis on individualized, meticulous, intimate caring for the patient. Where gardens are a part of the spirit of the place, it is the patient, not just patients, who are cared for. Whether Catholic, Quaker, Feng Shui, or secular, these centers not only provide humane care but attend to the intensely human needs of each patient. They strive to be homes rather than fortresses. At Monterey, towels are warmed and kimonos are provided as nightwear. At the Queen of Peace, residents' rooms contain pieces of the aged patients' own furniture from home—often a set piece re-creating a

portion of their former abode—so that their environment occasions as few dislocations as possible. How extraordinarily sensitive—and how unusual!

At each place where restorative gardens are valued, the interior and exterior are an integrated whole. In each case, not only is the garden associated with more intimate care, but it seems to help humanize the institution. Our restorative garden places are not primarily research institutions or great urban teaching hospitals (though Rusk is certainly part of one) but often quite the opposite. Monterey actively chooses to be a small community hospital providing general medical-surgical care. It also specializes in oncology and orthopedics and cardiology with highly individualized rehabilitation programs. It is not "high-tech," but it is intensely personal.

Contemporary hospitals and clinics are growing ever larger, competing to encompass the most "lives" (the new code word for people who may require medical care) within their so-called catchment area. Nursing homes similarly exert every legislative and economic effort to expand their capacity. The Queen of Peace Residence stands as a lovely exception. It reduces the number of its residents to give more meticulous individual care and closer attention to each resident.

Where restorative gardens appear, the emphasis is not on machinery or advanced technologies, though they are often in place, but on the intimacies of patient care. In settings where patients' contact with nature is a priority, heightened emphasis also seems to be placed on the role of caregivers—whether nurses, physical and occupational therapists, aides, physicians, or volunteers—who are frequently very active. Of course it might be expected that gardens would be most valued in these settings. Person-to-person, humane interactions and cures are most evident where patient-nature and patient-garden interchange are the modus vivendi. The presence of the natural environment energizes the staff as well as the patients.

How do we universalize this feedback cycle of patients to nature, nature to patients and staff, and staff to patients? How do we extend the humanizing effect of natural views and gardens to the fortresses of modern medicine? How do we integrate the natural into the institutional? And, of course, should we be pressing this agenda at all?

The last question lies at the heart of this book. Extreme economic pressure is being exerted on health care, medical research, and teaching facilities of every kind. Surely, many would argue, it is *not* an appropriate time to be considering the financial and programmatic commitments a restorative garden requires. Existing restorative gardens—often remnants of a more secure time—demand the attention of hospital administrative staffs, landscape professionals, and often skilled volunteers. Attention takes time and money. How can we suggest that the restorative garden should, in fact, command the interest of all these groups and drain time and increasingly scarce economic commitments from more compelling needs?

We argue in this book that this is a critical moment for restorative gardens. As we outline their history, we find that such gardens have played an integral role in the evolution of humane medical care. Gardens have a mythology, a poetry, and a history, strongly linked to life cycles and the processes of healing, renewal, and ultimately dying. The persistent appearance of healing gardens in places and times of medical innovation suggest that beyond the aesthetic human beings feel a biological need for contact with the natural.

In each of the six cases we study, the garden has a history, a context, and a specific role to play in the institution. Each provides us with clues about why gardens are meaningful in these particular settings and what importance they have for patients, families, and staff. From history and landscape design we proceed into less clearly charted waters. Much of the considerable medical-psychological literature on nature and healing is still speculative. Yet this literature and the insights garnered from the evolving fields of neuropsychoimmunology, psychobiology, evolutionary biology, and psychology inform this study. They add weight to the argument that healing landscapes exert a powerful and positive effect on recovery and healing. And a garden may ultimately offer a unique balm for the dying and those beyond medical help.

We conclude the book with a plea for considering the essential role of the garden when planning, designing, or renovating health facilities of every type. It is desirable and needful for health care professionals to be cognizant that all patients—inpatients and outpatients, the healthy and the moribund—will benefit from some contact with nature. Staffs work better, and families feel better, in a setting in harmony with nature. It takes little more effort to plan for views, to landscape for greenery, and to remember that the tradition of gardening, and of restorative gardens especially, persists in our lives and history because they provide an essential element in the healing of the human body and psyche.

Oberrheinischer Meister, *Das Paradiesgärtlein*, c. 1415, Städelsches Kunstinstitut, Frankfurt am Main. *(Photo: Artothek)*

The History

🌿

The restorative garden is one among the many varieties of gardens that humans have planted since taking up agriculture ten thousand years ago. From that faraway time until at least the nineteenth century, gardens were everywhere—behind houses, inside and outside city walls, and interspersed with buildings throughout the cities and towns. Only with the building of the nineteenth-century European and American cities did human settlements become so densely crowded with buildings that structures overran most green spaces and gardens disappeared. During the thousands of years when gardens were ubiquitous, their meaning was by no means uniform or constant. Even in contemporary culture, the ever-present psychological possibilities of gardens have sometimes been reinforced but sometimes neglected or even denied.

Sun and moonlight and the plants and water of gardens have always afforded human beings psychological orientation and sensations important to maintaining the sense of self. Such personal feelings, however, are forever being modified by the setting of the garden and by the meaning that current culture imposes on the visitor's experience. A garden may afford a familial retreat or offer a theater for social display or serve as a religious link between the visitor and the deity. In some places and eras, gardens have been heavily freighted with intense personal emotions; at other times they have been subjected to the cool winds of science or fashion. During times when intense feelings and the religious experiences of nature receive cultural acknowledgment, gardens are employed as a means of therapy: as places for the relief of pain, places to assist the patient's struggle

for orientation and equilibrium. Under these conditions, gardens may properly be labeled restorative.[1]

The restorative garden is intended to provide an ordered place where its occupants will experience a sense of well-being and wonder that will alter their mood. The order derives from the gardener's art, practiced in rich variety. The wonder of the garden must be furnished by the visitor.

Restorative gardens are meant for the healthy as well as for the sick. For the healthy, such gardens encourage sociability among companions, promote relaxation and contemplation for the solitary visitor, or create a sense of community among residents who live in quarters around the garden. For the sick of body or troubled in spirit, the same garden relaxes and soothes and thereby encourages the body and the mind to restore themselves.

The restorative garden as a reflection of individual emotion, cultural training, and social support originated in Persia, Egypt, and the Orient, where its existence has continued unbroken since the birth of history. Such gardens first appeared in Europe during the Middle Ages, and subsequently took on altered forms around the middle of the eighteenth century. In our own time they have been given still other embodiments in rehabilitation programs, cancer and AIDS treatment facilities, nursing homes, mental hospitals, and hospices for the dying.

A confusion of possibilities obscures the precise origins of the European restorative garden, because it was one type among the myriad medieval courtyards. Gardens adjoining institutions for the care of the poor, sick, and infirm may well have been commonplace in the thousands of Christian charitable foun-

RESTORATIVE GARDENS *The Healing Landscape*

dations that flourished from the tenth through the fourteenth centuries. Among these many foundations, hospitals and monasteries nursed the sick, but the multiple meanings of *hospital* and *hospice* confound any attempt to make a precise identification of the origins of the Western restorative garden.

The medieval hospital offered hospitality and charity, but religious motives, not medical practice, animated such establishments.

[This] . . . charitable foundation [Saint Bartholomew's Hospital, London] so well devised by that famous and renowned King Henry VIII, hath since the times of the Gospel been much augmented: and is by the wise governors of the house as faithfully employed to the comfort of many poor members of Christ, which by the charity of that house, have been healed of divers diseases otherwise incurable. We read that an angel stirred the pool of Bethesda and made it apt to cure all manner of diseases: but here not only the angel of God goeth in and out among them, but Christ himself is present, assisting them in such charitable works, and giving a blessing thereunto.[2]

The very word *hospital* derives from the Latin *hospes*, meaning host, and *hospitium*, designating the good feelings that should flow between host and guest. During the fourth century, Christian usage altered the meaning of *hospitium*; it came to mean the place where such feelings were experienced. The thousands of such institutions in turn owed their creation to the Christian obligation to charity and to give mercy to the poor. "In so far as you did this to one of the least of these brothers of mine, you did it to me," Christ admonished his listeners in speaking of the Last Judgment.[3] Kings and queens, nobles and wealthy churchmen, merchants, guilds, and municipal corporations established hospitals. Most took the form of small endowments for five or a dozen residents, although a few, like the ninth-century Hôtel Dieu in Paris, grew from modest beginnings to become large all-purpose relief and medical institutions.[4]

Most hospitals sprang up within towns and near churches, and there they catered to the impoverished: orphans, pilgrims, vagrants, the disabled, the aged,

the infirm, and the insane. Despite the poverty of the residents, charity did not flow only in one direction, as it does today. Instead, the donors expected their benefaction to be reciprocated by the residents, with prayers for the souls of the founders and their families to speed them through Purgatory.[5] Often hospital residents lived according to some rule, like that of Saint Benedict or Saint Augustine; sometimes food and lodging were gifts outright and no routine pertained. Above all, variety and small size were the hallmarks of medieval hospitals.

Some endowed refuges set aside rooms for pilgrims and travelers, and often a place was made at the entrance for giving alms to nonresidents. Since both the poor and travelers often fell sick, many hospitals offered nursing, and it would be sensible to surmise that the courtyards functioned as restorative gardens. A few European hospitals, such as the great hospitals of Byzantium, Muslim Egypt, and Spain, even specialized in health care and had resident physicians. Early in the thirteenth century, Parisian physicians began regularly to attend the Hôtel Dieu, an all-purpose foundation that dispensed charity for every human misfortune from mental illness to starvation. At Florence's famous Santa Maria Nuova, founded in 1288, the beds for patients far outnumbered the twelve spaces set aside for the poor.[6]

According to a functional classification of 858 English hospitals established between the tenth century and Henry VIII's suppression of them in 1547, only an estimated 6 percent were specialized health care hospitals, 61 percent succored the poor, and 33 percent were leprosoria.[7] Leprosoria, or lazar houses, were always located at some remove from towns because both the Bible and contemporary laws enjoined banishment of these feared sufferers. Very often, leprosoria took the form of a scattering of small houses in a field, without a formal courtyard or enclosing wall.

Perhaps the most unusual of all the medieval establishments was the colony of mental patients who gathered at Gheel in Belgium. Gheel, like many

8

medieval villages, grew upon the story of a miracle, but centuries after its foundation, its practices served as models for modern boarding-out programs for the mentally ill.

According to the legend, a seventh-century pagan Irish king and his Christian queen bore a daughter, Dymphna, a devout girl who planned to devote her life to the Church. Before she could do so, however, her mother died. The king, after searching all Ireland in vain for a new queen as beautiful as his first, proposed to marry his daughter. Thereupon Dymphna fled to Antwerp and thence to a forest twenty-five miles inland. Her father pursued her and in his rage slew her near Saint Martin's Chapel in Gheel.

The story of the atrocity spread; and believing the king to have been insane, people imagined that Dymphna must have been assigned by God to assume a saintly role toward those suffering from mental illness. Pilgrims began to come to Saint Martin's Chapel to make novenas. Soon the chapel added a room to accommodate them, and then village families took the visitors in as boarders. By the fifteenth century, the village operated a regular system of religious cure and family boarding. Later, in 1852, the Belgian government nationalized community services, and ever since, Gheel has served as a model for home care supplemented by a facility for medical supervision and emergency hospitalization.[8]

Wherever a little wealth appeared during the Middle Ages, whether in a town, a manor, a church, or a monastery, walls rose in response to the pressing need for security. Because walls were everywhere, many hospitals enclosed gardens and yards with walls and lines of buildings. For example, Saint Mary's Hospital in Winchester, founded in 1158, surrounded a large courtyard in the manner of a college, and Saint Nicholas of Salisbury, a thirteenth-century establishment, had an arcaded court. There must have been many such hospitals wherever town land had not already been so built upon that a hospital had, like Saint Mary's of Chichester, to be squeezed onto a long narrow city lot.[9] Whatever the form of these enclosures, they all offered their residents the universal pleasures of shelter, sun, and shade, but it is doubtful if the gardens of charitable hospitals could draw upon any religious energy as powerful as the religious faith that animated the monastic cloister.

Saint Bernard (1090–1153) wrote a definitive description of the purpose of the restorative garden when he described the courtyard garden of the hospice at his monastery in Clairvaux, France:

> Within this enclosure, many and various trees, prolific with every sort of fruit, make a veritable grove, which lying next to the cells of those who are ill, lightens with no little solace the infirmities of the brethren, while it offers to those who are strolling about a spacious walk, and to those overcome with the heat, a sweet place for repose. The sick man sits upon the green lawn, and while inclement Sirius burns the earth and dries the rivers, he is secure, hidden, and shaded from the heat of the day, the leaves of a tree tempering the heat of that fiery star; for the comfort of his pain, all kinds of grass are fragrant in his nostrils. The lovely green of herb and tree nourishes his eyes and, their immense delights hanging and growing before him, well might he say, "I sat down in his shadow with great delight, and his fruit was sweet to my taste" [Song of Songs 2:3]. The choir of painted birds caresses his ears with sweet modulation, and for the care of a single illness the divine tenderness provides many consolations, while the air smiles with bright serenity, the earth breathes with fruitfulness, and the invalid himself with eyes, ears, and nostrils, drinks in the delights of colors, songs, and perfumes.[10]

The central cloister was the monastery's core open space and therefore the most important symbolic garden. Generally, the monastic church itself formed the north wall, and the dining hall, dormitory, kitchen, and cellars completed the enclosure. An arcade, the direct descendant of the Roman peristyle, connected all these rooms and sheltered the passage from sun and rain. The garden itself was divided into four squares, as in the Persian tradition and also according to the Garden of Eden legend. At the intersection of the four paths that divided the garden plots stood a well or fountain. Often the monks planted a juniper or other evergreen to symbolize the Tree of Life of

Genesis. Sometimes, too, they placed statues of the saints or the Holy Family in the enclosure. The plantings consisted of grass and flowers.[11]

As with all closed gardens, the cloister was designed to present the onlooker with a highly ordered and selected view of nature. The sky and the plants themselves recorded the passing of the seasons, while the bounded and restricted view was intended to encourage a reflective mood. The most earnest wish was for the spiritual transformation of the viewer. Saint Bruno (1033–1101), the founder of the Carthusian order, wrote that "he hoped the beauty of the place would lead the monks to feel that already here below they could perceive, through senses quickened by spiritual insight, the outlines of a golden paradise, lost to sinful man in Eden."[12]

The monastic hospice served three different clients: people traveling on pilgrimages, many of whom were sick and exhausted, the local poor and helpless, and visitors who came to the church to see its relics and to pray at its shrine. In the ideal ninth-century Benedictine plan of Saint Gall, there were to be two hospices: one a large room, like a barn, for the poor and the pilgrims, the other a guest house on the other side of the church for distinguished visitors. There was also an infirmary for sick monks and an herb garden for medicinal plants.[13]

In preparation for the Last Judgment, all Christians were enjoined to do good works. Monasteries thus had a duty to provide hospitality and care for the sick.[14] Their medical practices, in turn, derived from the larger setting of medieval medicine. In the centuries between Saint Benedict and Saint Bernard, no single group dominated medicine as licensed physicians do today. Instead, many different people offered specialized services: nurses and midwives, magical healers, apothecaries, barbers and surgeons, lay brothers, monks, and clerics. Most of these specialists mastered their craft through apprenticeship and by trial and error, but the learned few, university-trained clergymen and scholarly monks, sought guidance in Christian and ancient texts. It is possible, therefore, to imagine monastic practice as combining the popular herbal remedies of the day with some Greek ideas about the harmony between human beings and nature, and dietary prescriptions. The monastic rhythms of prayer, work, and mealtimes can be viewed as a sort of *regimen sanitatis* of rest and recuperation for the exhausted pilgrim or the sick or injured guest.[15]

A special element of the monastic establishment, the paradise garden, demands attention because its history records the rise and decline of enclosed restorative gardens. The replacement of the Christian symbolism of Paradise with the secular symbols of forest, knight, and hunter signaled the end of the contemplative monastic garden.

The medieval paradises were walled, often circular, places for meditation. Generally, the monks placed them outside the church at the east end, behind the main altar. The sacristan, as the monk responsible for the church, tended the garden, raising flowers, especially roses and lilies, to decorate the altar, the shrines, and the statues. The symbols of this garden derived from a fusion of two traditions that appear in the Old Testament.

Genesis tells the story of the Garden of Eden twice. In the second telling, a river flowed from the Garden, whence it subdivided into four streams, two of which were named the Tigris and the Euphrates (Gen. 2:10–15). From this imagery came the medieval cloister's crossed pathways arranged in a mandala pattern. The garden itself found meanings in the erotic language of the Song of Songs, which had been read by the Church Fathers and by such authorities as Saint Thomas Aquinas (around 1225–1274) as symbolizing the soul's union with God. The garden in the Song is not large and open like the forest Eden, but an enclosed place. The bridegroom sings:

> She is a garden enclosed,
> my sister, my promised bride;
> a garden enclosed,
> a sealed fountain. [Song of Songs 4:12]

And the bride describes herself:

Breathe over my garden
to spread its sweet smell around.

Let my Beloved come into his garden,
let him taste its rarest fruits. [4:16]

This medieval paradise garden is thus a place of love, sacred love at first, and later sacred and secular love. The merger of the Genesis and the Song of Songs versions of Paradise occurred during the seventh century, at the same time as the invention of the cult of Mary. As a consequence the monastic paradise garden became Mary's garden, a place of roses and lilies, the rose symbolizing her love, the lily her purity.

I am the Rose of Sharon
the lily of the valleys,

the bride sang [Song of Songs 2:1].[16]

During the twelfth century, the garden and the forest settings for the experience of love coalesced with the contemporary secular fashion of courtly love. In that construction, the ardor of the gallant for his lady would ideally be transformed by charity and wisdom so that the lover himself would experience some of the perfection lost after the Fall. For a time, the monastic lady chapel and lady garden and the secular love garden of the knight and his lady flourished together.

Against these religious and courtly conventions stood an alternative vision. Many medieval Christians imagined the Garden of Eden to be a forest, an extensive, if not boundless, place where the trees bore abundant fruit. "Shadowy glades and pathless depths" also abounded, as they did in northern Europe at the time, and these dim places "conjured up an atmosphere of mystery and suspense which effectively blurred the dividing line between reality and fantasy." Such legendary figures as King Arthur and his knights and Tristan and Isolde dwelt there.[17]

During the late Middle Ages, mysticism and the impulse toward monasticism declined, and as they did, the institution of the enclosed meditative space withered away. During the thirteenth and fourteenth centuries, the old myth of the unicorn and the virgin was added to Marian lore. The unicorn, symbol of Christ, and the virgin, Mary, were placed in an enclosed paradise garden. Yet public faith in the old allegories was fading, and soon hunters and all manner of wild animals seized the foreground in the unicorn imaginings. The paradise garden, the virgin, and the allegory of the soul's longing for union with God fell away, and the garden itself became a mere moral testing ground for knights and their ladies.[18]

Decline of the Restorative Garden

Once divested of their mystical religious meanings, the courtyards and open spaces within and surrounding the hospitals of Renaissance and Reformation Europe became subject to accidents of local wealth and architectural tradition. Hospital open spaces were no more than that: spaces where the ambulatory could stroll or sit and catch the sun. The grounds were no longer charitable adjuncts of monasteries, hospitals, and hospices. Although Renaissance humanists stressed the influence of environment on human development, their enlightened ideas did not alleviate the plight of the poor. Moreover, during the fifteenth, sixteenth, and seventeenth centuries, the corruption of old charitable foundations and the emergence of political and religious conflict deprived many of the established foundations of their economic resources. As a result, it often proved impossible for the old institutions to provide a decent environment for the sick and disabled poor. A 1414 English statute attempting to reform the existing foundations before the London merchants took charge of that city's hospitals spoke of the contemporary perception of pervasive corruption. "Many hospitals . . . be now for the most part decayed, and the goods and profits of the same, by divers persons, spiritual and temporal, withdrawn and spent to the use of others, whereby many men and women have died in great misery for default of aid, livelihood, and succor."[19]

Nevertheless, these same centuries contained the seeds that would later germinate and blossom into the modern restorative garden. The proliferation of the nursing orders, improvements in the care of the insane (in Spain, for instance), progress in science and the spread of a scientific approach to medicine, the introduction of statistics and political economy into statecraft, and the better ordering of military medical facilities in France and England all prepared the way for the later re-establishment of restorative gardens.

The arrival of the bubonic plague in 1347 coincided with a further decline in monasticism and a revival of towns and commerce. Fourteenth- and fifteenth-century towns accordingly experienced sudden gains and losses. In the face of periodic epidemics, crop failures, and waves of migrants, the many small refuges of the poor were overwhelmed. Yet the revival of cities and commerce required that thousands of young people leave their farms and villages to work and settle in the towns. There, spoiled food and contaminated water took a relentless toll, especially on infants and children. In no large city in Europe could the resident population reproduce itself. For Florence, Rome, Naples, Paris, Amsterdam, Barcelona, Lisbon, or London to grow, armies of newcomers had to arrive each year.[20]

These waves and eddies of migration, influxes greater than those of the pilgrimages or the Crusades, inevitably cast up populations of the sick, the poor, the itinerant, the disabled, and the unfit. At the same time, periodic outbreaks of bubonic plague added panic and crisis to the suffering and need that were a daily reality. The European response to all these demands for public care was a hodgepodge of punitive laws, quarantines, pesthouses, poverty relief, and general and specialized hospitals. From the vantage point of the present, it is possible to detect in the multiplicity of responses the roots of our modern instititional structure: secular and religious charities, municipal free hospitals, and private acute-care and public chronic-care hospitals.

No government in the fourteenth and fifteenth centuries was capable of administering national wel-fare and health programs on the scale necessary to cope with the exigencies of migrations, crop failures, and plagues. The princes and parliaments of Europe placed the burden of responsibility on civil and ecclesiastical authorities. Municipal and parish officials, in turn, attempted to maintain order by suppressing begging, driving off vagrants, and providing relief for the local indigent population. The periodic plagues convinced city fathers that contagion of all kinds came from the poor. And once cities and towns instituted house quarantines and built pesthouses, the hazards of poverty increased.[21]

Important differences marked the adaptations of Catholic and Protestant nations, and these differences affected the design of hospitals and the treatment of their residents. In Catholic countries, continuities in form and administration prevailed through the Renaissance, the Reformation, the Counter-Reformation, and the Enlightenment.

During the fifteenth century, Spanish hospital design and practice was the best in Europe. Following Arab tradition, Spanish hospitals continued the courtyard style. In addition, they often placed the kitchens and service rooms on the ground floor, thus allowing light and air to stream into the upstairs wards. In the rest of Europe, such hygienic benefits were uncommon until the eighteenth-century medical concentration upon fresh air.

The hospital at Zaragoza, Spain, founded in 1409, instituted a system of patient care that influenced the eighteenth-century reformer Philippe Pinel (1745–1826), who adopted its practices and popularized its methods. At Zaragoza, instead of being whipped and confined, as was the custom of the time, mental patients followed a regular routine: they ate in a common dining room and then followed a full day's routine of household chores and work in the vegetable gardens, farms, vineyards, and orchards. Only the "furious" patients remained locked in their cells, isolated, but unchained. The Zaragoza method of socializing patients came to be known in the nineteenth century as the Moral Treatment.[22]

Vincent van Gogh, *A Corner of the Asylum Garden*, Saint-Rémy, 1889, Museum Folkwang, Essen, Germany.

In France, the energies of the Counter-Reformation called forth a nursing order whose work later influenced the twentieth-century movement to establish hospices for the dying. Saint Vincent de Paul (c. 1580–1660) was a peasant's son who as a young priest served convicts in the galleys. He organized laypeople for charitable work and founded a society of priests to do missionary work in rural France and train ill-educated clergy. In 1633, together with the wife of a royal official, Saint Louise de Marillac, he founded a noncloistered nursing order, the Sisters of Charity (Filles de la Charité). This order, which by 1660 had set up forty houses in France, offered home care nursing, and shelters for sick and impoverished women, in many parishes of Paris. Most important for its future influence, the order staffed the modernized military hospitals of France.[23]

Some of the old Catholic establishments maintained their gardens and courtyards as part of their patients' regime, and the architectural traditions of arcades and interior courtyards remained strong. When Louis XIV built a hospital, the Invalides, in Paris for his veterans in 1671, the huge building encompassed numerous courtyards planted with rows of trees to fashion *promenoirs* and *cours des infirmeries*.[24] The Brothers of Saint John of God, who ran the finest hospital in pre-Revolutionary Paris, the Hôpital de la Charité, catered to paying patients and offered all sorts of amenities, including a garden quadrangle.[25]

When the English prison and hospital reformer John Howard (1726–1790) toured Europe at the end of the eighteenth century, he described hospitals with gardens for patients in Marseilles, Pisa, Constantinople, Trieste, and Vienna. He especially commended the garden and open arcade of the hospital of Santa Maria Nuova in Florence. In all these hospitals he admired the flow of fresh air, the chance for patients to see gardens through their windows and doorways, and the opportunity for convalescent patients to walk in the gardens. A century later, in 1889, when the painter Vincent van Gogh entered the provincial asylum of Saint-Paul-de-Mausole at Saint-Rémy, he found himself in a former monastery with a deserted garden and buildings set amid wheat fields.[26]

Most of the new Renaissance and Reformation Catholic hospitals, however, walled their patients off from the outside sun and gardens. In 1456, for example, the Milanese constructed a vast and influential hospital, Ospedale Maggiore, according to a cruciform design, with the wards arranged in the shape of a church nave and transept. The patients lay, two or more to a bed, along the walls. At the ends of these long rooms stood altars where priests said Mass. The windows were so high up on the wall that neither patients nor nurses could see the formal grounds outside. Such churchlike designs prevailed for a long time in Catholic hospitals.[27]

Patients at most Protestant charitable hospitals during these centuries had no access to gardens, either. Commonly, a town converted an old house to receive the indigent sick, although a few towns adopted the alternative home care strategy of paying one poor person to take in and care for another, or set up dispensaries with outpatient services.[28] When urban growth created the need for something more ambitious, philanthropists solicited subscriptions to construct free-standing hospitals whose facades resembled those of large mansions. Inside these buildings, then as now, the hospital proprietors endeavored to manage the poor as inexpensively as possible. Often two or three wards extended from one nurse's station. In his tours of the 1770s and 1780s, John Howard reported only two gardens associated with the hospitals of the British Isles: one at Saint George's Hospital for the Sick and Lame, and the other at the British Lying-In Hospital. Both were London establishments, and both were eighteenth-century foundations. The British pattern, he observed, was for hospitals to be designed with all the patients' rooms opening out onto interior corridors.[29]

The then prevalent trends in gardening did not draw attention to the contribution the environment could make to health. Merchants and princes in Italy, France, Holland, Germany, and England rediscovered the villas of ancient Rome and began to elaborate on them. They added their own heraldic devices and family allegories to the garden symbolism of the ancients. Topiary work, fountains, mazes, statues, and formal patterns, hedged, walled about, and arranged for theatrical effect, became the dominant fashion, from the Villa d'Este at Tivoli to Versailles, Het Loo, and Hampton Court.[30] The gardens of the seventeenth and eighteenth centuries reverted to the meaning that they had held in ancient Greek and Roman times. People understood them as places of rest and retreat from the cares of everyday life. Andrew Marvell's "The Garden" (1681) nicely captured the secular meanings of the era: "Society is all but rude, / To this delicious solitude."[31]

Hygiene and Hospitals

The late eighteenth-century restorative garden, in both its hygienic and therapeutic goals, owed its invention to the convergence of certain ideas and institutions born in previous centuries. Two intellectual currents, both initially far removed from gardens, ultimately gave strong impetus to the hygienic component of eighteenth- and nineteenth-century restorative gardens: the statistical movement of the seventeenth and eighteenth centuries and the new governmental practice of employing scientific experts.

During the seventeenth century, curious men in England, Germany, and France began scrutinizing death registers and also gathering and estimating all manner of economic data. Poverty, sickness, and death figured prominently in their tables and ratios. Consequently, the statisticians argued that starvation, sickness, and death robbed the state of its wealth. If the health of sheep and cattle could contribute to the store of a prince's wealth, why not regard the health of his human subjects in a similar fashion? The statisticians theorized that in the rivalry among kingdoms, the prince who took good care of his people would prosper most. Not only was the systematic assembly of data a novel procedure, but the compilers' assumption that public measures could be taken to avoid sickness and speed recovery constituted a fresh idea. Their campaign bore fruit in the seventeenth and eighteenth centuries in the new state management of granaries, the ordering of military hospitals and medical services, and the efforts to impose national standards on local hospitals and charities.[32]

The statisticians were taking part in the seventeenth-century initiation of modern science. In medicine, this new outlook prescribed careful observation of the patient, the application of the new discoveries in physics and chemistry, and wariness about generalizations. During the seventeenth century, Leyden, Holland, flourished as the center of this new scientific medicine, and its innovative approach soon spread to Germany, France, Scotland, England, and ultimately the United States.[33]

One concomitant of the diffusion of these ideas was experimentation in new designs for hospitals, designs that paid special attention to hygiene. It was supposed that infection was spread through the air by noxious vapors that arose from rotting material, stagnant water, animal waste, and putrefaction of all kinds. Abundant fresh air and much washing and attention to cleanliness promised the best defense against the infectious miasmas, as they were then called. New hospital sites accordingly had to be well drained, with ample grounds, open to the play of sun and wind.[34] So, for example, when Peter the Great of Russia imported a Dutch physician to be the director of the first hospital in Russia, Dr. Nicholas Bidloo built his hospital in Moscow with a large formal Dutch garden.[35] When the physicians of Edinburgh established a hospital in 1729 to care for the sick poor, they built it on a hill and in a U shape to catch the air and sun, and they also set aside two acres for a garden—thus modeling their arrangements on those in Leyden.[36]

The Royal Naval Hospital at Stonehouse, near the naval base at Plymouth, was the most notable of the eighteenth-century hospitals. From Stonehouse both France and England were to take the inspiration for the pavilion hospital, with its emphasis on gardens, which was to dominate nineteenth-century hospital architecture throughout the world.

Constructed in 1765 for sick and injured sailors, Stonehouse could accommodate 1,200 patients. It consisted of three-story buildings arranged around a large rectangular lawn, in the manner of a college campus. A continuous open exterior colonnade joined each building to its neighbor. Each of the five buildings that contained the wards had a large, square floor divided in half by a partition; each ward consisted of twenty-five single beds in a room lit and ventilated on one long side by a full row of windows. When French commissioners visited Stonehouse in 1787, they found there a design that accorded with experimental findings on the benefits of ventilation.[37]

During their inspection of Parisian hospitals, one of the leading French investigators, the surgeon Jacques Tenon, had noticed that the largest, the Hôtel Dieu, was so crowded with beds, and its interior spaces were so large, that it could not be adequately ventilated, even if it were renovated. He concluded that it ought to be torn down and a new hospital ought to be built in its place. Tenon's plans called for a series of twenty-four-bed wards joined together at their ends, much like the teeth of a comb, by a long service corridor. After many years his suggestions were adopted by French royal commissions, and pavilion wards of this kind became the standard for good hospital design throughout the nineteenth century. The first full realization in France came with the building of the Hôpital Lariboisière in 1846–1854, which soon served as Florence Nightingale's model in the reform of hospitals in England.[38]

One happy consequence of the pavilion building design derived from the spaces between the pavilion wards. When hospitals were limited to two or three stories, the open space could be given over to gardens that could be used by the patients, if the hospital directors included gardens in their therapeutic regimen. Indeed, when the Hôtel Dieu in Paris was rebuilt in 1865 with twenty-four-bed pavilions, formal gardens were laid out in the open spaces between the wards. To be sure, a bedridden patient could not see the gardens, but there was abundant air and sunlight, and a patient who could walk about had at least a near view of the gardens.[39]

Florence Nightingale (1820–1910) appreciated the fact that the new hygienic hospital plans also provided substantial therapeutic benefits:

Second only to fresh air . . . I should be inclined to rank light in importance for the sick. Direct sunlight, not only daylight, is necessary for speedy recovery. . . . I mention from experience, as quite perceptible in promoting recovery, the being able to see out of a window, instead of looking against a dead wall; the bright colors of flowers; the being able to read in bed by the light of the window close to the bed-head. It is generally said the effect is upon the mind. Perhaps so, but it is not less so upon the body on that account. . . . While we can generate warmth, we cannot generate daylight.[40]

Therapy and the Revival of the Restorative Garden

The new medical science with its emphasis on hygiene and pavilion hospital designs offered the possibility of gardens for hospital patients but did not draw any direct therapeutic link between patient welfare and the use of gardens beyond the commonsense notion that sitting in the sun and walking about feels good. The therapeutic connection between the nursing and medicine within the hospitals and the gardens without came from the eighteenth-century Romantic movement's revival of pastoralism. With the popular spread of this attitude, nature and gardens came to be thought of once more as places of bodily and spiritual restoration.

In many ways the eighteenth- and nineteenth-century contrasts between the man-made and the natural, and the projection of intense emotions onto views of nature, whether in gardens or in the wild, resembled ancient Hellenic attitudes. In modern times, however, the attitudes were not limited to a literate elite. Romanticism constituted a broad popular movement that flowed into all aspects of life from science and medicine to child-rearing and domestic life. Froebel's kindergarten, the highly illustrated seedsmen's catalogues, city parks, and hospital gardens were all elements in a pervasive cultural attempt to unite human emotions and morality with nature.

Alexander Pope is credited with combining the English words for the intensified interest in pastoral landscapes with the art of gardening. Pope gave the word *landscape* its modern meaning: landscape is something a person makes and does, not merely something art or religion does to people. In its old meaning, *landscape* had referred to a moralized portrayal of nature in art, as in Milton's *Paradise Lost* or Poussin's *Four Seasons* or the Hercules theme of the gardens at the Villa d'Este. For Pope, the new attitude meant that landscape was something everyone experienced, not something poets and artists constructed for the edification of others. The Romantic landscape, including its gardens, was based on what any person might take in at a glance—see from an overlook or contemplate while sitting within the landscape or observe while walking through it. As in Pliny's time, the emotional intensity of the scene now came from the viewer's projection of personal sentiment onto nature, not from the teachings of the Church and the Bible.[41]

Pope landscaped his five acres in the Romantic way. His friend Horace Walpole wrote a garden essay urging the estate owners of Britain to adopt the fashion for open expanses. Walpole particularly took delight in the pulling down of the hedges and garden walls and the opening up of rural England to the carriage and to the walker's view. He urged owners of country estates to give up their parterres and instead to "deal in the colors of nature," to catch its "most favorable features," and thereby to see, as the architect William Kent and his clients did, "a new creation" opening before their eyes. Thus the new style of gardening was not to order nature as in formal gardens. Instead, "the living landscape was chastened or polished."[42] To be sure, the new open landscapes of the British estates were as contrived as any of their walled, hedged, rectangular predecessors, but the open forms and pastoral elements suited the Romantic taste for seemingly wild and unplanned designs.

Accordingly, in England the gentleman-parson Gilbert White studied the rural landscape with the sort of enthusiasm common to the age: his curiosity was a mixture of wonder and observational science. Jane Austen's families walked and drove about in the kind of landscapes encouraged by Horace Walpole. In sum, by the middle of the eighteenth century in England, the emotional temperature of people's relations to the natural world was rising once again, and gardens became—and would remain during the nineteenth century—places as emotionally significant as they had been during the Middle Ages.[43]

During the entire period, the English Romantics participated in a lively exchange of ideas with their counterparts on the Continent. Samuel Richardson's popular sentimental novels *Pamela* (1741) and *Clarissa Harlowe* (1747–1748) were quickly reinforced by Jean-Jacques Rousseau's *La Nouvelle Héloïse* (1761) and Johann Wolfgang von Goethe's *The Sorrows of Young Werther* (1774). The literary exchange made a quick progress from a beginning in which emotions were solicited for their own sake to a more mature and

complex view of the relation among human emotions, the many aspects of nature, and varieties of religious experience. Modern humankind, modern nature, and modern gardens and landscape thus all emerged at the end of the eighteenth century.

In Rousseau's *La Nouvelle Héloïse*, the heroine builds the new kind of Romantic paradise garden, an artful yet artless-seeming garden where native plants flourish.

With ecstasy I began to wander through the orchard thus metamorphosed, and if I did not find any exotic plants or any of the fruits of the Indies, I found those natural to the country, laid out and combined in a way to produce a cheerful and agreeable effect.... I followed winding and irregular walks bordered by these flowery thickets and covered with a thousand garlands of woody vines, wild grape, hops, convolvulus, bryony, clematis, and other plants of this kind, among which honeysuckle and jasmine condescended to twine. These garlands seemed as if negligently scattered from one tree to the next, as I had sometimes observed in forests.[44]

The informal garden was carefully contrived to provide a place of contemplation and emotional transport through its imitation of elements found in untended nature. In such a place, as in a forest, or on top of a hill or mountain, a sensitive soul could experience an emotional connection with spiritual forces. For Rousseau and his Romantic readers, nature offered a bridge that could join personal emotions, the moral order, and the world of the spirit.

Goethe continued this tradition but elaborated on it to include in man's relation to nature all the conflicts that characterize the modern understanding of the world. His novel *Werther* was a powerful study of depression. In it the hero falls in love with a maternal young woman who is not free to marry him. Obsessed by his passion, Werther declines into deep depression and commits suicide. The young man does not merely suffer the conventional melancholy of refused lovers in contemporary sentimental fiction; he becomes mentally ill. In Goethe's treatment, nature takes on the aspects of his shifting moods. When Werther is happy, he delights in nature, and nature reflects his mood. When he is depressed, nature reveals its destructive side. The multiple and contradictory qualities of nature and God's creation—of life and death, good and evil—are thus portrayed as part of the human condition. The wellspring of mature Romantic expression in all the arts was thus a rich fusion of science, commonplace facts, emotions, and religious experience. Goethe translated this outlook into quite specific ideas about landscape in his *Elective Affinities*.[45]

These popular Romantic attitudes toward nature once again endowed gardened spaces with heightened emotional force and religious power. So revitalized, gardens rejoined the therapeutic enterprise.

No text illuminates the cultural union between horticulture and medicine better than the prescription for hospital siting and hospital garden design written by the German theorist Christian Cay Lorenz Hirschfeld (1741–1792):

Hospitals are to be situated outside and away from cities, to allow for garden space. Hospitals should be located away from busy urban areas in a healthy and positive and inspiring location, not in valleys . . . but on sunny, warm, hilltops protected from the wind or on southern slopes on dry soil.

A hospital should lie open, not encased by high walls, not fenced in by looming trees. The garden should be directly connected to the hospital, or even better, surround it. Because a view from the window onto blooming and happy scenes will invigorate the patient, a nearby garden also invites patients to take a walk.

The plantings, therefore, should wind along dry paths that offer benches and chairs. Clusters of trees are preferred to alleys of trees, which through the years will mature and meet at the top so that air will not circulate. . . . Sad conifers should not be used but trees with light and colored leaves and flowering and fragrant shrubs and flowers. A hospital garden should have everything to encourage the enjoyment of nature and to promote a healthy life. It should help forget weakness and worries and encourage a positive outlook; everything in it should be serene and happy. No scene of melancholy, no memorial of mortality should be permitted to intrude. The spaces between the three groups could have beautiful lawns and colorful flower beds.

Noisy brooks could run through flowering fields, and merry waterfalls could reach your ear through shady shrubbery. Many plants with fortifying fragrances could be grouped together. Numerous songbirds will be attracted by the shade, peace, and freedom. And their songs will rejoice many weak hearts.

As decorations you could . . . build seats with a roof or a gazebo from which the view is magnificent.[46]

Few hospitals in Europe or America received such generous landscaping, but sites on the edge of town and on large lots were commonly chosen for nineteenth-century hospitals. Also, the spaces between the pavilions offered at least a view of sunlight and lawns and often of tended gardens as well. At the end of the eighteenth century, individual interpretations of this common design formulation diverged in accordance with the therapeutic goals of the hospitals. Those treating mental patients placed greater therapeutic demands on their gardens than did the acute-care hospitals. The mental hospitals initiated patient programs in what today we call occupational and horticultural therapy, while the acute-care hospitals encouraged their convalescents to sun or exercise in the gardens.

The conjunction of the Romantic movement with the egalitarianism of the American and French Revolutions also worked a profound change on the design of mental hospitals. For example, both Romanticism and the new egalitarianism played a role in the building of the new Schleswig Asylum, 1792–1820, the first mental hospital built for that purpose. Ultimately, the plan and building took the form of a country hospital with gardens planted in the open English manner.

The old Saint Hans Hospital, built in 1619 and managed by the Copenhagen Poor Board, was a filthy, overcrowded refuge, typical of its era. Those suffering from mental illness were tied to chairs and beaten, as had been the practice for centuries. The "furious" were often confined to boxes as well. A reformer, Neils Ditter Riegels (1755–1802), who called himself "the voice of the silent of Saint Hans," led a campaign for the building of a new country asylum. "How can anyone dream," he questioned, "that the mad, repulsive, abandoned who cannot speak for themselves, do not now send up their shrieks to the ears of people that their conditions are not better?"

In 1797 Riegels proposed that a new Saint Hans be located at a farm, with a separate house and garden for each type of sufferer. "It would ideally be in the teaching of these gardens that the very best medicine would be found." Here, far from the city, a Copenhagen citizen would become a "gainful, healthy country man." To help defray the cost of the new facility, the farm would offer separate accommodations to paying patients. Riegels's ideas eventually prevailed, and in 1820 a rural asylum with gardens, flowers, lawns, trees, and some amusements was built.[47]

The new therapeutic regimen of Dr. Philippe Pinel at the Bicêtre, a refuge for 4,500 men, and the Salpêtrière, a refuge for 5,000 women, both in Paris, like the parallel work of the Quaker William Tuke (1732–1821) at his York Retreat in England, began the sustained modern movement for the humane and effective treatment of mental patients.[48]

Pinel called his methods the *traitement moral*, meaning a psychological treatment as opposed to a physical one. English translators used the word *moral*, and in England and the United States the new methods subsequently came to be known as the Moral Treatment despite the unfortunate and inappropriate overtones of moralizing.[49] The goal of the *traitement moral* was to socialize the patient, and to do so by creating a social and physical environment that would allow the patient's own resources for reasonable behavior to reassert themselves. The new approach proposed a threefold reform: first, the abolition of all forms of physical punishment, and the use of physical restraints (straitjackets) only on very specific occasions and for short periods of time; second, careful observation and classification of patients according to their symptoms; and third, a regular routine in a restful setting that resembled many of the activities of the outside world.[50]

Dr. Pinel's book, *A Treatise on Insanity*, is an argument built out of many specific cases and hospital events. As he tells his stories, he gives a wonderful sense of the flowing together of science, politics, and the reforming optimism of his era. First and foremost one notices a profound respect for his patients as human beings, a respect that seems deeper than the egalitarianism promoted by the French revolutionaries.

A large gathering of madmen inspires an indefinable thoughtful tenderness when one realizes that their present state derives only from a vivid sensuality and from psychologic qualities that we value highly. I find that truth ever more convincing and confirmed by my daily notes. Here is the father of a family whom unexpected losses have thrown into despair; here a son exhausted by work and vigils to provide for his parents' subsistence; elsewhere a passionate and sensitive young man, victim of unrequited love.[51]

In the lunatic infirmary, which is insulated from the body of the hospital, and which is not subject to the control of the governor, it has frequently happened that lunatics, who were perfectly composed and in a fair way of recovery, have, in consequence of the silly raillery and rude brutality of their attendants, relapsed into the opposite condition of violent agitation and fury. Maniacs, on the other hand, who have been transferred from the infirmary to the asylum, and represented upon their arrival as more than commonly furious and dangerous, rendered so no doubt by severe treatment, have, upon being received with affability, soothed by consolation and sympathy, and encouraged to expect a happier lot, suddenly subsided into a placid calmness, to which has succeeded a rapid convalescence.[52]

. . . The domestics and keepers are not allowed, on any pretext whatever, to strike a madman, and the straight waistcoats, superior force, and seclusion for a limited time are the only punishments inflicted.[53]

Pinel and his staff sought to make elements of the patients' life resemble those of life beyond the hospital. They arranged a work program and gardening whenever possible.

I was one day deafened by the tumultuous cries and riotous behavior of a maniac. Employment of a rural nature, such as I knew would meet his taste, was procured for him. From that time I never observed any confusion nor extravagance in his ideas. It was pleasing to observe the silence and tranquility which prevailed in the Asylum de Bicêtre, when nearly all the patients were supplied by the tradesmen of Paris with employments which fixed their attention, and allured them to exertion by the prospect of a trifling gain. . . . I made, at that time, every exertion in my power to obtain from the government an adjacent piece of ground, the cultivation of which might employ convalescent maniacs, and conduce to the re-establishment of their health. The disturbance which agitated the country in the second and third years of the republic, prevented the accomplishment of my wishes.[54]

Pinel's and Tuke's proposals for the Moral Treatment spread quickly across Europe and to America. The first mental hospital in the United States, the Friends Asylum in Philadelphia, built in 1817, resulted from the founders' visit to Tuke's York Retreat.[55] As in Europe, the therapeutic regimen of the new American asylums rested on a particular hypothesis concerning the origins of mental disorders. This hypothesis was based on the assumption that some constitutional factor, perhaps some damage to the brain tissue, predisposed the patient to insanity. The onset of mental disorder was thought to be connected with the stresses and traumas of the patient's social life among family members and associates. The cure, therefore, proposed removal of the patient from all familiar surroundings so that the patient could relax and be taught new patterns of behavior. Like Pinel, the American hospital superintendents of the first half of the nineteenth century believed that many of their patients could be cured. The staff of the Friends Asylum spoke of patients as "deprived of the use of their reason," and because each individual contained the "divine principle," no one was without the possibility of return to health.[56]

The designers of the building and grounds sought to create a protected, sanitary, homelike, easily supervised, and restful environment. The superintendents in those days wanted the grounds outside the buildings to perform several functions. To promote privacy and quiet, the grounds needed to be protected from the bustle of contemporary life and the intrusion of the curious. This goal could be accomplished by locating a new asylum outside the city, and also by screening the grounds with a band of trees, a fence, or ideally a high wall. The great authority Thomas S. Kirkbride of the Pennsylvania Hospital for the Insane recommended a minimum of a hundred acres, and two hundred acres for a hospital with a full farm program.[57] Next, the grounds should open onto vistas that the patients would experience as soothing and beautiful. In this era, beautiful grounds meant an artful improvement on the open cattle-grazing and dairy landscapes that then existed everywhere in the northeast United States. Patterning the grounds on eighteenth-century English aristocrats' estates, American gardeners laid out lawns with specimen trees and clusters of trees whose foliage directed attention toward the best distant views. The goal was to plant something that would be in harmony with the views of nature represented in the Hudson River School painting of the time. Accordingly, the Friends Hospital features a screen of forest around the circumference and undulating lawns with artfully placed clusters of trees.[58]

Finally, a regular routine of work was prescribed as the core element in the routine for recovery. Patients might choose to work at cooking, housekeeping, or simple crafts, but gardening and farming were encouraged because they were outdoor activities. In a well-run asylum, the patients cared for the grounds, tended the kitchen gardens, and worked the hospital farm. "Without sufficient provision for out-door exercise and occupation for the patients and an ample supply of means of amusement and employment," Kirkbride wrote,

the excitement in the wards, and the violent and mischievous propensities of their inmates, will be apt to be such as to require modes of management that might otherwise be easily dispensed with. . . . The farm and garden offer admirable means of useful occupation to the insane men, at certain periods of the disease, for valuable as they are to a large number, no greater indiscretion can be committed, than the attempt to set all insane men to work in every stage of their malady. To those accustomed to such pursuits, as well as to many who have been differently occupied, regular, moderate labor in the open fields or in the garden, in certain stages of their disease, contributes most essentially to their comfort, and tends to promote their recovery. Labor, then, judiciously used, is one of our best remedies; it is useful in improving the health of the insane, as in maintaining that of the sane.[59]

So long as its crucial therapeutic methods could be maintained, the Moral Treatment enjoyed a remarkable success. To succeed, the methods required a small institution of not more than two hundred patients, a community of well-trained and -supervised attendants who lived and worked among the patients to create a rich environment of therapeutic relationships, and, in addition, careful individual observation and attention. A follow-up study of the patients discharged from the Worcester State Hospital in Massachusetts between 1833 and 1853 showed a remarkable success rate. Of those discharged, 45 percent went on to live successfully in their cities and towns: they did not commit suicide; they did not become welfare cases; they did not require further hospitalization.[60]

Unfortunately, such good works were soon overwhelmed, much as the medieval hospitals had been. Waves of poor immigrants flooded the hospitals. The poverty, foreign ways, and unfamiliar religions of these new patients were in conflict with the small-town Yankee Protestant culture of their caretakers. At the same time, Dorothea Dix (1802–1887), imitating the Englishman John Howard's (1726–1790) earlier exposés, led a campaign to get the mentally ill out of the jails and poorhouses of the United States and into state-run asylums. Governors and legislatures responded by building massive institutions, now misnamed asylums. Appropriations were consumed by bricks and mortar and graft, while the parsimonious legislators actually reduced the appropriations for patient care. The state asylum thereby ballooned into a storage place for hopeless cases, and the Moral Treatment was reduced to custodial care.[61]

By the 1880s the states stopped voting adequate funds, the wards grew overcrowded, and most, if not all, the horrors Dorothea Dix had campaigned against returned.

What the leading hospital historians have written about the old Bethlehem Hospital of London, the notorious "Bedlam," now fit the late nineteenth-century mental hospital scene: "Hospitals have a way of being conceived in glory," Thompson and Goldin wrote, "executed with ingenuity and humanity, then subjected in use to misuse and abuse, finally to be overcrowded and understaffed and always forever plagued by insufficient funds. A hospital before death can become more decrepit than a man. The man dies, but a moribund hospital may live on for decades, and what is so terrible, filled to capacity."[62]

The Pavilion Hospital

The fortunes of the pavilion hospital unfolded in a fashion quite the opposite to those of the garden-equipped mental hospital. While the mental hospital moved from decades of early success to overcrowding and failure, the acute-care hospital began with decades of crisis from epidemics of infection. Then, toward the last quarter of the nineteenth century, physicians mastered antiseptic practice, and the acute-care hospital triumphed to become the seedbed of modern scientific medicine.

As we have seen, the Anglo-French pavilion hospital drew its inspiration from the principles and practices of hygiene. The theory of hygiene, in turn, rested upon the miasmal hypothesis about the origins of disease; commonsense habits of washing, meanwhile, transformed the theory into everyday practice. Physicians familiar with the great epidemics of plague and cholera reasoned that disease spread from the emanations of decaying matter: from the wounds and wastes of invalids, from rotting human and animal filth, and indeed from decay of all kinds. Since the Renaissance, the public defense against these emanations had been the isolation of the sick through quarantine and the cleansing of streets, alleys, and houses. It followed that clean, airy, well-kept, sunlit hospitals, such as those being established for the military, should promise the least contagion and the lowest mortality. And so they did during the eighteenth century.

Both the physicians who observed the treatment of soldiers following the Battle of Waterloo and Florence Nightingale caring for the wounded during the Crimean War (1854–1856) found confirmation of eighteenth-century practices in the surprising differences in mortality experienced by soldiers put up in barns and tents as opposed to those confined to conventional hospitals. The least sheltered fared the best.[63] These dramatic demonstrations set the program for nineteenth-century pavilion hospitals: wide spacing between long, low buildings to afford abundant sunlight, and plenty of windows and ventilators to flood the wards with fresh outside air.[64]

The intervening green spaces called forth by these arrangements were sometimes intentionally arranged to form parklike spaces for convalescents, hospital staff, and visitors. They thereupon became adjuncts to the therapeutic process in the wards. The medicine of the day, whether descending from the Parisian scientific school or from older traditions, stressed the role of the environment in the patient's well-being. The goal of both the science-oriented physicians and the traditionalists was to help the patient recover his or her natural state, understood to be a condition in which the human organism had found some equilibrium with its environment. Thus, the garden formula of the pavilion hospital was easily adopted into the care-giving process.[65]

Unfortunately, the pavilion hospital failed to fulfill its promise until after the acceptance of the germ theory of disease and the subsequent change in surgical practices during the 1870s and 1880s. "Hospitalism," the spread of cross-infections from one patient to the next, rose to alarming levels during the nineteenth century because of the hospital overcrowding that attended the rapid waves of urbanization, and because of lax and ignorant procedures of surgery, pathology, and autopsy. Surgeons grew alarmed when amputations and surgical wounds of all kinds failed to heal as they had formerly, and deadly infection often followed these incisions. Many surgeons limited their interventions to the most desperate cases, and some even questioned whether hospitals ought to be closed altogether. They guessed

that the bad air somehow caused the infections to spread. Then in 1867 Joseph Lister (1827–1912) published his essay in which he reasoned from Pasteur's studies of fermentation that there existed particles in the air that caused the infections. A bit later, Pasteur himself reported on the bacteriological basis of hospitalism.[66]

It was in this confused climate of discouragement and discovery that the Johns Hopkins University trustees set about building their new hospital and medical school. Johns Hopkins (1795–1873) had been a very successful Quaker wholesale grocer and banker in Baltimore. In his deed of gift, he imagined his new institution to be a public charity, a free hospital.

The indigent sick of this city and its environs without regard to sex, age, or color, who require surgical or medical treatment . . . and the poor who are stricken down by any casualty, shall be received into the hospital without charge . . . and a limited number of patients who are able to make compensation.[67]

Hopkins had lived very much in the style of the merchants of his era, with a townhouse in Baltimore and a large suburban estate, "Clifton," on the Harford Road. Here he maintained an elaborate garden that had become a Baltimore showplace to which the public was "admitted by card and shown the garden by attendants." We may imagine a Victorian spread with bedded plants and bright ornamentals and exotics.

In his deed of gift he wrote: "I wish the large grounds surrounding the hospital buildings to be properly enclosed by iron railings, and to be so laid out and planted with trees and flowers as to afford solace to the sick and be an ornament to the section of the city in which the grounds are located."

He also imagined that a convalescent center would be built near the city, so that the long-term patients would not obstruct the admission of acute cases to the hospital.[68]

In 1875, when the building committee members considered their alternatives, they worried about the extreme differences in patient mortality that existed

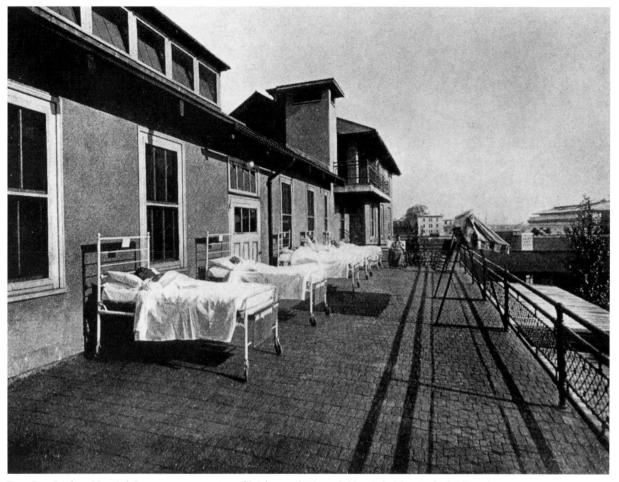

Peter Bent Brigham Hospital, Boston, c. 1913, courtesy of Brigham and Women's Hospital. *(Photo: Bradford F. Herzog)*

between hospitals and private practice. The committee saw three alternatives for the management of "hospitalization": (1) "Open air treatment, or (2) tents, barracks, and destructible pavilions," or (3) a compromise, "pavilion hospitals of which well built and well managed examples exist . . . in England, and the 'Roosevelt' and 'Presbyterian' in New York, with others in Philadelphia and Boston."[69] In addition, the participants imagined that some still newer design might be even more effective than the three alternatives they had identified. The committee thereupon canvassed four American experts, asking them to comment on the relative merits of barracks that

would be periodically destroyed versus the common two-story English permanent pavilion.[70]

John Shaw Billings (1838–1913), assistant surgeon of the U.S. Army, replied with a long essay on the prevention of the "hurtful influence of hospitals" owing to the spread of infections, as well as on the need for four-year medical schools and the promise of scientific exploration.[71] The committee thereupon hired Billings to supervise the construction of Johns Hopkins Hospital.

Billings's plan specified a hospital campus of detached special-purpose buildings arranged around a central garden and fountain. There were to be eight one-story ward buildings, a dispensary, an operating theater, a nurses' home, a pathology building, a laundry, an administration building, and two buildings for private patients, which would offer single rooms. Billings also proposed that a "bridge," or arcade, with a roof-walkway, should connect the buildings. Since the wards would be aligned north to south with their narrow ends bordering the central garden, the garden would be invisible to patients or staff in the wards. He intended, however, that his bridges be placed where "the ward patients could have the benefits of sunshine and fresh air." In these times, good nursing practice at Johns Hopkins and elsewhere called for helping ambulatory patients to get outdoors, and for wheeling the ward beds out onto sunporches and roofs.[72] Indeed, the fashion for the fresh-air treatment rose to a peak before World War I. A physician writing on hospital management in 1910 noted: "Physicians insist that patients with certain diseases be treated out-of-doors—not only in cases of tuberculosis, but cases of pneumonia, whooping-cough, anemia, insomnia, and all those convalescing from almost any acute medical or surgical trouble."[73]

The prestige of Johns Hopkins Hospital and its medical faculty made Billings's essay and design a standard to which hospital builders referred during the great wave of American hospital construction at the turn of the century.[74] Yet just as the pavilion style with its accompanying gardens, sundecks, and sunroofs triumphed, powerful events converged to transform general acute-care hospitals inside and out. Knowledge of germ theory and antiseptic practice allowed efficiency engineers to replace the land- and heat-consuming low-rise pavilion hospitals with compact multistory buildings.[75] The stunning advance of medical science from bacteria to vaccines to x-rays to pharmaceuticals, along with the growing safety and complexity of surgical practice, brought ceaseless demands for ever more-specialized hospital spaces. These successes also lured paying patients into hospitals. Together, the specialization and the new patients revolutionized the institution, completely altering its internal environments and its relations with the outside world.

Inside the hospital, specialization according to patients' particular conditions began to replace the former all-purpose wards. In 1880 the contagious had been isolated from the others; by 1918 the grouping of patients into distinct categories—acute surgical, chronic medical, tubercular, pediatric, contagious, and psychopathic—had launched the unending process of differentiation of hospital units into diagnostic clusters and treatment procedures that characterizes today's general hospital. Such functional clusters erased all trace of the long-standing tradition of the hospital as a place of all-purpose medical charity and made it resemble the hive of trade and business specialties which then flourished in crowded American city centers.

At the same time that the hospital ceased to be the domain of the twenty-four-bed charity ward, it began to mirror the class hierarchy of the city surrounding it: dispensaries, emergency rooms, and wards for the poor and working-class; two- and four-bed wards, even singles as the standard for the middle class; and luxurious single rooms and private physicians for the well-to-do. Sometimes, as at the Johns Hopkins Hospital, Massachusetts General Hospital, and Columbia-Presbyterian Hospital in New York City, the class divisions were carried further: patients from different classes were housed in separate buildings.[76]

The Design Revolution

The sum of these changes, all under way in acute-care hospitals during the first decade of the twentieth century, amounted to a transformation as revolutionary in its consequences as the Renaissance charity hospital's supplanting of the monastic hospice. The Renaissance transformation had marked a sharp decline in care-giving because it replaced an all-class institution with a welfare institution for the sick poor.

The twentieth-century revolution was not all a loss with regard to care. The classes were at least partially reunited, if not on the same floors, at least within the same institution. The steady advance in treatment practices, surgery, and medicines also brought cures where before there had been only care. The losses came from the effects of specialization and the focus on the patient as an organism with a specific pathology. As patients thus became components, not entities, the hospital itself more and more resembled the environment of the office and the laboratory. Patients became diseased entities, not self-healing humans who sought the assistance of scientifically trained physicians and nurses in order to recover. In acute-care hospitals, the design emphasis shifted toward saving steps for physicians and nurses, and away from attending to the patients' environment. Gardens disappeared, balconies and roofs and solaria were abandoned, and landscaping was restricted to entrance beautification, tennis courts for the staff, and parking lots for employees and visitors. These trends which so possessed the twentieth-century American acute-care hospitals spread, after World War II, to long-term and chronic-care facilities, to the hospitals of the Veterans Administration, to mental hospitals, and to nursing homes. The prestige of the big urban teaching hospitals with their gardenless patient environments set the style for all the others.

The early twentieth-century boom in hospital construction encouraged a Boston architect to write a series of books on good design, and through the successive editions from 1918 to 1928, it is possible to follow the onset of the design revolution. Edward F. Stevens (1860–1946), Massachusetts Institute of Technology Class of 1883, had developed a successful hospital practice and served during World War I as a designer for the U.S. Army's overseas hospitals. He introduced his first edition with a vision common to his time: the ambitions of factory engineering efficiency. "Food, together with the treatment, are the processes of manufacture. The hospital planner must seek to eliminate all lost motion and unnecessary waste."[77] Most of his discussions of efficiency appeared in his sections on equipment, cooking, heating and ventilation, and the specifications for sanitary

management. The hospitals he admired, however, were pavilion hospitals like Billings's Johns Hopkins and his later Peter Bent Brigham Hospital in Boston, and their German equivalents. Environmentalism remained in the forefront for Stevens. In writing about site planning for a hospital, he held the same concept of nature as an escape that had animated the writing of the eighteenth-century garden commentator Christian Hirschfeld, although Stevens stated his goal in the businesslike terms of keeping the hospital filled with patients. "Avoid noise, provide the patient freedom from disturbing elements," he wrote. Seek "an environment that will be an uplift to the patient . . . sunlight and ventilation and the modern fresh air balcony, these items . . . are factors toward increased hospital capacity."[78]

The Rudolph Virchow Hospital in Berlin (built in 1907) served as Stevens's leading example. It was a hospital of two thousand beds, and one-story pavilions arranged in a park. "The beautifully laid-out grounds and parks, with their walks and drives, become the ideal place for convalescents. One of the roles of these parks is that every third day they are for the use of the patients, every third day for the sole use of the staff, and every third day for the sole use of the nurses."[79]

Stevens also adhered to the practice of having the patients sun. "The ward or bed patient should be so placed that it is possible to have *sunshine* in the room and near the bed some part of the day. All necessary inside doors and windows giving access to porches should be *wide enough* for the patient to be moved in his bed without any change and without any discomfort or inconvenience, to any part of the building, porches, or roof" (italics in the original).[80]

Stevens offered the example of a suburban hospital which most nearly realized his environmental ideas. The Newton Hospital, situated at the outer edge of a comfortable Boston suburb, had been built over a number of years through a collaboration of Stevens's firm and a landscape architect. The result was a kind of hospital estate, with an artful scattering of small buildings, patient gardens, and planted grounds for visitors and staff.[81] Today the Newton-Wellesley Hospital (as it is now called) has squeezed itself into a series of factory-like additions and has given up all its gardens. But elsewhere across the nation, a good many small community hospitals continue the tradition of gardens for hospital patients.[82]

Stevens's 1918 edition also revealed the beginnings of revolutionary trends. He discussed the departmentalization of wards, the needs of special children's units, the arrangement of contagion wards, and the multiplication of private rooms. In design terms, Stevens's treatment of private rooms was influenced by the achievements of Ellsworth M. Statler (1863–1928), who was then enjoying immense business success, thanks to his construction of a hotel chain in which each hotel room was furnished with a private bathroom.[83] In class terms, Stevens in his treatment recognized the entry of the fee-paying middle classes into a former charity institution. He also devoted a good deal of attention to the new psychiatric wards of general hospitals and the new acute-care psychopathic hospitals just then coming into being. Finally, in a chapter given over to tuberculosis hospitals, he addressed the isolation and loneliness of the patients.[84]

His last edition (1928) recorded the further advance of the design revolution. Private pavilions composed entirely of single rooms multiplied, while public wards subdivided into two- and four-bed units had become the norm. The new units were often planned as "Rigs wards" in which the long pavilion was divided by partitions and two or four beds were placed with their heads to the partitions to form small self-contained areas.[85] Stevens also offered more multistory exemplars to replace the low-rise alternatives. The criteria of sunshine and fresh air, however, had not yet disappeared from his big-city acute-care hospital designs. The 5th Avenue Hospital in New York City, for example, featured all private rooms, but it still had airing balconies.[86]

The most pronounced change during the 1920s hospital building boom was the shift from one- and two-story pavilions to multistory blocks in which communications were carried from floor to floor by elevator. Saving on the costs of high-priced city land, reducing heating costs, and confining everyone to interior living constituted the new efficiency. The exteriors showed off popular historical styles: Spanish, Georgian, Jacobean, and Gothic. Inside, the old pavilion merely became the nursing floor. The nurses' station moved from the end position it had occupied in Florence Nightingale's plan to the center, next to the elevator stack.

The core assumption of hospital management remained the single patient in a bed, a person who required only the services of skilled general nursing and the periodic visits of a physician. The hotel booking system, another efficiency measure, placed incoming patients in any empty bed. As a result, a hodgepodge of symptoms was now represented on any given hospital floor.[87] Privacy for the new fee-paying patients, however, remained the dominant theme of contemporary design books. "The comfort of the patient, with freedom from annoyance, will have much to do with the process of his recovery. . . . Privacy is another factor that adds to the patient's comfort. It is so important that it can be classified as a necessity, and as much privacy as possible must be provided."[88]

Yet the privacy of the multistory acute-care hospital and the growing demands of medical practice for specialized diagnosis and treatment did not mix well. Already in the 1920s Sigismund S. Goldwater (1873–1942), the superintendent and director of Mount Sinai Hospital in New York City from 1903 to 1929, objected to the effects of the elevator. He thought the mingling of patients and visitors, contagious and noncontagious, posed hazards.[89] Moreover, the ever-growing need to wheel patients about contravened completely the ideal of patient privacy. The design authors Butler and Erdman highlighted the contradiction. "Patients are wheeled great distances, taken up and down in elevators, and wait in corridors and lobbies for their turn to be propelled elsewhere for treatment or an operation."[90]

The steady reduction of gardened spaces in twentieth-century acute-care hospitals, and especially in big urban general hospitals, where they are perhaps needed most, constitutes a major loss to the quality of patient environments in the United States. Chronic-care hospitals, however, have experienced gains as well as losses. The continued elaboration of occupational therapy, from its nineteenth-century beginnings in mental hospitals, the development of the subspecialty of horticultural therapy, and the popularization of milieu therapy have worked together to expand the possibilities for gardens for all kinds of patients.

By 1960 the garden options available to any health care facility included a rich traditional array of outside gardens for walking, sitting, sunning and airing, sunlit inside rooms, and greenhouse-like corridors. It also included active gardening for disabled adults, children, and patients of all kinds in the form of horticultural therapy in patients' rooms, hospital corridors, special greenhouses, and gardens on the hospital grounds.

Here was a broad menu of garden settings and activities awaiting adoption by all health care facilities, from the waiting rooms of clinics to big urban general hospitals and state and federal chronic-care hospitals. Unfortunately, such is the dominance of the architectural fashion of the enclosed air-conditioned office and hotel room, and the "cure, not care" focus of American medicine that both garden traditions and garden innovations have been neglected. Everyone has moved indoors. There are exceptions, however, and it is these exceptions among health care settings and their achievements and possibilities that are the subject of the case studies in this book.

The recent history of America's chronic-care hospitals demonstrates the possibilities of garden environments at both extremes: repeated, un-looked-for failures, and innovations of promise. On the side of failure, the tuberculosis hospital holds up a warning flag to anyone interested in the restorative effects of patient gardens.

Tuberculosis declined steadily during the late nineteenth century in the United States, yet it continued to flourish among the urban poor. As a result, it came to be popularly identified as a tenement disease.[91] Well-to-do Americans had been treating the disease with environmental measures, moves to the country, and especially removal to the dry mountain air of Colorado. In Germany, physicians reported achieving successes by combining the national pleasure in spa-going with the ancient regimen therapy. According to the German method, tuberculosis patients were to remove themselves from the cares of everyday life, take mild exercise, follow the spa rhythms of promenades, bathing, music, gardens, and meals. The element that the German doctors reintroduced was the close supervision of the spa regimen by physicians.[92]

Dr. Edward Livingston Trudeau (1848–1915), a New York City tuberculosis sufferer who had sequestered himself in the town of Saranac Lake, New York, popularized the German system in the United States. In 1882 Robert Koch identified the tuberculosis bacillus and, in so doing, made reliable diagnosis by physicians possible. Two years later, after studying Koch's methods, Trudeau opened his Adirondack Cottage Sanitarium (operated 1884–1954). Trudeau shared the belief that tuberculosis could be treated to good effect by altering patients' ways of living. He set up a colony of small cottages and trained his patients to lead an all-outdoors life. This German-American hybrid treatment of rest, open air, and medical supervision came to be the model that U.S. sanitaria followed. In 1900 34 sanitaria for tuberculosis were in operation, with 4,500 beds; by 1925 their number had grown to 536 sanitaria with 673,000 beds.[93]

Because they were out-of-doors living places and pesthouses, sanitaria were located in the country, or at the edge of the city. So New York City sited its huge Sea View facility on Staten Island, and the state put its tents and cabins in Otisville.[94] Such settings did not lack for lawns and gardens, but the locations were lonely, and the regimen of rest, light tasks, and supervised social life proved intensely boring. At the same time, false messages about progress toward a cure set nurses and doctors in conflict with their patients. Some physicians went so far as to say that recovery from tuberculosis was a matter of self-discipline, and in making that pronouncement they placed the burden for healing on their patients. They implied that those who followed the regimen exactly would get better.[95] In some sanitaria, ambulatory patients worked on farms and in shops and did housework, as mental patients did; in others, shop work and light activities were offered to counteract the boredom, while in still others, rest was paramount.[96]

Architect Stevens suggested that the loneliness might be relieved if every patient were provided with a small heated closet in which to store possessions and enjoy some moments of privacy.[97] Dr. Thomas S. Carrington, an expert on the design of tuberculosis hospitals, hoped that the natural beauty of the hospital surroundings would keep the patients from checking out. "The problem of holding tuberculosis patients at sanitaria grows more serious each year, and as institutional care of certain classes of cases seems to be an absolute necessity in order to control the disease, every effort should be made to place patients upon sites that have natural attractions which will help amuse and make them contented."[98]

A patient of Trudeau wrote home to the contrary: "I do nothing all day but lie here staring at the mountains. I wish they would rearrange them a bit."[99]

The lesson of the tuberculosis hospital is a complicated one. Gardens, scenery, and closeness to nature abounded, yet the clinical process and institutional discipline militated against whatever restorative uses patients might have discovered for themselves. Everything conspired to create a climate of anger and frustration.

Commonly, patients checked in and then served an indefinite term of confinement, to be discharged only on the physician's advice. The medical staff, in turn, felt under pressure to cure patients, or at least to be able to report some progress toward health. When frequent examinations revealed no progress or a worsening condition, the results were often concealed from the patients, lest they become discouraged. Dying patients were isolated; the presence of death in the sanitaria was denied. The idea of hospice service had not yet entered American hospital culture. In addition, the fear of tubercular infection among inhabitants of the outside world made the patients feel like pariahs. Overall, 12 to 30 percent of the patients fled within a month, and those who stuck it out had to endure an atmosphere heavy with frustration, control, anger, and denial. The gardens of twentieth-century American tuberculosis hospitals were thus hardly gardens at all; they were places whose potential restorative functions could not be realized, because of circumstances within the institutional setting.

Innovations in Occupational Therapy

Gardening as a planned activity linked to patients' therapeutic regimen found its role when occupational therapy came into its own in the twentieth century. Occupational therapy in the form of work and recreation had long been a practice at mental hospitals that established regular programs of work, games, storytelling, or music. As such, it had a commonsense rationale as an antidote to boredom, and in this capacity it had been the subject of repeated medical rediscoveries and endorsements.

During the 1790s, for example, Dr. Philippe Pinel had revived the practice recorded at Zaragoza during the fifteenth century. Dr. Benjamin Rush, physician during the American Revolutionary era, wrote in his 1812 essay on the diseases of the mind: "Man was made to be active. Even in paradise he was employed in healthy and pleasant exercises of cultivating a garden. Happiness, consisting in folded arms, and in pensive contemplation beneath rural shades, and by the side of purling brooks, never had any existence, except in the brains of mad poets and love-sick girls and boys."[100] And in the 1870s the Jacksonville, Illinois, State Hospital formed a patient and staff band to play for the other patients and the townspeople, an imitation of Arabic and ancient Greek medical praxis.[101]

In the early twentieth century the popular revival of interest in crafts provided a stimulus for experiments and teaching that enlarged the scope of former work and recreation programs. Within two decades, occupational therapy organized itself into a distinct therapeutic specialty.

In 1906, at Gloucester, Massachusetts, Dr. Herbert Hall set up a workshop where mental patients and craftsmen worked side by side. Five years later his observations were published. He found that when a series of graded work assignments were given to patients who had formerly been either idle or overworked, a strong rehabilitating effect was observable. About the same time, a Boston nurse, Susan E. Tracy, began teaching craft techniques to her nursing students. She likened a bedridden orthopedic patient— an alert mind confined by pain, casts, and traction— to an animal caught in a trap. In such circumstances, occupational therapy offered both palliative and remedial benefits. Soon quite a few hospitals offered courses in occupational therapy. Then, in 1917 at a gathering at Consolation House in Clifton Springs, N.Y., an institution that instructed the disabled about ways to become gainfully employed, those early practitioners assumed their modern-day professional name: occupational therapists. Thus, at the moment of American entry into World War I, the three components of occupational therapy—palliation, remedial work, and employment—had fallen into place.[102] Moreover, several of the manuals published by these pioneers mentioned gardening as one useful mode of therapy.[103]

Physical therapy had its roots in the ancient practices of massage, baths, and exercise, but it had undergone a nineteenth-century reformation in response to emerging knowledge about the stimulation and relaxation of muscles. A Swedish fencing master, Peter Henry Ling (1776–1839), invented a course of exercises for developing specific muscles. Gustav Zander (1835–1917) put Ling's course into effect by designing exercise machines to which he added scales and removable weights so that their use could be carefully gauged. These machines were imported into the United States and further perfected by Dudley A. Sargent (1849–1938) of Boston and R. Tait McKenzie (1867–1938) of Philadelphia, who also prescribed the exercises to be performed.[104]

After World War I, in response to the needs of returning veterans, physical therapy and occupational therapy entered into collaboration. The physical therapists concentrated on building up the returning veterans' damaged and surviving muscles, while the occupational therapists concentrated on the small-motor coordination necessary for everyday life and gainful employment. In Europe, rehabilitation hospitals added garden work to their occupational therapy programs to help the wounded turn their thoughts from the experience of destruction toward acts of creation. Red Cross volunteers in the United States imitated these precedents by setting up a number of truck gardens next to veterans hospitals, and in 1920 the Federal Board for Vocational Education gave disabled soldiers courses in garden work.[105]

During the subsequent interwar years, occupational therapy, which included handicrafts, music, art, and sometimes gardening, continued in mental hospitals and was introduced in the many tuberculosis sanitaria. In the general hospitals occupational therapy, in tandem with physical therapy, responded to the new epidemics of poliomyelitis (nationally, the first of these epidemics occurred in Vermont in 1894, the last in 1951), as well as to waves of automobile casualties. Notable within the therapeutic enterprise were Elizabeth Kenny's methods of muscular re-education for paralytics.[106]

By the twenties, the number of auxiliary services provided to hospital patients had multiplied sufficiently to pose problems in clinical coordination. In addition to doctors and nurses, a general hospital now employed social workers, psychologists, physical therapists, industrial therapists, and occupational therapists. It was the private mental hospitals, however, that addressed this multiplication of specialists as something more than an administrative problem.

The innovation stemmed from the work of psychiatrists who reasoned outward from their understanding about the causes of mental illness to theorize about environments that might prove therapeutic. Dr. Harry Stack Sullivan (1892–1949) of Sheppard and Enoch Pratt Hospital and Chestnut Lodge in Maryland proposed a theory of interpersonal relations. Accordingly, in his work with schizophrenics he took great pains to create an atmosphere of warmth and sympathy for his patients. He observed that in such an attentive social setting the patients could be resocialized to behave in a different way.[107] Karl and William Menninger, inspired by Freud's drive-oriented psychoanalytic theory, also began to prescribe particular social environments for the patients at their Topeka, Kansas, clinic.[108] In the creation of their therapeutic environments, these early "milieu therapists" formed teams of many specialists. Karl Menninger (1895–1990) called all those who were not R.N.'s or M.D.'s teachers. "We prefer," he wrote, "the honored name of 'teacher' for all these fine and useful people, who teach the art of living to persons who may never have quite learned it or, if so, have lost it for a time."[109]

By World War II, the joint practices of paying careful attention to all aspects of mental patients' social environment and of having all staff for a particular patient consult together had come to be known as milieu therapy. Its contribution lay in the revival of concern for patients' environments and for the details of their social interactions. In such a climate, horticultural therapy arose as a subspecialty of occupational therapy.

Horticultural Therapy

Horticultural therapy, the active involvement with plant materials and gardening within an integrated clinical program, had many inventors, some amateur and some professional. Mental hospitals had a long tradition of farmwork, often sustained because operating the farms lowered the food costs of the institution. Some tuberculosis sanitaria had similar work programs. The precise date and manner of transition from the old farming therapy to the new horticultural therapy are not recorded. The occupational therapy manuals suggest that gardening was taught in some chronic-care and veterans hospital settings during the 1920s and 1930s.[110]

During World War II and its aftermath, horticultural therapy as we now know it came into being. Volunteers at military and veterans hospitals provided a major stimulus. Fragmentary reports tell of garden club volunteers' setting up gardens, greenhouses, and garden programs at Camp Edwards, Cushing General Hospital, and Chelsea Naval Hospital in Massachusetts, and at Camp Callan in California; and at the Battle Creek, Michigan, hospital, retail florists offered training.[111] This volunteer activity continued for many years, because after 1951 the National Council of State Garden Clubs made work with the blind, disabled, elderly, and mental patients one of its major activities.[112] One of the most original of these volunteer projects, at least at its genesis, was one at the neuropsychiatric hospital of the Veterans Administration in Los Angeles. Staff members were given three and a half acres of undeveloped property, where with patient volunteers they made a vegetable garden, a fish pond, a lath house, and chicken and rabbit houses. Subsequently, a local philanthropist began a public campaign for support of the garden, and the patients carried it on as an ambitious landscaping project.[113]

The professionalization of horticultural therapy took place in stages, at several different places. In 1942, Mary Tingley began teaching a course on horticulture to her occupational therapy students at Milwaukee Downer College (now Lawrence College in Appleton, Wisconsin).[114] Then Rhea McCandliss, the head gardener at the Topeka army base where Karl Menninger was serving as director, began offering therapy to the soldiers. Dr. Menninger, who brought to his Army hospital practice the enthusiasm of his family for gardening and the emphasis of his clinic on multiple activities, asked McCandliss to take patients into her greenhouse. From 1946 to 1953, she managed a horticultural therapy program at what became Winter Veterans Hospital, and then, between 1959 and 1972, she established a similar program at the Menninger Foundation.[115] In time, her work there led to the establishment of an undergraduate degree program in clinical psychology and horticultural therapy at Kansas State University (in 1972).[116]

Pontiac, Michigan, proved to be another important center of professional innovation. There Alice Burlingame, a psychiatric social worker and occupational therapist, started a group of volunteers in 1951 to teach flower arranging to elderly women confined to the hospital. Soon she realized that her workers needed both psychiatric and horticultural training. The next year she and Dr. Donald Watson began a series of workshops at Michigan State University that in 1953 became the university's horticultural therapy master's program. In 1960 Watson and Burlingame published the field's first textbook, *Therapy Through Horticulture*, in which they stressed the role that working with plants could play in raising patients' morale and motivation.[117]

A year earlier, the Rusk Institute for Rehabilitation Medicine in New York City had received the gift of a greenhouse and a small garden from Enid Haupt. In 1964 Howard Brooks joined the staff to establish a horticultural therapy program there. As at the Menninger Clinic, the effort was to design horticultural activities that would relate to the specific needs of individual patients, but at Rusk the emphasis was on reinforcing the physical gains patients were making.[118]

Meanwhile, in 1969 Clemson University in South Carolina built a prize-winning garden for the blind that attracted attention and funds for its horticulture program. Soon thereafter, it was able to send its students to teach at schools for the deaf and blind, mental institutions, and juvenile homes. By 1973 Clemson too was offering a graduate degree in horticultural therapy.[119]

In 1968 Rhea McCandliss sent 500 questionnaires to hospitals of all sorts. More than 200 replied, and of those, 140 had some type of horticultural pro-

gram. The teaching staff in many of those programs comprised both volunteers and professionals, either professional gardeners, occupational therapists, or horticultural therapists. As in the past, the chronic-care hospitals for the mentally ill, the elderly, and veterans were the most active. "Very few general hospitals or acute treatment centers offered any horticultural therapy," McCandliss reported.[120] Finally, in 1973 the pioneers of the field formed a professional association, the National Council for Therapy and Rehabilitation Through Horticulture.[121]

Thus, by the mid-1970s in the United States, the development of milieu therapy and horticultural therapy offered new ways of integrating gardens into many different clinical settings, from hospitals offering acute care and rehabilitation to those specializing in long-term palliative care. In addition, a few hospitals continued the long tradition of providing gardens for patients, staff, and visitors to look at or in which they could sit and walk. Never had the opportunities for gardens at health care facilities been so various. Yet such was the design and management bias of the time that the concept of employing plants and nature to directly transform patients' environments and treatments was relegated to the hinterlands of medical practice and research.

Environmental Failure

The most recent half-century of vigorous American hospital development and hospital building has constituted an environmental failure. The environments provided for patients, staff, and perhaps even physicians continued the long decline initiated by the efficiency movement. The drive for patient privacy came to a halt. To be sure, the open ward of twenty to thirty beds disappeared and was replaced by floors of double and single rooms. But care no longer took place primarily at the patient's bedside. Instead the patient had to move from specialist to specialist, submitting to special treatments. Formerly, doctors were mobile; now the patient had to make the "house" calls. At the same time, hospital expansion made for long corridors, and the multiplication of hospital functions led to the proliferation of rabbit warrens and cubbyholes for technicians and many caregivers. The art and science of medicine flourished, but health care environments failed to keep pace.

The environmental failure is particularly frustrating when reviewed from the perspective of the 1990s. After World War II all the necessary elements were in place for the reassertion of the clinical wisdom of providing sunlight, fresh air, and gardens. The federal grants under the Hill-Burton Act (1946) made available funds for new construction. For many years the Blue Cross and corporate and union insurance programs provided adequate fees for all innovative medical procedures. In 1966 federal Medicare and Medicaid funneled still more resources to hospitals, clinics, and nursing homes.[122] By the 1960s, hospital consultants and architects had mastered the issues raised by increasing specialization within medicine, with the attendant demands for a constant flow of medical supplies and for more efficient internal traffic circulation. At the same time, the popularization of modern architecture freed designers from the constraints of inherited forms. Finally, postwar developments in occupational and horticultural therapy spoke eloquently for the efficacy of gardens, while at the same time popular suburban styles of domestic landscaping offered fresh ways to link indoor and outdoor space.

Such elements could well have been combined to create truly humane environments for patients, staff, and visitors. Unfortunately, hospital administrators and insurance carriers focused on semiprivate and private rooms as the improvement that patients deserved, while physicians focused on putting new procedures into place. As a result, the post–World War II American hospital commonly imitated the air-conditioned office building and failed to realize or even to propose its own unique environmental requirements.

Isadore Rosenfield (1893–1980), an architect and professor of medical architecture at Columbia University from 1945 to 1970, fully understood the contradictions in postwar hospital designs. The solutions he proposed would have combined interior reorganization with outdoor access for patients, staff, and visitors. In *Hospital, Architecture and Beyond* (1969), he concentrated on two aspects of the environment and social life in health care buildings. First, he evaluated the decision between building up (the elevator choice) and building out (the corridor choice). The building of multistory hospitals represented a victory for elevators.[123] Yet studies showed that the delays caused by elevator trips, both in the ride and in the wait for the elevator, consumed a great deal of everybody's time. In the time required to take the typical ride (one and a quarter minutes, not counting time spent waiting for the elevator), it was possible to walk the distance—275 feet—and a person need not wait for the elevator before starting to walk. From this analysis Rosenfield concluded that low-rise hospitals would be more efficient. People would move along corridors and take stairs, and the elevators would be reserved for the disabled and bedridden.[124]

Second, he addressed the new clinical circumstances. Specialists and specialized services were multiplying, and physicians and staff needed to have a way to consult quickly and easily with one another. Rosenfield likened resultant clusters to a city, a dense hive of activity with easy contact from door to door. He therefore proposed gathering all the medical services together: emergency, x-ray, surgery, pathology, psychiatry, cardiology, and social service. Such a core would not only facilitate conversations among physicians, it would also reduce the trips that patients had to undertake.[125]

The union of these two principles, the low-rise institution and the high-density medical core, made Rosenfield's final floor plan resemble a crab: the medical core is the stout body, and the patient rooms and nursing stations the claws and legs.

Such general design principles, of course, offered the potential for vastly improved health care environments. Because the buildings would be low-rise, the long corridors of the tall block hospital could be pierced with windows and views of exterior gardens.

The Boston architect Thomas Payette, for example, uses small gardens at the intersections of corridors to make these walking journeys pleasant.[126] By the same token, patients' rooms and nursing stations could be sunlit and have fresh air and access to exterior gardens.

The ubiquitous ranch house was the suburban contemporary of this hospital design alternative. In some cases domestic picture windows faced the street, not the garden, but the low-rise house with easy access to exterior lawns and backyard gardens was the norm of the times. In fact, a brilliant landscape architect, Thomas D. Church (1902–1978) of San Francisco, planned and built many ingenious gardens for domestic settings. His was not the big institutional garden of a Frederick Law Olmsted or Jens Jensen, but rather the small garden that bespoke a new kind of indoor-outdoor living.[127] In the rest of the country this came to be known as the "California style." Church trained several important practitioners, and he wrote regularly for popular home and garden magazines. Consequently, his ideas came to be widely known.[128] The applicability of his design ideas to health care settings can be seen in the Stanford Medical Plaza, the work of his protégé, Lawrence Halprin.[129]

Patients, staff, and visitors at more of our hospitals could have enjoyed such gardens, sunlit corridors, and fresh air. That prospect never materialized, however, because hospital administrators, insurance executives, and physicians failed to take into account the restorative possibilities of their institutional environments.

Today, the mistake is being repeated. Just as mid-twentieth-century hospitals imitated the office building, health care facilities in the closing years of the century are imitating the commercial hotel and retail mall, with their multistory entrance atria, their arcades of shops and restaurants.[130] To be sure, such spaces are familiar enough to patients, staff, and visitors, and in that sense the replicas of commercial designs will make them comfortable. But they ignore the special emotional needs of a health care facility. The patients are anxious, afraid, in pain, and often drugged and disoriented. If they are resident for long, they soon feel alienated from their setting. A garden, even the view of a garden, unlike either an atrium or a mall, can allow patients to make their individual space into their particular image of a home space. Likewise, the staff are inside the institution, often working under stress, all day long. To be outside in a garden, or inside in a glassed-in garden, is a feeling that far transcends the opportunity to grab a pizza or a coffee in the arcade. And so too with the visitors, whose fears and anxieties must be respected. A garden can be for them, too, a place to collect their feelings and thoughts. In the winter, when in many regions the gardens are frozen and it is too cold to linger outside, they still offer sunlight and the marvels of the natural world.

Not all medical institutions in the United States have ignored the importance of gardens for their caring environments. There were exceptions, and some of these exemplars are the subjects of the case studies of this book. It is important to realize, when thinking about who continued or elaborated upon the garden tradition, and who did not, that the major exceptions appear in two groups: One group consists of medical settings in which modern medicine can offer no quick cure; the other group consists of small community hospitals where the hospital environments are expected to mirror the values of the surrounding community.

Enid A. Haupt Glass Garden, Howard A. Rusk Institute of Rehabilitation Medicine, New York University Medical Center. *(Photo: © 1996, Karen S. R. Balogh)*

Toward a Theory of the Restorative Garden

Let us state this at the outset: there is no *firm* scientific proof that gardens or horticulture have therapeutic value. Virtually no research would satisfy the medical scientists' need for double-blind controlled studies, nor are there crossover studies in which the data are reproduced and reaffirmed in a variety of experimental settings. In studying the role of gardens—or any psychological or aesthetic therapeutic agent—satisfying the demands of statistical certainty is well-nigh impossible. Despite this lack of experimentally irrefutable ground to stand on, however, a steadily accumulating body of evidence compellingly suggests that nature and gardens fill a critical niche in the approach to patients. To ignore these data because they are "soft" would be akin to saying that Mozart may not be exalting because we have no proof of it. What we propose is to consider whether the present data will support a theory of the restorative garden that takes us from the realm of the ineffable into the domain of the plausible.

As we approach this task, we should also clarify a second issue. We do not propose restorative gardens as an alternative mode of therapy. Restorative gardens are not replacements for medical interventions. They are not cures. We see hospital gardens as essential enhancements to the medical encounter, and we shall argue that restorative environments contribute so profoundly to a sense of well-being, to improved body function, that they must perforce be considered vital components of the medical therapeutic milieu.

Remarkably, only a single study directly addresses the question that animates our book: Does the environment affect recovery and healing? Both before and since Roger Ulrich's "View Through a Window May

Influence Recovery from Surgery," the literature on plant-person interaction has focused primarily on how nature makes us feel generally. In this oft-quoted and elegant study Ulrich showed, with very good control for numerous variables, that patients with a view of nature had statistically significant shorter hospital stays, lower analgesic use, and fewer complaints during recovery.[1] Quite simply, patients in rooms with views of the natural world got better more quickly and easily.

Ulrich's study built on several earlier "window studies" showing that the mere presence of windows with a view to the outside seemed to reduce the delusions and depression that often accompany prolonged stays in the intensive care unit.[2] Steven Verderber's interviews with hospitalized patients suggested that windows, whatever the view, connected patients with the flux of the outside world, whether natural or urban, and eased their stay in the hospital.[3] As to the particular view, environmental preference studies have repeatedly shown that in virtually every society, natural settings, "green nature" as Charles A. Lewis calls it, is the view of choice. As little of nature as flowers in a patient's room may enhance recovery.[4] From these observations have sprung a considerable literature and numerous theories about why contact with nature plays a particularly critical role in psychological well-being and healing.[5]

At the broadest social level, learned cultural influences may determine our response to nature and to gardens. There may be differences in the particular flowers we know or the garden styles we enjoy, but virtually every society cherishes nature, and gardens in some form, as part of its tradition and culture.

Whether through an interest in individual flowers, their lore, the horticultural act, or the garden as a work of art, all humankind interacts with nature in complex and varied ways.[6] As Mirabel Osler lovingly puts it: "The spirituality of gardens has spanned the world. In time and in geography. The mystical quality that a garden throws off is as powerful as the scent of flowers."[7]

Not surprisingly, the very universality of our response to nature suggests that it is not purely a cultural or a learned one. The intensity and extent of our preference for nature suggest that a *need* for nature arises in far deeper well-springs of our collective psyche. As Ulrich aptly points out, cultural theories may explain how responses are maintained, but the belief in nature's healing power seems almost genetic.[8]

Stephen and Rachel Kaplan have crafted a psychological theory of the restorative environment that takes us beyond culture and into the realm of individual psychology.[9] They see contemporary society as burdened by ever-increasing stress. The requirements and blandishments of highly technological societies force us into "directed attention"—the kind of attention that requires concentration, effort, and ultimately, if it continues unabated, produces stress and fatigue. Indeed, survival—in any society, during any historical era—requires intense concentration that can be physically and mentally exhausting. Recovery from this fatigue can be facilitated by the "restorative experience." Although that experience may be any activity that relieves directed attention and allows for effortless or involuntary attention, it turns out that contact with nature—in nearly every form, from the casual stroll in the park to full immersion in the wilderness, or even a view out a window—is among the most potent of restorative experiences. That nature is the restorative environment of choice is supported by the popularity of gardening, camping, and wilderness experiences in general. Nature most readily satisfies the Kaplans' criteria for a restorative event. Their first requirement is a sense of *being away*, in a setting removed from the routine demands on our

attention. This environment must be perceived as *extensive* yet connected to a larger, but comprehensible, whole. This environment must evoke our *fascination*— this is critical—if we are to experience the involuntary, effortless attention that provides psychic relief. And finally, the restorative environment must be *compatible* with the needs of the individual.

It is apparent that a garden or wilderness can give one the sense of being away and that its extent is considerable (whether in reality, or seemingly, by good design), but in what way do nature in general and gardens in particular awaken our fascination and satisfy our needs (the second two Kaplan criteria)? The mere prospect of nature, as mentioned, seems to have beneficial effects. Workers who can enjoy views of nature routinely report less job pressure and fewer ailments. Rachel Kaplan describes the phenomenon of "thereness": that is, the mere *availability* of nature seems to have beneficial and restorative effects, whether or not one actually takes advantage of it.[10] Prisoners with proximity to green nature made fewer visits to health care providers, and even Alzheimer's disease patients with dementia seemed to show some functional improvement when their environment included "green nature" and gardens.[11] Our enjoyment of where we live seems in part to derive from proximity to nature, and nature is where we seek to go when troubled.[12]

The Kaplans see nature as providing coherence, legibility, complexity, and mystery.[13] In many ways this is a recipe for garden design: the best of our gardens possess all the elements that entice our interest—coherence, our ability to make sense of the landscape; complexity, the richness of the scene; legibility, our ability to read, understand, and decipher it (in essence, to render the complex coherent); and mystery, the final dimension—a promise of more to come. And as another garden writer has said, "The quest for this relationship between our minds and the universe makes us first organize natural forms into easily grasped patterns and to re-arrange them into new compositions which please us by opening up fresh and less obvious fields of comprehension."[14]

The Kaplans' conception of the restorative experience provides one psychological explanation for what constitutes gardens' invigorating, refreshing, and *healing* power. But when a patient sees a garden, what occurs on the physical level to allow enhanced well-being and perhaps faster recovery from illness? What bodily events chart the restorative effect? With these questions we move into the realm of psychophysiology and neuropsychoimmunology.

Illness and hospitalization are among the most profound stresses of human life—this is a given. Stress produces several physiological events: elevation in blood pressure, increased heart rate, measurably increased muscle tension, and changes in brain wave function and mental concentration.[15] These physiological occurrences prepare us for coping with stress, but they also take a toll and, if unchecked, can have deleterious effects on health and recovery time. Even when the source of stress is unaltered, however, we can think ourselves into relaxing. The built-in "fight-flight" reaction can be diminished through learned behaviors or (in the current jargon) by "relaxation techniques."[16] More important, what emerges from the psychophysiological studies of Roger Ulrich is that views of nature seem to provide the preferred form of physiologically measurable stress reduction. This relaxation occurs remarkably quickly—almost within minutes. What Ulrich found was that after exposure to a defined stressor, people shown videotapes with color and sound of natural settings recovered dramatically faster—measured by heart rate, muscle tension, skin conductance and pulse transit time (which is in indirect correlation with systolic blood pressure and hence an effective measure of stress)—than a group shown urban scenes. Not only did the group exposed to natural scenery recover faster physiologically, but within four to six minutes, they *felt* better. They were less angry, less fearful, and had generally more positive attitudes. It is noteworthy that in these and other preference studies, not only were scenes with vegetation significantly preferred to urban scenery, but scenes of vegetation and water together were the most pleasing and affect enhancing.

This research steers us toward somewhat deeper reaches of human response, beyond those of conscious or learned control. The rapidity of response to nature and its mobilization of so many physiological responses suggest that the parasympathetic nervous system—that is, the component of the nervous system thought not to be under conscious control—must also be involved in the calming effects experienced in response to nature.[17] These findings have been confirmed quite directly in studies of dental and medical patients. Patients lying down in stretchers in a presurgery holding room who were exposed to ceiling pictures of nature scenes had substantially lower blood pressure than patients looking at blank ceilings or other pleasant scenes.[18] Verderber concluded from hospitalized patients' responses to questionnaires that views to nature made the patients feel better; Wilson showed that delirium among intensive care patients could be substantially reduced if they were allowed views to the "outside"; and Ulrich showed reduced anxiety in cardiac surgery patients.[19] Thus, physiological events beyond conscious control must be taking place. Ulrich has convincingly argued that such responses are unlikely to be cognitive or based on purely cultural or learned influences.[20] Intuitively, we know that when such responses so persistently cross cultural and social boundaries, they must have far deeper physiological origins.

We have known for some time that stress affects virtually every organ system. Physiological responses have evolved from the adaptive need for heightened arousal of our senses and body functions in response to danger. Hans Selye, in his classic studies that defined the "fight-flight" syndrome, showed that in times of stress or perceived danger, our endocrine systems go into overdrive, stimulating heart muscle and nervous system.[21] Mental alertness, anxiety, stomach cramps, cold and sweaty palms, and rapid heartbeat are probably the symptoms we most commonly experience consciously in reaction to stress.

More recently, a body of evidence has extended Selye's work to suggest that not only is the endocrine system mobilized during periods of stress, but our central nervous system and immune systems become galvanized and are intermittently linked and interdependent. In other words, the endocrine, central nervous, and immune systems are in multidirectional communication with one another. The pituitary gland, which has been called the "master gland" of the endocrine system, controls the production of the thyroid, the adrenal, and growth hormone, all of which are involved in stress reactions. The pituitary gland sits *in* the brain, bathed in and fed by chemicals called neuropeptides, which are made by a brain stimulated by the vicissitudes of consciousness.[22] Here the mind-body connection is not only biochemical but anatomical as well. The work of Gerald Edelman on the nature of mind describes how brain cells and their vast connections respond to immediate inputs but are modulated by previously selected evolutionary patterns of response.[23] This "neural Darwinism"[24] becomes important in the consideration of humans' evolutionary response to nature and its effect on the brain and on the neuroendocrine and central nervous system response to the stresses of patienthood.

The brain and the entire central nervous system send messages to the endocrine system via neuropeptides and to the immune system via neurotransmitters. The endocrine system sends its controlling hormones back to the nervous and immune systems. The immune system acts as a sensor as well when it sends cytokines (another chemical messenger) in dynamic, continually adjusting feedback to the endocrine and nervous systems.[25]

Again, we have known for some time that stress causes endocrine and nervous system production of epinephrine and norepinephrine, which give us the numerous felt and observable responses to stress described by Ulrich. We recognize these as the "adrenaline rush." Only recently have scientists understood how intimately connected our immune systems are with neural and endocrine responses. Very often our felt response to stress is translated into activities in our very cells. Evidence from the emerging field of psychoneuroimmunology lends credence to the supposition that what we feel influences body function not only on the organ system level but on a cellular and molecular level as well.

We know, for example, that human lymphocytes (the warriors of our immune response to disease) have receptors on their surface for numerous hormones (thyroid, growth hormone, growth hormone releasing factor, and others), as well as for such neuropeptides as endorphins.[26] This was a very early and surprising finding. It was unexpected because we know that our bodies rarely have unnecessary receptor sites; their presence therefore meant that these hormones had to interact with the highly specific lymphocyte receptors on a molecular level. The implications of the discovery that central nervous system peptides and endocrine hormones had an effect on immune function are profound. We know that stressors can suppress both T-lymphocyte transformation into killer cells and B-lymphocyte differentiation into antibody-producing cells. We need both kinds of lymphocytes and their products to fight off various infections and cancers. The recognition that beta-endorphins, or β-endorphins—narcotic-like peptides in the brain that may reduce pain—and lymphocytes interact at receptor sites raises questions about the role of the immune system in distraction from pain, pain relief, and peacefulness of dying. That β-endorphins have been found in all these instances suggests that their narcotic-like effects play an important role in stress reduction and general well-being. It has been proposed, for example, that the "runner's high" experienced after vigorous exercise and the calm experienced after injury may both be generated by such endorphins.

The web of infinitely complex interactions between environment and consciousness is mediated by the molecules and structures of our neural pathways, which in turn control macromolecules that mediate both the sensed and the myriad unconcious physiological responses of our bodies. Our acutely felt responses to stress can, for the present, be defined only in laboratory test tubes. The molecular responses are no less potent than our perceived stress reactions, and, more important, they may be the pathways through which nature works its restorative power. What is it that makes our molecules respond—how does nature relax us and soothe our senses—and why have our physiological responses evolved in this way—to be so sensitively attuned to the natural world?

When we are tranquil, all the biological hubbub is quieted down and reversed. Any decrease in stress can bring this about, but nature, uniquely and with singular rapidity and consistency, restores us to physiological and felt homeostasis. Edward O. Wilson's *Biophilia* suggests that our ties to nature are in fact biologically based and part of our evolutionary heritage.[27] Wilson believes that our humanity derives in large part from our connectedness to other species, both flora and fauna. For our purposes the biophilia hypothesis is important because it traces the roots of our response to nature, and hence gardens, back to the same evolutionary soil in which consciousness and culture evolved.[28]

We began as a sentient species on the African savannah—grassy plains dotted with trees and groves of vegetation, and denser woods near rivers and lakes—and whenever we can, we choose to be in savannah-like places.[29] We make our parks and our gardens look like the savannah. The attraction of the savannah, though, is not merely fortuitous but intimately linked with our capacity for survival. Survival of early *Homo sapiens*, like that of all animal species, depended on the ability to read the landscape to detect clues that would enhance survival. Jay Appleton suggests that our present responses to landscape derive from the biological necessity of habitat selection.[30] We had to choose habitats for their safety from predators and their ability to provide sustenance. The savannah provided the key elements that satisfied our survival needs—prospect and refuge:

prospect, the ability to see threats coming; refuge, places that were safe from predators and offered sources of food. At this point in our evolution, habitat selection for most of us is no longer key to survival, yet the neural pathways selected and evolved over eons still respond to such settings. It is likely that this evolutionary residue is precisely what makes contact with nature so important and so soothing. Habitat selection has been transformed from an imperative for survival to a source of pleasure and relaxation. Our brains may no longer be poised to recognize every beneficial or threatening nuance in the landscape, but they certainly derive a biological balm from contact with the natural. As Ulrich and his colleagues have shown in "Stress Reduction," in virtually every study of contact with nature, people mention stress reduction as one of the most important benefits. There are exceptions, however: the bush cannot be too dense, lest we get lost in it; the trees cannot be so high that they offer us no protection. Perhaps that explains why forests too dense and too dark induce biophobia—Ulrich's term for those aspects of nature we find threatening, preserved in our biological responses and in our myths.[31]

Our response to nature, to landscape specifically, whether positive or negative (biophilic or biophobic) occurs in two stages. The first is the near-instantaneous decision either to explore a place or to move from it. The second stage of response occurs after we decide to stay.[32] In health care settings the first stage is the crucial decision to stay and to be calmed. What in a garden helps us make that decision?

The elegant studies of Gordon Orians and Judith Heerwagen on landscape aesthetics confirm the evolutionary bases for our choices.[33] When we choose the contours of our gardens, parks, and cemeteries—our places of respite—our choices are made in response to needs molded by our evolutionary past. To survive, we needed food and water, places where we could see and not be seen, climbable trees offering prospect and escape, and room to move. When budget and location are not limiting factors, we choose to live on open tree-studded prominences overlooking water.[34] Wilson has called this the savannah gestalt.[35] Orians and Heerwagen have shown these choices of savannah-like habitats to be remarkably consistent in detail. In preference studies using paintings, photographs, and video, people prefer open, distant views with scattered trees and copses, water and tame grazing animals, refuges and paths that suggest ease and movement. Landscape paintings with these ingredients are by far our favorites.[36]

Even beyond landscape as a whole image we prefer individual trees to remind us of savannah. The trees we like most have short trunks (easier to climb), broad canopies (greater protection from sun and rain), and flowers (sources of food). In other words, they resemble the acacia, the icon of the African savannah.[37] In our visual arts, in our garden art, in our places of refuge and tranquility, we select these forms.

We evolved in the savannah; and it is the savannah that entices us and soothes us. Whether we turn to Appleton's hypothesis about habitat selection for prospect and refuge, the Kaplans' thesis about the interaction between coherence and mystery, Orians and Heerwagen's view of the selection preferences imposed by evolution, or Wilson's biophilia hypothesis, it is clearly rooted in our evolutionary memory that particular trees, this particular open landscape, provide respite from the harshness of a dangerous, wild earth. In the savannah gestalt, all these theories come together.

It has been proposed that art may have the same biophysical evolutionary origins. Ellen Dissayanake has suggested that there is an inherent biological need to "make special."[38] Initially, acts of art were associated with important human events—birth, death, transition, and they evolved into a more purely aesthetic expressions as their link to life's rhythms became less powerful. We would argue, however, that landscape is a much more potent connection to our evolutionary past. For while art may have been associated with important moments, being sensitive to the nuances of landscape was *essential to survival*, and it is

more than likely that the neurobiological vestiges of a vitally necessary impulse toward habitat selection remain intact. The fact that people who have never seen an acacia or a savannah are uniformly attracted to savannah-like settings suggests some precognitive basis for the preference. That great gardens, certainly of Western and Eastern cultures, consistently propose landscape designs with savannah-like features and views confirms the consistency of choice and suggests origins more distant than those of learned response. The work of Appleton and Orians and Heerwagen has extended such concepts to general aesthetics; and surely the symbolism we see in gardens and nature inspires our art. Without a doubt, the savannah gestalt has played an evolutionary role in shaping our sensibilities.

But it is more than just aesthetics that evolution colors. It forms our biophysical and biopsychological response to nature. Here we are speaking of something other than the "good vibes" of paramedical or alternative therapies.[39] While numerous therapeutic modes—meditation, for example—influence our psyches and relax our bodies, none act as directly as contact with nature. To experience the healing effects of the garden requires no special preparation: we are all evolutionarily prepared for its benefits, even if we have never seen a garden.

We know from the Kaplans' work that our responses to gardens are a balancing act between diversity and complexity and the need for coherence and legibility, not forgetting the elusive sense of mystery. When these are not in balance, we may suffer from the biophobia that Ulrich describes, but it appears that little is required to achieve the minimal balance: contact with nature quickly has a positive effect. As Rachel Kaplan has pointed out and as numerous "window studies" have confirmed, the sheer "thereness" of green nature is enough to soothe us. Charles Lewis gives us numerous examples, from slums to arboretums, of places where contact with nature makes us feel better.[40] The key point is that it is noncognitive. We need not have learned about gardens or landscape aesthetics, we need no prior nature experience to be calmed by a garden. This soothing takes place at the most basic physiological levels. Our brain synapses seem prepared for it. The neural Darwinism proposed by Edelman would certainly prepare our modern brains for the ministrations of the garden. The atavistic need for habitat selection assuredly determines the evolution of the synaptic pathways in the brain that modulate our responses to nature. Savannah is the image that appeases the brain. When we see, hear, smell, or touch nature, those synapses are stimulated by the pulse of recognition.

When nature puts our nerves at ease, the complex interaction of neuropeptides and endocrine hormones that relaxes us takes place. Nature's balm begins in our evolution-prepared central nervous systems; it fires our neuroendocrine and neuroimmune systems. Ulrich's measurements of blood pressure, muscle tension, and alpha-wave activity are just the macrobiological tip of the iceberg. We know that after contact with nature, our immune system works better, hormones that promote healing are activated, neuropeptides that ease pain are produced, and we simply and immediately feel better.

Gardens accomplish this uniquely, because they are savannah brought home. A garden is not just green nature, with its subtle variations alternately inspiring aversion and attraction. Rather, a garden is a preselected habitat. It is nature tamed, nature brought down to a human scale. A garden is pure refuge. Laden with the biological symbolism of safety, a garden elicits from us the opposite of the fight-flight reaction to stress and arousal: nature stimulates the physiology of serenity and recuperation. Gardens help us heal, and where healing is not possible, gardens can bring peace to the dying.

At the Rusk Institute, the Enid A. Haupt Glass Garden pool (left) with its plants and fish welcomes visitors to the greenhouse and its connected gardens, used for therapy, recreation, and relaxation. *(Photo: © 1996, Karen S. R. Balogh)*

Howard A. Rusk
Institute of Rehabilitation Medicine

New York, New York

The practice of the art of medicine is always a cooperative undertaking: the success of medical interventions reflects on the knowledge and skill of the healers and depends on the constitution, will, and restorative powers of the patient. Nowhere does this interdependence of caregivers and patients stand out more clearly than in a rehabilitation hospital, whose patients suffer from deformities, paralysis, loss of muscle and nerve functions, and loss of limbs. Here the caregivers and the cared-for must have a common vision of a life freed from total dependency while they work at the task of building up surviving bodily functions and developing new skills.

Dr. Howard Rusk fully understood the many elements that must work together in any successful course of rehabilitation. He stressed the need to attend to "the whole person," and this outlook, in turn, led him to build gardens at his hospital. The gardens were a reflection of his concern to provide restorative environments for his patients, children and adults.[1] There are four gardens at the Howard A. Rusk Institute of Rehabilitation Medicine of the New York University Medical Center: a children's play yard, the Enid A. Haupt Glass Garden for patient visits and horticultural therapy, and two sitting and strolling gardens for patients, visitors, and staff—the Enid A. Haupt Perennial Garden and the Alva and Bernard F. Gimbel Garden. This cluster of four gardens functions as an important element in the clinical processes and the environment of the Rusk Institute. In their diversity they demonstrate what can

be accomplished even in a hostile urban site of high-rise buildings beset by automobile traffic, noise, and polluted air and lacking in sunlight.

The Rusk Institute of Rehabilitation Medicine is but one small element in a vast medical complex that stretches along 1st Avenue in New York City from the Veterans Hospital at 23rd Street, through the Bellevue Hospital of the City of New York, and on to the New York University Tisch Hospital and ends at the Rusk at 34th Street. Rusk is a 152-bed rehabilitation hospital within a confederacy of institutions. The New York University Medical Center, its clinics, hospitals, special services, and medical school, is responsible for managing its own facilities and also for staffing many of the services at Bellevue and the Veterans Hospital in its capacity as supervisor of the teaching beds in these two giant affiliates. Since World War II the thrust of the New York University Medical Center has been toward keeping up through research with the most advanced techniques. As a rehabilitation center, the Rusk takes an approach to patient environments based on much longer patient stays than elsewhere in the confederacy. The average patient stay at New York University's Tisch Hospital in 1993 was 8.7 days; at the Rusk it was 35.3 days.[2]

History

The Rusk Institute and its programs grew out of the convergence of two events: the push for expansion by the New York University medical leadership, and the experiences of a St. Louis physician during his wartime service in the U.S. Army Air Force.

Howard A. Rusk (1901–1989) left his St. Louis practice of internal medicine in 1942 for an assignment to the U.S. Army Air Force hospital at the Jefferson Barracks in the same city. Characteristically, at the outset of his military career he saw medical problems as connected with psychological and social ones. First off, he confronted the problem of how to manage a pack of bored nineteen- and twenty-year-olds, patients too weak for military drill but too strong for hospital confinement. After a series of misadventures, Rusk developed a Convalescent Training Program for physical training and military instruction that helped the young men to manage the transition back to active duty (1–16). Next, as those injured during the war began to return to the United States, Rusk witnessed planes discharging men who had lost limbs and others who had suffered horrifying burns. These broken men reminded Rusk of the terrible record of World War I casualties and of his own helplessness with the stroke patients in his former private practice.

I recall someone asking me how paraplegics had lived up to that time. The answer was, except in extremely rare cases, they usually died—their life expectancy in those days was often less than a year. They got terrible bedsores, developed kidney and bladder problems, and simply lay in bed, waiting for death. It was almost the same with strokes. The old wives' tale was that you had one stroke, and then you sat around waiting for a second one, or a third one, or however many it took to kill you. If you had any kind of brain injury affecting your locomotive functions, everyone assumed your life was finished. [42–43, 79]

The need to respond to this suffering led Rusk to the discovery of the world of rehabilitation. In 1943 the specialty was a patchwork of efforts, all far removed from the center of medical attention. Rusk's own medical school, the University of Pennsylvania, had appointed a professor of physical medicine, but his work attracted little attention from the faculty or community. During World War I the Red Cross had funded the Institute for Crippled and Disabled, and several states and the federal government offered limited aid, but the work of all these specialists was divided between the provision of prosthetics and the adjunctive physical therapies of massage and exercise. As late as 1943, the Veterans Administration had no organized rehabilitation programs (44).

Initially, Rusk focused on retraining the least damaged so they could be placed in useful Air Force jobs. Then he turned his attention to the harder task: "to bring the severely injured man back to mental as well as physical health." He thought it essential that these patients be taken out of the environment of military hospitals and placed in surroundings "that would improve their outlook." He located a corporate recreation center in Pawling, New York, where he set up his pioneer rehabilitation program (44–45).

The Air Force, however, had no doctors or therapists trained for such work. Fortunately, Rusk learned that during that summer of 1943 Columbia University would offer a course on the care of the disabled, and through that listing he met Dr. George G. Deaver of the Institute for the Crippled and Disabled. Deaver immediately set up a training program for the Air Force personnel and later joined Rusk in his projects (48). Rusk's approach had always been to personalize treatment as much as he could, and one of the unique features of the Army Air Force rehabilitation service was its assignment of an individual physician to each patient (69).

Later he recalled with pride the success of his convalescent and rehabilitation programs. "We discovered that we had saved at least forty million man-hours of duty time, and that we had gotten more sick or injured men back on duty than any branch of service had done during any war in history. More important, we had prepared thousands of boys for useful roles in civilian life after the war who might otherwise have wasted away for years in veterans hospitals" (75–76). Later on, when General Omar Bradley took command of the Veterans Administration, he made Rusk's programs for rehabilitation a regular part of the Veterans Administration services (73).

When Dr. Rusk returned to St. Louis he began canvassing his colleagues about the possibilities for setting up a rehabilitation service for civilians. He knew that during the war 17,000 servicemen had suffered amputations, but that during those same years 120,000 civilians had lost limbs and 350,000 Americans were being permanently disabled every year (85, 97). The orthopedists he spoke with felt that they had already addressed the problem, but Rusk, as always, saw rehabilitation as something more than retraining people to move their limbs: "It was true that they had adopted some good methods of therapy. But they failed to see my point: the whole person needed rehabilitation, not just the part of him that had been damaged. They had no concept of the emotional problems which follow disability, or the problems of job placement, or the other fundamentals behind our philosophy" (77).

In 1941 Bellevue Hospital established a department of rehabilitation medicine in cooperation with the nearby Institute for the Crippled and Disabled (23rd Street and 1st Avenue), then an affiliate of Columbia University. This institute had been founded during World War I to give vocational training to the disabled. Aided by a small grant from Bernard Baruch, the New York University Medical School incorporated the Bellevue unit into a new department of physical medicine in 1945. Thereupon, the dean, Donald Sheehan, began a search for a man to direct the new training and clinical unit (77).[3]

In December 1945 Dr. Rusk moved from St. Louis to New York to become the director of the New York University (NYU) Department of Physical Medicine and to work with Dr. Deaver in managing two wards at Bellevue Hospital. Here they moved beyond the traditional therapies of heat, light, water, and massage. Rusk credited Deaver with placing the emphasis in rehabilitation on the necessities of independent daily living, and with developing detailed measures and practices to help patients master the specifics. At Bellevue, for example, they set up practice curbs and moved in half of an old bus so that

Dr. Howard Archibald Rusk, M.D. (1901–1989), in a photo taken in October 1986. Known as the father of rehabilitation medicine, Dr. Rusk developed rehabilitation procedures that have become part of standard medical practice throughout the world. *(Photo courtesy of New York University Medical Center.)*

people could regain skills essential to city living (87–88, 90).

Because Bellevue was a municipal hospital offering its services to residents of New York City, it could not treat outsiders, many of whom wanted to take advantage of the new methods. At this time, too, Dr. Rusk had met with representatives of the United Mine Workers Welfare Fund, an organization that had a long list of severely injured coal miners waiting for help. Rusk's goal now became to establish a permanent rehabilitation service attached to a university medical school and training hospital. Fortunately, by 1947 New York University had purchased for one dollar the cleared Urban Renewal site of eleven acres between 30th and 34th Streets, 1st Avenue and the East River.

Enid A. Haupt, a friend of Dr. Rusk and benefactor of the Rusk Institute, standing in the Enid A. Haupt Glass Garden in the 1960s. Mrs. Haupt funded the construction and left an endowment for the Glass Garden, as she would do decades later for the Perennial Garden. *(Photo courtesey of Enid A. Haupt)*

NYU was planning to build a new medical campus there. Rusk began by opening a temporary facility while he raised funds for his permanent hospital.

In 1948, with money raised from the Milbank Memorial Foundation, the supporters of the old Institute for the Crippled and Disabled, and a loan from NYU, he was able to open a temporary forty-bed hospital on 38th Street. Rusk proudly wrote that the new facility offered "physical therapy, occupational therapy, physical rehabilitation, social service, vocational guidance and testing, plus prosthetic services." They even had the first model kitchen designed by Lillian Gilbreth to teach disabled housewives how to keep house from a wheelchair (113).

Rusk proved to be more than a successful medical administrator; he was an evangelist for rehabilitation and a compelling fund-raiser. In 1951 he opened his brand new Institute of Physical Medicine and Rehabilitation (later called the Howard A. Rusk Institute of Rehabilitation Medicine) with a four-story building at 34th Street and 1st Avenue, the first unit to be located at the new New York University medical campus. In 1954 he added three more floors on top to bring the facility up to its present 152 beds—117 for adults and 35 for children. By 1968 he was able to open an eight-story research building adjacent to his hospital.[4]

These Rusk buildings, triumphs of his engaging optimism and solid medical achievements, were built according to the fashions of the 1950s and 1960s and were fueled by the contemporary enthusiasms of New York City's federal Urban Renewal projects, as were the New York University Hospital buildings that followed.

Taste at that time directed architects to build simple forms, ideally elegant architectural masses. Far from exploiting the landscape to make the buildings habitable, they ignored the natural features of the sites in favor of hard surfaces, sculptural buildings, and the latest mechanical equipment for elevators, heating, air-conditioning, and ventilation. The East River is not a focus of the Rusk hospital despite its historical significance to Manhattan Island and the pleasant views from the 1st Avenue site. The river and the island lie along the Atlantic flyway, but birds and bird habitats were not taken into account. Similarly, the underlying rock, the foundation for the tall buildings and the railroad tunnels beneath the site, has been ignored. Nature was forgotten in the initial designs. It required a sponsor for its presence to be once again recognized.

Dr. Rusk had been raised in rural Missouri and had spent his days in a country suburb of St. Louis. He believed that natural settings promoted a return to health. As a result, over the years of his directorship he built four gardens to promote the well-being of his patients, visitors, and staff and to support the physical and occupational therapy programs. Since his death in 1989, a fifth garden has been built to replace one of the original four, an open-air rooftop space that has been abandoned.

The first garden was a greenhouse located near the 34th Street entrance to the hospital. The records indicate that its founders, Dr. Rusk and Enid A. Haupt, the donor, intended to combine the pleasures of visiting a garden space with some possibilities for patient gardening. A dozen years after its founding, Dr. Rusk referred to the greenhouse as the Therapeutic Greenhouse. He recalled a dinner party in which he asked for Mrs. Haupt's aid in constructing a greenhouse.

The Institute had just been built and we were already crowded with severely disabled and distressed human beings. I told her that I felt the erection of a therapeutic greenhouse would be of incalculable inspiration to those courageous people who were actually fighting for their lives. To work in it would be to help them live with dignity and independence. She liked the idea and the Therapeutic Greenhouse was born. It included a beautiful reflection pool [and] . . . wide aisles so that wheelchairs could go between the benches; planters with bright flowers, and also birds and fish.[5]

On May 13, 1959, the Enid A. Haupt Glass Garden opened. The greenhouse is located on the northwest

The Alva and Bernard F. Gimbel Garden at the Rusk Institute was designed by Martin H. Cohen, FAIA (Fellow, American Institute of Architects), of Skidmore, Owings & Merrill. It can be seen from the outpatient physical therapy department and is used for ambulatory therapy sessions. Staff members often eat lunch in this garden, and inpatients and their families also use it, especially on weekends. (Photo: © 1996, Karen S. R. Balogh)

side of the hospital, in a place that, since the building of the research wing, is shaded. No papers survive today indicating why this site was chosen in preference to a roof garden, although it seems that the builders intended the greenhouse to give a cheerful and welcoming effect to the entrance.[6] From the outset a gardener tended the plants and supplied plants to the patient floors. It took some time, however, for the Occupational Therapy Department to teach its staff and others about how to use the greenhouse.

In the fall of 1959 Elizabeth Hannesson of Occupational Therapy started a program for brain-damaged patients that lasted two hours per day.[7] By July 1960 the decision seems to have been made to place the greenhouse under the supervision of the Occupational Therapy Department, an arrangement that continues to this day. The staff at that time consisted of a gardener, an occupational therapist, and volunteers. Volunteers helped keep the greenhouse open from nine to four, and half a dozen or so children regularly visited for therapy. Adults, however, shied away from the greenhouse, being reluctant to brave the cold to cross the small space between the greenhouse and the front hallway.[8] The idea of a horticultural therapist combining the skills of a gardener and an occupational therapist had not yet reached New York City.

By October 1960, however, Clark and Hannesson had worked out a modern program for multiple garden use. Their long memorandum to Dr. Rusk was directed against a prevalent idea that "the garden is not real therapy," that it is a passive recreational space and "an evasion of more dynamic treatment." They countered their fellow staff members' reluctance to prescribe greenhouse activities for patients by proposing three overlapping functions for the facility.

First, the supply of flowers and greenery to otherwise drab window sills is important in creating a relaxed and living atmosphere throughout the Institute.

Second, . . . the healing properties of work with plants and soil have long been recognized and have been used intermittently in this setting for diversional and avocational purposes with adults and as a children's play area.

This recreational work relates directly to one of the central occupational therapy goals: "to animate psychic energies."

Finally, the bulk of the memorandum devoted itself to lists of specific physical therapy and occupational therapy tasks, ranging from "general strengthening of the upper extremities through hand-eye-arm coordination to fine dexterity."[9]

About a decade later, the practices recommended in this memorandum were published by Howard D. Brooks and Charles J. Oppenheim in an influential Institute of Rehabilitation Medicine Monograph that was to advance the profession of horticultural therapy.

The late 1960s and early 1970s were also a time when Dr. Rusk built three more gardens. At the dedication of the greenhouse Dr. Rusk spoke with Enid Haupt and Bernard Baruch about establishing a children's play yard. In 1970, as part of the general landscaping that accompanied the building of the research wing and the establishment of the Gimbel Garden, the small Jessie Stanton Playground was built.

The Alva and Bernard F. Gimbel Garden was a gift from that couple, who had long been supporters of Dr. Rusk and the New York University Medical Center. Their garden is a sheltered place, facing east, next to the East Side Highway. It opened October 3, 1969.[10] Like the greenhouse, the children's garden, and the Gretchen Green Rainbow Roof, the Gimbel Garden was to contribute to Dr. Rusk's goal of a lively atmosphere combining energy and repose. "The place does not look like a hospital. It is a tempest inside four walls, with wheelchairs flying past, people on crutches, kids on tricycles—doctors, nurses, and visitors rushing up and down the halls. Nobody spends the day in bed unless he's actually ill. Disability is no excuse for inactivity. The patient goes to work the minute he arrives, and that's what accounts for the high-spirited atmosphere. We don't give people time to brood about themselves. . . . It's a happy place."

Rusk went on to write of the Gimbel Garden: "On the East River side of the institute is another garden—trees, fountains, comfortable benches, where patients can sit in the sunshine in the beautiful quiet atmosphere that seems far removed from the hustle and traffic noises of First Avenue" (87–88, 90).

The different gardens were to have their reinforcing functions: the greenhouse and the children's play yard for therapy and play, the Gimbel Garden for rest and quiet, and the roof area for parties and play. The roof garden was a gift of Gretchen Green, a longtime volunteer. It opened in 1970 on top of the seven-story patients' building. The province of the Recreation Department, this garden, the Rainbow Roof, featured umbrella-shaded tables, lounge chairs, crab apple trees, and flower boxes. A brochure described it as a "tiny sky park which affords a beautiful view of the East River and Manhattan Skyline."[11] For some reason, the roof garden was not kept up, and by 1986 it had lost most of its trees and flowers. That year a leak was discovered in the roof; the garden was torn up and not replaced.

In 1991, after Dr. Rusk had died, Enid Haupt gave another garden to the hospital. This time she arranged for the planting of a four-thousand-foot open space next to the greenhouse—as a perennial garden overlooked by a glassed-in room off the main entry hall. This garden not only supplements the greenhouse but offers some of the same recreational activities as the old Rainbow Roof.

The Gardens

When gardens exist in health care settings, they, like gardens everywhere, fuse culture and place in ways that meet our most basic needs. They express what we are and what we want to be. Gardens shelter, protect, and nourish us. Usually there is a natural place from which to begin, a place that inspires and challenges, one that is reflected or enhanced in the garden's design. But a garden can be built even in a hostile set-

ting, in a place where nature has been obliterated, under the most challenging conditions—as long as someone has the vision and the will to do it. A few individuals can accomplish great things—and bring the personality of the place to life.

SENSE OF PLACE

The sense of place at the Rusk Institute is determined by several powerful forces; the City of New York, the culture and form of the health care setting, and the individuals who champion its gardens. New York is to some a harsh, aggressive place, dirty, noisy, and overwhelming. To others, it is a vibrant, energizing place brimming with life and culture. The scale of high-rise buildings, the unrelenting paved surfaces and pace of life can make its inhabitants feel insignificant and disadvantaged even if they are in the peak of health. At the same time, few places offer such richness and variety of experience found in so small a geographic area. To be ill and facing long-term disability in this city is almost unimaginable, yet life can again be full once a person has the opportunity to convalesce, relearn to ride public transportation, and regain access to shops, museums, concert halls, and parks. At the Rusk Institute, this recovery is made possible slowly and gradually. The gardens and their horticultural therapy program play an important role in advancing patients from often complete dependency to complete independence, if they are fortunate.

As part of New York University Medical Center, the Rusk Institute occupies an unusual niche. Known as a tertiary-care hospital, NYU Medical Center delivers specialized high-intensity patient care, pursues basic science and clinical research, and trains health care specialists. It and others like it are at the top of the health care hierarchy, garnering copious government and philanthropic resources. The teaching at these bastions of technology has shaped American medicine, molding the thoughts and values of nurses, physicians, and therapists around quantitative analysis and scientific methodology. Rarely do these institutions have a link to nature that seems to "soften" the cool, rational, sterile (superior) scientific mission and imagery these institutions generally convey. When found in tertiary-care settings, gardens are usually either grandiose statements of institutional power or presentations of nature as a set piece or art object. Patients, family members, students, and even staff members are expected to be impressed by the size, control, and good taste of the institution. Patients are assumed to be too ill, and the staff too preoccupied, to experience "domestic" comforts on a human scale.

As a rehabilitation center, the Rusk Institute occupies one of the lower ranks in the health care hierarchy. Rehabilitation centers are generally characterized by long patient stays, low technology, and low expectations. The goal is restoration and accommodation rather than cure. The limiting factor is the human healing process, both physical and mental, which proceeds at an "untechnological" pace. The very intensity of acute-care hospitals makes lengthy rehabilitation prohibitively expensive and drives patients into less prestigious chronic-care hospitals. It is in these settings, where a return to normalcy is the ultimate goal and where the patients' psyche and motivation count for so much, that domestic-scale gardens are found. Gardens in these centers are often the places most evocative of life before illness or injury, for they often adapt suburban elements to the institutional setting. The gardens allow escape from the clinical realm and serve as a safe means of progression from the hospital room to the outside world. When horticultural therapy programs exist and gardens are staffed professionally, the added dimensions of program development and expertise in the care of plants make them especially rich experiences. They are often in constant use and can have great power and meaning.

The Glass Garden and its two attached outdoor spaces at Rusk Institute are examples of how nature is dealt with in a modern scientific community. As a rehabilitation hospital under the umbrella of a tertiary-care center, the Rusk Institute is limited in its

ability to command attention and resources. But this has both positive and negative aspects. The gardens exist in a small space not otherwise needed for institutional priorities. The garden staff must make an unremitting effort to maintain a link to the rehabilitation services of the Rusk Institute. The gardens and garden staff are tolerated, not embraced. But where the garden culture at Rusk does not receive attention or significant monies from the administration, neither does it feel the impact of scrutiny or intervention. As long as it furthers the broad mission of the institution, does not challenge the supremacy of the scientific approach, and does not cost too much, it is allowed to function in its own sphere. Thus the institute is a place of innovation and experimentation, where new clinical, educational, and research programs flourish like its plants.

Ultimately, gardens express the personality of the gardener, and at the Rusk Institute a strong belief that contact with nature is a universal and primal need has been translated to both physical form and program development. Nancy Chambers, director of the Enid A. Haupt Glass Garden and Horticultural Therapy Program since 1986, has developed gardens and horticultural programs to sustain all at the Rusk Institute—patients, visitors, and staff. A large and diverse collection of plants, with birds, fish, and amphibians living among them, serves as a touchstone to individuals of diverse cultures. Chambers says that whether they are from suburban Long Island, the Caribbean, or the Philippines, garden visitors "find a piece of their hearts here" (interview with Nancy Chambers, March 28, 1997). This is a magical place, a totally encompassing garden world in which to find quiet recreation, relaxation, and refreshment. The Glass Garden can transport its inhabitants out of the city, out of the clinical setting, perhaps even out of the ill or injured bodies that have so consumed their recent attention. The Rusk Institute gardens are also civilized places, though removed from harsh realities and proffering rare pleasures. In addition, horticultural therapy for patients, training for health care professionals, a vocational rehabilitation program, and research in areas like integrated pest management and stress reduction in cardiac patients also take place in the garden. The gardens may seem remote from illness, work, and the surrounding city, but in reality, they are designed to be fully linked with the lives and needs of the people at the Rusk Institute.

There are four gardens at the Rusk Institute and several more in the New York University complex. Each has a different purpose and style. The Rusk Institute gardens are relatively small, and three of the four—the Glass Garden, the perennial garden, and the children's play yard—are connected, occupying one site. Horticultural therapy takes place in the greenhouse and perennial garden. Their design is domestic in scale. The ambience is subdued but intense, with the exuberant plant displays and quiet social activity. The fourth, the Gimbel Garden, occupies a separate location. It is not seen from the public areas, and no corridors lead directly to it, so its existence is almost a secret. This sublime space offers visitors a troughlike pool with bubbling fountains and the dappled shade of rows of honey locust (*Gledtsia tricanthos*) trees. Its forms are geometric and its colors subtle, and despite the noise from the nearby Franklin Delano Roosevelt Drive, it is a remarkably contemplative space. The physical therapy department, whose wall of windows looks into the garden, employs it as a training ground for walking. Staff members hold informal meetings and eat lunch in this garden.

Other gardens at the health care center may have a stronger visual presence, but their designs are less suited to direct use. Opposite the glass-walled front entrance to the New York University Medical Center is a large garden of simple but strong design. Light streams down between the buildings and illuminates a lawn and a few trees. It is striking—a large and elegant city space that can be seen from 1st Avenue through the glass walls of the building's large lobby. A contained vision of a landscape park, beautiful but not intended for direct use, it establishes an almost corporate presence. The grass and trees are in a raised area, surrounded by steps and loose crushed stone. Even if physical disabilities did not prevent the patients from using it, the garden has been framed in a way to imply that it is something to be looked at but not touched. People do make use of it, of course, but crowded in the corner by the glass doors, often smoking, they diminish the integrity of the garden's "hands off" design.

Another, smaller garden nearby occupies a site at the entrance to the New York University School of Medicine. It is of modern design, a good geometric composition featuring a few plants. It could be a museum courtyard. It has little to do with living, growing, changing things. It is about art, perfection—difficult themes to represent in a garden. Were it more private, it could assume the role of a contemplative garden. In its present location, however, it is a pleasure to look at in passing.

Still another garden, although undistinguished and noisy, is heavily used, for it is adjacent to a cafeteria. Medical students and staff swarm to its tables in good weather.

Each of these gardens has a role to play. Each makes a contribution to the life of the medical center. The variety of their designs suggests an attempt to move beyond the obvious need for something to fill the space between buildings and take a step toward meeting the complex needs of the medical center and its people.

SITE HISTORY

The land on which the Rusk Institute sits was created from wetlands developed over a period of two hundred years, then obliterated and redeveloped after World War II under an urban renewal program. As with most such urban renewals, all that existed before was lost and is now almost impossible to imagine. Only the name Kip's Bay survives as a reminder of another time and place. Massive towers surround the Rusk Institute, casting shadows and ensuring a high population density in the neighborhood. A ventilation stack for the Long Island Railroad tunnel forms a wall of the perennial garden. Marshland near the shoreline was filled in, and a highway, the Franklin Delano Roosevelt Drive, was constructed beginning in 1936 to connect the newly opened Triborough Bridge to the downtown. The presence of the drive, projecting both shadow and noise, is strongly felt, especially in the Gimbel Garden.

Yet it was the natural conditions that shaped the development, beginning in the seventeenth century. Jacobus Kip owned a farm in this area, "a goodly estate, covering one hundred and fifty acres, and comprising meadow, woodland, and stream."[12] His land extended eastward to a bay subsequently named Kip's Bay. He, along with Peter Stuyvesant, was one of the few landowners of Manhattan at this time. In 1655 Kip built a mansion of imported brick for his young bride, Marie de la Montagne (the house remained standing for almost two hundred years). During the Revolutionary War, it was at Kip's Bay that British frigates anchored on September 15, 1776, to take over Manhattan Island, and there they remained for the duration of the war.[13]

In the early nineteenth century this region was the site of the country estates of many prominent New Yorkers, among them the editor Horace Greeley.[14] Although the land was low and marshy, it was mapped in 1851 as part of a grid of streets, numbered as they are today, and was developed in the cheapest fashion. "Much of this low land has been filled in; and wherever the original course of the stream is obstructed, the tendency of the water is to percolate through the loose soil thus making it damp and insalubrious. . . . On First Avenue and the grounds adjoining . . . the water penetrates to the cellars when the tide is high."[15] Essentially a service area to midtown, Kip's Bay was developed with breweries, laundries, foundries, carriage factories, slaughterhouses with their attached holding pens, coal and wood yards, and later, power plants. Densely populated, squalid, and inhabited by the poorest of the city's population, in 1865 it was declared a slum by volun-

teer sanitary inspectors.

Because of these slum conditions, the neighborhood had no defense against large-scale construction projects. Big transportation projects in particular shaped both the neighborhood and the hospital site. For many years, from the beginning of the nineteenth century until the construction of the FDR Drive, the Rusk site shoreline served as the link between ferries to Hunter's Point, Queens, and Manhattan streetcars. By 1908 the Bromley map shows this transportation node to have been relocated underground in what is now a Long Island Railroad tunnel. A short distance away, the block on which Saint Gabriel's Church sat was demolished to construct an entrance ramp to the Queens-Midtown Tunnel, and two power plants were built just to the north of the Rusk site.

Bellevue Hospital was long a part of the neighborhood, having been relocated to 27th Street and 1st Avenue in 1816 from what is now City Hall Park. One of the major municipal hospitals, affiliated with what is now New York University School of Medicine, it grew steadily and expanded its services. As it did so, the need for more land became a pressing issue. After World War II the New York City Redevelopment Authority cleared the nearby area from 1st Avenue, and the FDR Drive from Bellevue to 34th Street. The first structures built for the expanding New York University medical community on this unused land were the Rusk buildings.

SITE PLANNING

Rusk Institute occupies a site on the south side of 34th Street between 1st Avenue and the FDR Drive. Designed in the late 1950s, it is a glazed white brick complex with two major wings—a six-story wing for patient care and an eight-story wing for basic scientific research. The buildings form an L with open space on the corner at 1st Avenue and 34th Street. This is the location of the three contiguous gardens, all fenced or walled off from the streets. The Enid A. Haupt Glass Garden is a greenhouse that extends into the center of the open space. On either side of

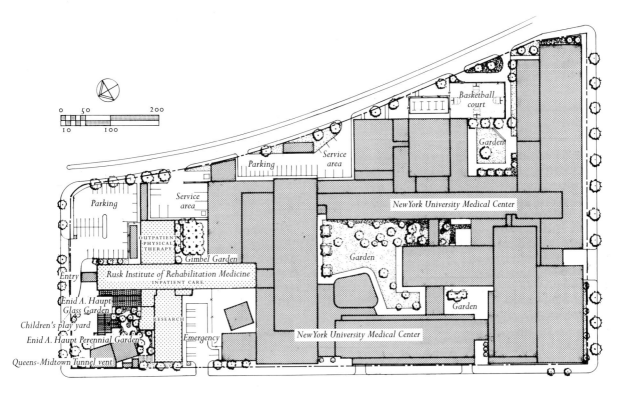

Rusk Institute site plan *(by David Kamp)*.

the conservatory are the two outdoor gardens. The perennial garden, the equivalent of a backyard space, and the play yard for children are now in the process of reevaluation; a new design has been completed and a fund raising effort is almost complete. A fourth garden, the Gimbel Garden, is located on the FDR side of the patient care wing.

The Rusk Institute itself is unmistakably clinical in appearance. Long tiled hallways and hospital beds, wheelchairs, and other equipment dominate the lives of all here. The few domestic touches—artwork, stuffed animals, flowers—are more decorative talismans than the stuff of daily life. Even if one comes to this place of superior reputation with hope of cure or restoration of function, it may be hard to accept that the intensity of the therapeutic regimens allows little pause, little connection with the larger world.

Enid Haupt and Howard Rusk seemed to have realized this at the time of the greenhouse donation. Both had experienced the pleasures of nature and knew that gardens would enhance the institution.

The gardens were not included in the plans for the Rusk Institute, though, and were built in leftover spaces between buildings. They were afterthoughts in a process dominated by the needs of clinical medicine and rigorous therapy. Thus they are gardens built in adverse conditions, and it has required great effort to overcome their settings. Their most basic problems—lack of sunlight, poor ventilation and soil conditions, and inadequate rainwater collection—have been mitigated by the knowledgeable professional garden staff. Plants have been selected for their tolerance of low light and poor ventilation. The soil has been amended, and where it was structurally necessary,

The production-style greenhouse of the Glass Garden is fully wheelchair accessible. The garden has wide aisles and plant benches of varying heights and is filled with plants and animals that could otherwise not live in a temperate climate. Conceived as a place of respite, the Glass Garden has evolved into one where patients receive therapy and go to escape the rigors of the clinical setting. *(Photo: © 1996, Karen S. R. Balogh)*

put into raised planters. Irrigation and hand-watering are routine. Other problems are more difficult to solve. Traffic noises remain audible, despite walls, fountains, and chimes. And because inside the building neither circulation patterns nor important windows reveal the gardens, they are difficult to find. Although the gardens could be a prominent feature and a part of the lives of all at the Rusk Institute, instead, only those who seek them out enjoy their pleasures.

The isolation of the gardens was hardly accidental. It was, in fact, predictable. Modern architecture and planning since World War II has been dominated by mass, not space. Each building is designed to maintain its own integrity, to be viewed as a sculpture, preferably on an open site. Unlike during the late nineteenth and early twentieth centuries, when buildings in great urban spaces were designed to work in concert, during the modernist era relatively little thought has been given to the juxtaposition and interaction of buildings. When the ground plane is used as a pedestal on which to display architecture and space between buildings is ignored, domestic-scale gardens are squeezed onto sites. In this era of cheap energy and climate control, building designs have increasingly denied the natural environment.

Porches and balconies are omitted, now that people no longer sit outside to catch summer breezes, and windows are often sealed. But the denial of nature by the scientific, technological world of health care and by the planning and architecture professions combined could not obliterate the need for gardens. The richness of the garden experience has continued to challenge the contemporary habit of divorcing ourselves from the natural world. Even without a commitment on the part of hospital planners and designers to incorporate nature into the planning process, the gardens which fill the leftover spaces at the Rusk Institute have added a dimension that promotes the goals of the institution as a whole.

If the Rusk Institute is an example of how very useful and pleasing unanticipated, unplanned garden spaces become, other New York City gardens, both large and small, that were designed and built with more forethought in other eras enhance the urban environment considerably. Rockefeller Center affords fine outdoor spaces amid its tall towers. Other spaces throughout the city, from Central Park to Paley Park, from Columbia and Rockefeller Universities to Battery Park City, provide space for both intense activity and quiet contemplation.

THE GLASS GARDEN

Often relying on primitive methods, cultures around the globe have manipulated the environment for millennia, trying to mitigate the harshness of the elements and enhance the pleasant natural effects, pushing the growing season, and extending the plant zone. Erecting edifices to face the sun or putting up barriers to the wind can indeed change the microclimate, but to limited effect. It was not until the eighteenth century, when the technological innovations of the wrought-iron glazing bar and a metal supporting structure were fitted with glass to produce greenhouses and conservatories, that wholly foreign climates could be introduced. Built in northern cold-weather regions and often dramatic in shape and size, greenhouses offered access to an astounding array of tropical

and subtropical plants otherwise never seen. Greenhouses offer more than just an opportunity to view plants, to inspect exotic shapes, textures, and colors at close range. The structures have become so well loved because they provide a total, almost other-worldly experience: warmth, diffuse yet often intense light, humidity, scents, and often birds or small animals.

As the first garden built at the Rusk Institute (and in fact the first altogether at the New York University Medical Center), the Glass Garden holds a special position. Others have been developed over the years and are much appreciated, but this garden remains the heart of the Rusk garden culture. Enid A. Haupt and Dr. Rusk conceived of this hospital garden, a pioneering concept at the time, as a respite, an antidote, a place to escape the rigors of the clinical setting. Since its opening in 1959, it has retained its original character as a place of relief, even as the hard work of therapy is carried on there.

It is open every day and receives more than 100,000 visits per year by people who come to enjoy and learn about plants, to purchase them, or to work with them in their therapy sessions. Approximately 25,000 patient treatments take place each year, of both children and adults, who often share the same work table. Weekends and evenings, the gardens are open for strolling, sitting, talking, and entertaining visitors.

Although it is unclear who ran the conservatory in its earliest years, professional management is usually essential to the success of a greenhouse operation. By 1964, horticulturalist Howard Brooks was named director. Esteemed within the profession, a member of numerous horticultural and ecological societies, he cultivated interests extending beyond plants and nature to classical music and watercolor painting. In his efforts to create an interval of pleasure in the lives of those bound by difficulty, he integrated his other interests as well into the activities in the garden. Concerts were held weekly, and Brooks's own watercolors were displayed in the pavilion adjacent to the conservatory itself. His basic charge, however, was the greenhouse, and he and his undergardeners managed it as an estate or botanical garden conservatory where banks of plants in bloom—azaleas, hydrangeas, and orchids—were brought in, displayed, and then removed. *Vogue* magazine used the greenhouse for fashion photo shoots, and patients competed in the annual flower shows held there. Yet even in these early years, patients were brought down from the clinical units on the upper floors to the greenhouse on the ground floor for one-on-one occupational therapy sessions. The Rusk Occupational Therapy Program was, with the greenhouse managed by Director Brooks, developing and helping to define the profession of horticultural therapy.

Thus began the tradition of the donor and directors' defining and developing the purpose and form of the Glass Garden and building other, later gardens to fit the needs of patients and the institution as they conceived them. Over more than three decades, the greenhouse has been managed by a succession of five directors. Most were horticultural therapists who gradually changed the greenhouse from a display garden with therapeutic uses to a therapeutic garden with plant displays.

The current director, Nancy Chambers, has continued to shape the programs and space. She believes we are a part of nature and need nature in our lives, and these are the values that she interprets for the institution and its population. Aesthetics count for a great deal, but they do not drive the place. The garden is intended less as a visual experience than as an immersion in an all-encompassing environment. It is the life—plants, birds, fish, people—and change—movement of air, patterns of light and shadow, feelings of warmth and humidity, and sounds of nature—that are important here, and the complete sensory experience. Attention is paid to such design elements as contrasting leaf colors, shape, and texture, but a perfect, complete display is not the goal. It is the growth, the vitality that matter: the air is different here, both literally and figuratively. So are the quality of light, the smells, the sounds, the humidity, and the human activity and interaction.

The cornerstone of activity in the Glass Garden is horticultural therapy. Results of exit interviews and focus groups consistently show that patients find horticultural therapy to have been a positive experience, and suggestions for improvement are usually requests for more programs or for the gardens to remain open longer hours on the weekends. During the therapy sessions, the greenhouse work provides an opportunity for restorative manual labor and social interaction in the context of nature. To confront and challenge disability in the quiet company of others is viewed as an important part of the healing process. In addition, horticultural therapy allows patients to reverse the role of being cared for and become the caregivers. As one patient said, "I feel as if I'm creating something. I'm working with life." The plants are tangible proof of patients' productivity, capability, and self-reliance. The Glass Garden seems especially important to patients who were gardeners before they became disabled. "It gives them a big boost. It gives them hope" (September 12, 1996, interview with Nancy Chambers). Ultimately, the goal is to make therapy seem like a respite. Another patient said, "You come down here to get away from the hospital." And all the while, she was working with her hands, improving her upper body strength, coordination, and balance.

At Rusk, working greenhouses have been placed at right angles to each other to form an L shape. The pavilion is half a greenhouse with a shed roof, attached to the building wall, while the Glass Garden is a freestanding "production"-style greenhouse. At their juncture is a small conservatory that serves as an entry hall. These humble forms, architecturally undistinguished, house an ever-changing garden of plants and animals that could otherwise not live in a temperate climate. The stage for this place of enchantment is set by the small conservatory with its terrazzo floor and round terrazzo pool. The glazed walls of this square room are covered with tropical and subtropical plants, some touching the ceiling, others trailing along the walls, still others of more decorous

Horticultural therapy sessions take place in the Glass Garden treatment room in inclement weather and in the Perennial Garden in good weather. Groups often include both children and adults with different kinds of disabilities. *(Photo: © 1996, Karen S. R. Balogh)*

demeanor in pots here and there. The pool is occupied by plants, a fountain, and carp. Its sides are wide enough to perch on for a close look, as children often do. Chairs crowd the corners of the room, allowing intimate contact with the plants, their textures, colors, and scents. As is the case with all of nature, change is constant. Plants grow, overgrow, are pruned, relocated, and replaced. The fountain has been changed over the years from a pool with a modern sculpture at its center to an asymmetrical display of plants and water pouring from a bamboo pipe to a lava stone, surrounded by epiphytes and mosses, from which water

trickles. Nothing is static. Everything could be different again next year.

The sound of birds and music coming from the greenhouse beyond is alluring, yet the view is blocked. The visitor must go around the pool to experience the next pleasure, a tangle of plants on raised benches. Their varying heights allow patients to work on them from a wheelchair. The benches form aisles for viewing plants and birds and double as passageways to a small therapy area. An office, a storage area, and a sales display area are all accommodated within this 1,700-square-foot structure. One corner boasting an

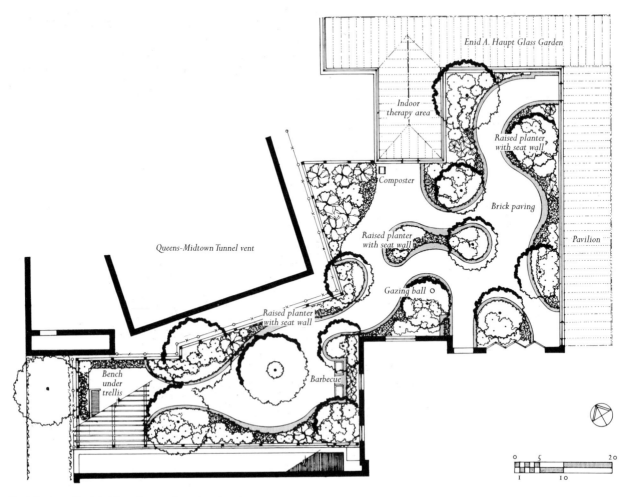

Rusk Institute Enid A. Haupt Perennial Garden plan *(by David Kamp)*.

orchid display is an especially pleasant place to sit and visit.

Both the perennial garden and the conservatory are full to overflowing, reflecting an endless desire to collect, grow, and display plants, which are the vital force in this environment. Each plant is selected for its beauty, interest, and contribution to the garden's variety. Each is known, understood, appreciated. In addition, the conservatory selection intentionally includes many tropical and subtropical plants that attract the attention of the diverse population of the city. Chambers's enthusiasm for plants and her devotion

to tending and sharing them are evident to all who visit—and are contagious. The focus of the collection is plants that can be grown in a New York City apartment, and any patient, visitor, or staff member can obtain the knowledge and materials to grow many of the plants at home. The Rusk Institute gardens as a whole cannot be reproduced, but anyone who is interested can take a part of this place home. Every patient is given a plant, and in the horticultural therapy program patients propagate and care for plants. When patients are discharged, they are encouraged to take their plants with them.

Chambers has begun a kitchen garden with coconut, banana, and pineapple plants. She believes that the more diverse the plants collected, "the more places you have to stop off, the more you hold people's interest." Several of the plant collections—the perennials, orchids, and cacti, for example—are maintained primarily by volunteers. A bonsai collection, once cared for by a bonsai master, was exciting and dynamic, and people gathered to watch him work. But now the plants will probably be removed because the garden, as Chambers says, "has lost the human dimension." Other plants include the Alamanda vine with its yellow blossoms and the Clerodendrum with its red and white flowers. Palms are grown because Chambers once lived in Southeast Asia and has "a special feeling for palms." Jasmine attracts the attention of Filipino staff. Many plants have signs to enable visitors to "read and reach another level of understanding" (all quotations taken from the September 12, 1996, interview with Nancy Chambers).

The conservatory is filled with birds, including zebra finches, Goffin's cockatoos, and diamond and banded-collared doves. Before long, butterflies may be introduced as well.

Chambers considers the Glass Garden's location near the main entrance to the Rusk Institute important to its success and has plans, when the new play yard is constructed, to have a more visible and welcoming entry built. At present, the lobby of the main entrance on 34th Street is small and dark. The garden entry on the side can go unnoticed, although a sign and small cart of plants for sale quietly announce its presence.

Oddly enough, the Glass Garden is a wholly artificial, energy-consuming environment where narrow temperature ranges, vigilant pest control, and continual watering, pruning, and feeding schedules must be carefully maintained. It was built by humans for humans and requires constant care. This is an abstraction of nature, built nature in a built context. This tight, enclosing, safe place, full of life, is a controlled environment in a world out of control. A green oasis

in a paved city, it is a place of both work and pleasure. The first greenhouse of its kind designed to be totally accessible to people in wheelchairs, it has served as a model for other facilities across the country. Newer, larger, grander gardens exist, but the Glass Garden at the Rusk Institute remains pre-eminent, if not in its design, at least in its programming and teaching. In addition to therapy, a broader educational program, the Horticultural Skills Program, is provided in cooperation with the Vocational Services Department. In the program, patients learn the skills necessary for later employment in interior plantscaping, and other plant-related occupations. The staff also lectures and provides workshops and classes on topics that relate to horticultural therapy and to making gardens accessible to the disabled. Chambers is working with a group to help establish minimal environmental standards for health care settings. Despite expertise and national recognition, however, the garden staff remains somewhat isolated within the New York University Medical Center. Chambers and her staff are rarely consulted when new building projects are planned or when existing gardens are redesigned. The institution as a whole is thus deprived of their knowledge and experience in urban horticulture and in dealing with patients, staff, and visitors.

THE PERENNIAL GARDEN

Perennial plants are a gardener's dream. Of endless variety and often bearing beautiful and dependable blooms, these long-lived plants are the mainstay of many gardens in temperate climates. Whether displayed singly as accents or massed together, perennials in combinations of sizes, shapes, textures, and colors can interest a gardener for a lifetime.

This outdoor perennial garden adjacent to the Glass Garden adds dimension to the greenhouse-based program and extends both the range of plants on display and the range of services available. It is a 4,000-square-foot garden, fully wheelchair-accessible, donated by Enid Haupt in 1991. Designed by landscape architects Bruce Kelly and David Varnell, it was

The perennial garden was opened in 1991, funded by Enid A. Haupt, and designed by Bruce Kelly and David Varnell. Its raised beds support dense plantings and provide wall seats on which to rest. The gazing ball (far left) in the perennial garden has its origins in fifteenth-century Europe. It has been seen both as a "wish ball" meant to attract garden fairies and as a "witch ball" intended to frighten off witches. Its mirrored glass reflects the garden. Physical, horticultural, and recreational therapy take place in this garden, and it is visited by patients, staff, guests, and volunteers. *(Photo: © 1996, Karen S. R. Balogh)*

conceived as the backyard space for the Glass Garden. It allows for such recreational functions as barbecuing and dining. Staff members wander through or eat lunch here. Volunteers can be found weeding or pruning. Physical therapists walk in it with patients, and in good weather the horticultural therapy sessions move out of the greenhouse and into the open air.

Raised beds curve throughout the brick-paved space. The planter walls are terra cotta—colored concrete of the right height, width, and texture for seating. The garden reflects the care and expertise of the horticulture staff, who have filled it with a wealth of plants.

Small trees, shrubs, and perennials selected to withstand the low light and harsh conditions of the urban environment fill the planters to overflowing.

Much of what is here is familiar, but the exotic is displayed and often labeled. To strike a chord of familiarity and then spark a new interest or inquiry is a piece of good design and it happens here with ease. Plants include crepe myrtle, amelanchier, dogwood, purple plum, Harry Lauder's Walking Stick, buxus, berberis, climbing rose, spurge, hosta, and astilbe.

The herringbone-pattern brick paving curves throughout the garden, sometimes narrow, other times wide enough to accommodate groups. A secluded arbor with a bench offers privacy difficult to find elsewhere. There is little garden ornament, but a gazing ball, or mirrored ball, occupies a rather prominent location. Although some might regard the ball as kitsch, Chambers can appreciate the gazing ball's historical roots and its playful reflection of the garden. Besides, more than a few patients and staff members will be reminded of the ones in their own yards.

Unlike many gardens in health care settings, those at the Rusk Institute, which aim to include as many facets of life as possible, encourage the visitors to have fun. A compost bin sits outside the potting shed door, and as people pass by, they give it a spin to mix the compost. Recently, Chambers has begun a collection of birdhouses at the Rusk, which will include the cute and the bizarre as well as the exquisite.

In sum, the gardens of Rusk Institute have great impact, in part because they contrast with the city, in part because they are part of a medical setting, but mostly because they are a rich, varied, fulfilling experience. They have the potential to provide physical restoration, social healing, and sustenance for the intellect and the soul. Both spatially and psychologically, they are a place apart, a place of therapy and enjoyment. They allow patients, visitors, and staff to connect with nature, with one another, with themselves.

To the experience of being ill, people bring their previous experiences, perceptions, expectations, and needs. The Rusk Institute affords them the opportunity to benefit from the best of scientific, technological health care without forgetting what is comfortable and familiar—and normal—in daily life. The Rusk provides this domestic component through that which is universally familiar—nature. The gardens were developed without the basic support of planning and architecture and have evolved as a result of need and potential. Innovative in concept and programming, these gardens have triumphed, making nature a part of life when planners and architects failed to. Together, the gardens and staff challenge contemporary notions about living apart from and in contrast to nature.

The gardens at Rusk Institute can be seen as a metaphor. The plants' growth and decay represent similar cycles in the human residents' lives, the times of illness and of vigor. Gardens show us that we can be strong, even when we are less than perfect. Like us, they need nurture and time, have limits and potential, and are buffeted by the forces of life. The staff members tend the plants as they do the patients, valuing the individual as well as the whole. In the end, it is the staff, the knowledge and compassion they bring, the programs they develop, and the gardening they do that make this place the city version of a calm in a storm.

Jeanne Jugan, founder of the Little Sisters of the Poor, portrayed by Leon Brun in 1855. At the time of her death in 1879, her congregation numbered 2,400 Little Sisters, who cared for aged poor of all denominations in ten countries. Today there are 3,000 Little Sisters caring for approximately 45,000 elderly people in thirty countries. *(Photo: J. A. Fortier, courtesy of the Little Sisters of the Poor, Queens Village, New York)*

Queen of Peace Residence

Queens Village, New York

In human affairs, innovations often take place at society's most troubled intersections, the points where a people's cherished values and their commonplace realities mock one another. Here accepted remedies fail and here the divisions between well-being and illth[1] call out loudly.

Thus, in the history of modern education, the needs of children who were not learning in conventional school sequences gave rise to the kindergarten and Head Start, and the deprivations of slum children called forth Montessori's training and the American progressive school movement. Likewise, modern medical practice owes many of its triumphs to its efforts to confront scourges like the epidemics of smallpox, typhoid, cholera, diphtheria, syphilis, tuberculosis, cancer, and AIDS.

The Little Sisters of the Poor are just such a social invention: a challenge to the heedlessness of the modern rush to mill towns and giant cities. The particular crossroads of wealth and poverty at which Little Sisters appeared was in the most ordinary of places, a poor fishing village on the coast of Brittany. There the usual town fathers dispensed the usual municipal relief, and the usual well-to-do women visited the poor. But such local responses could not succeed in the face of the tides of human migration and economic change that were sweeping Europe during the first decades of the nineteenth century. Often nothing seemed capable of counteracting roving bands of unemployed, riots in the countryside, and riots, revolution, and military repression in the cities. Change brought progress to some and dealt destruction to others, but always change bred more change. As Karl Marx wrote in 1848, "All that is solid melts into air, all that is holy is profaned, and man is at last compelled to face with sober senses his real conditions of life, and his relations with his kind."[2] These were times of unrestrained greed and abject suffering; times of the flowering of human ingenuity and the triumph of the spirit.

Two groups suffered disproportionately: children and old people. Historians who have reviewed the conditions of children during those decades allude to the slaughter of the innocents.[3] Such was the pace of the migrations of young people to the mills and mines and factories that the old found themselves stranded in the countryside, deserted by their families, and caught between the collapse of the old rural ways and the emergence of the new industrial culture.

The poverty of Brittany, and the poverty of Saint-Servan, the town where the Little Sisters of the Poor originated, repeated the poverties of a thousand other places in France and Europe. So, too, Jeanne Jugan's innovation can be understood as a fine contribution that reflects yet stands out from the more general humanitarian outpouring of the first half of the nineteenth century. The wide response of comprehension, sympathy, reform, and charity that made up this broad uncoordinated movement was both secular and religious. It was Catholic, Protestant, and Jewish, and its participants and leaders were women as well as men. Even 150 years after these events, we owe many of our institutions of education, health, and welfare to this spate of generosity and civic action.

One of the unique qualities of nineteenth-century humanitarianism derived from the widespread participation of women. Never before had so many women asserted themselves in sustained public action and cast aside their traditional family roles to devote their lives to the new humanitarian projects. Thousands of young women, from Poland to Ireland, from Sweden to Italy, left their mainly rural family settings to serve as teachers, nurses, and social workers.

In Catholic nations or communities, this humanitarian impulse often manifested itself in the establishment of new sisterhoods, and in the rapid rise of orders of noncloistered religious women, whose lives nourished a legion of new schools, hospitals, and charities.

In the general terms of modern humanitarianism, the story is a familiar one: first the initiatives of an exemplary leader, then her formation of a small group, and finally the response of hundreds of young women to her call for human sympathy and service. Although such was the common framework of the sisterhoods, each had its unique progress. In the case of the Little Sisters of the Poor, its founder's inspiration and the conditions of the congregation's founding help explain the continuing vitality of the institution.

Jeanne Jugan (1792–1879) founded the congregation. Much of her life remains obscure because she was not of the writing classes; her personal predilections ran to action and giving witness, not to written exposition. Some documents and recollections have survived from her time and have been gathered up in an official biography that can serve to sketch the nature of her responses and to delineate her enduring contribution to the the Little Sisters of the Poor.[4]

As with many of us, Jeanne Jugan's childhood prefigured the themes of her adulthood: the struggle against abandonment and poverty. Born in 1792 in the small fishing village of Cancale on the north coast of Brittany during the French Revolution, she was the sixth of eight children, of whom five survived for a time. Her father, a Newfoundland fisherman, disappeared, reported dead in 1796. Fortunately, the family owned a few animals and could survive in its one-room rented cottage thanks to the mother's work outside the home. Jeanne learned to read and write, but no record survives of any formal schooling (3–11).

At age sixteen, she found a position four miles from her village as a kitchen maid in the home of a wealthy woman. Toward the end of this domestic service, when she was twenty-two, Jeanne made a crucial decision, one that every poor woman used to face if she wished to pursue some alternative to the life her mother and sisters led. She refused a young man's offer and decided to remain single (15).

The marriage of her two sisters triggered a decision to break away from her home. She gave her sisters her fine clothes and moved to the nearby town of Saint-Servan, where she worked in the hospital of Le Rosais. The hospital functioned more as a poor house than as a medical institution; it sheltered 60 civilians, 217 sailors, and 35 foundling children (19). From 1817 to 1823, Jeanne Jugan worked as a nurse, although she lacked any training save the habit of hard work. It was in this occupation, however, that she began to discover a way for her religious training and impulses to give structure and meaning to her life.

A Eudist mission came to Saint-Servan during her first year at the hospital. The Eudists, wishing to secure some permanent outcome from their revival, established a number of associations, one of which admitted young women from the town. Jeanne joined this Marian congregation, the Third Order of the Heart of Mary, whose members celebrated the Feast of the Assumption with a procession. Jeanne Jugan was remembered as "austere." Surely, she was an outsider by class position and attitude. She told her young associates that she had chosen a life of poverty, and because she was a hospital nurse, she did in fact live that harsh discipline (23).

A few years later she joined the Third Order of the Eudists, a group that followed a regular timetable of prayer in an attempt to lead an ordered religious life at home. This membership and its devotions gave permanent shape and direction to Jeanne Jugan's later life. The Eudists were a seventeenth-century congregation of priests that had been founded by Saint John Eudes (1601–1680) to staff seminaries. They focused on love, first a loving relationship to Jesus, a devotion to his heart, and in addition abnegation of the self with the goal of forming a loving relationship of mutual assistance to all members of the religious society. The order had been reorganized and revived after the French Revolution (22–27). Jeanne Jugan's biographer stresses the Eudist connection because of its religious content and regimen, and because of its later institutional assistance to her.

Did she become exhausted or worn out psychologically? Jeanne Jugan left the hospital in 1823 to become a live-in maid for a spinster woman twenty years her senior, Mlle. Lecoq (1772–1835). A reasonable inference, looking back now to the undocumented past, would be that at this point Jeanne Jugan had the crucial experience of being loved. Nothing in her childhood and early life suggests much personal attention. For the next twelve years she and Mlle. Lecoq, the sister of a priest, lived a quiet religious life together. They attended Mass daily, taught catechism to the parish children, dispensed charity, and lived happily —a moratorium in Jugan's life. It is reasonable also to surmise that Jeanne Jugan came to experience the ideas, habit, and emotions of the love among companions that grounded her religious aspirations. In June 1835 Mlle. Lecoq died. She left Jugan a little money and some furniture. Jeanne Jugan was at that time forty-three years old (29–33).

Now began her seventeen-year mission. First she successfully established a poor women's social network. To support herself, she worked days in Saint-Servan doing housework, washing, and nursing. Many of her employers later became her first financial backers. Then she formed a friendship with another older woman, a former maid and cook for a priest, who had left her a small income. The two women rented a room and attic loft together. The roommate did spinning while Jeanne went out each day. Then the pair took in a fisherman's orphan, Virginie, a seventeen-year-old seamstress. All this time Jeanne Jugan continued her participation in the Third Order of the Eudists (35–40).

In 1839, at the age of forty-seven, Jeanne Jugan pulled together the threads of her life into one coherent pattern. As she did so, she experienced a tremendous release of energy, hope, and empowerment. Her biographer reported that she felt a sense of "thanksgiving and joy" that came from "her renunciation of all self-centeredness, in communion with Jesus, and [her submission] to the Father's will" (40).

At the outset she quit her job, telling her employer that she intended henceforth to devote herself to a life of charity. She said that every day, as she had done her errands in the town market, she had seen the old women begging there and that she felt called to help them. Her mistress gave her the first donation. A few days later, with the consent of her roommates, she took into their rooms an old blind widow who had formerly been cared for by a sister, but the sister had taken ill and died in a hospital. The widow stood abandoned. Next came a maid who had served her masters even after they had lost their money. She had supported them first with her money and then by begging for them. They died and she too remained penniless and alone. Then came a young friend of Virginie's, and next a woman they nursed back to health (43–45).

In these first two years, 1839–1841, Jeanne Jugan set forth the guidelines for what later would become the Little Sisters of the Poor: first, the service of caring for the elderly poor and the abandoned; second, the gathering of a little community of religious women to establish a community home and offer care; third, some religious rules to direct the lives of the community; and fourth, the practice of begging to support their enterprise.

Jeanne Jugan's initiatives were, however, a woman's mission in a man's world. Men dominated nineteenth-century France as powerfully as men anywhere in the world. As a result Jeanne Jugan depended upon men for much of her income and for her place within the organization of the French Catholic Church. Like other social innovators of her era, she attracted men to help her, even men who were willing to assume the role of a men's auxiliary. Conversely, she had to deal with men who wished to control her movement, to dominate the institution she fashioned. Both types appeared from the start of her enterprise.

The Brothers of Saint John of God, a sixteenth-century Spanish order that managed the famous Charité hospitals in France, were a mendicant order. Jeanne Jugan met some of the brothers as they passed through Saint-Servan raising money. One, Brother Claude Marie Gandet (1806–1884), encouraged her to beg for her poor. He lent her his confidence, introduced her to some donors, and gave her a first begging basket. Later, Jugan would model the Rule for the Little Sisters of the Poor on that of the Brothers of Saint John of God.[5]

She was not so lucky with Abbé Auguste Le Pailleur (1812–1895). At the outset he encouraged the little band of women to adopt some of the measures of the Third Order of the Heart of Mary. These rules called for regular morning and afternoon times of silence, the sacrifice of personal will, and "withdrawing spiritually into" the Heart of Jesus (45–46). Later the Abbé would seize control of Jugan's new organization, appoint himself father superior general, and even promulgate a story that he had invented the movement (102, 142–146).

Starting in 1841, Jeanne Jugan found ways to spread her vision and to attract recruits to her community. During the summer of 1841 the little group moved to a former barroom to accommodate the nine women in their care. Here she instituted the practice of giving work to those who were able to work. The residents pulled apart scraps that Jeanne Jugan collected to spin the wool into fresh thread. The next year they purchased a former convent that had been suppressed by the state. By November 1842 twenty-six old women were in their care.

Success bred official opposition. The town fathers cut off the municipal aid they had been providing, because Jugan's organization ran counter to the established charitable structure of a French town. In that era, charity was the province of well-to-do families.[6]

The town fathers stated that Jeanne Jugan's program ought to have been in the charge of the ladies who ran the local foundling home. Fortunately, the Bishop of Rennes intervened in behalf of the "young persons consecrated to the care of the infirm aged in the parish of Saint-Servan." But the municipal relief continued to be withheld (49–51, 59–60).

Trouble arose within Jeanne Jugan's little community as well. In May 1842 the group gave itself a name, the Servants of the Poor, and they adopted the hospitaler's code, "to share the distress and penury of those they sought to help." The little band then elected Jugan their superior and took a vow to obey her. A year later, in December 1843, when they re-elected her as their superior, Abbé Le Pailleur interposed his authority as a priest, canceled the election, and appointed a young girl as the mother superior (52–53, 74).

Jeanne Jugan accepted this power play, just as ten years later she would accept the Abbé's order that she retire to the mother house. Nothing in her background suggests that Jeanne Jugan was a bureaucratic power-seeker, or that she possessed either the will or the skills for institutional in-fighting. A good analogy might be the difference between a boss and a workman. For the boss, the pleasure flows from power and control over others; for the workman the pleasure comes from picking up the tools and making the object.

Jeanne Jugan proved herself to be a brilliant worker at her self-appointed task. Almost every day from 1840 to 1852 she walked about the towns of northwestern France, from Rennes to Angers to Tours, begging, speaking, and enacting her version of the Gospel. Her vision, to be sure, was an institutional one. She imagined communities of religious women like herself coming together to care for the aged and abandoned poor. It seems likely that in begging, in approaching strangers and being refused, she was carried forward by her special combination of secular and religious love. It seems most likely that the nursing and caring acts that the old people required nourished her religious orientation and that her religious orientation, in turn, supported what she had learned of love among companions. Begging was hard work, and many of the old people were difficult. Some were alcoholics. Early on, the Servants of the Poor had some success with these addicts by giving them a regular life, regular meals, friendly attention, and work to do, much as the monks of the exemplary hospital at Zaragoza, Spain, had succeeded with their imposition of monastic routine centuries before.

A surprising emergence into national prominence came in 1845. The mayor of Saint-Malo presented a petition to the French Academy in behalf of Jeanne Jugan requesting that she be awarded the Prix Montyon. The award offered not only money but an Academy pamphlet setting forth the merits of her work and the reasons for her winning the prize. This recognition gained Jeanne Jugan national prominence, but more immediately the pamphlet enabled her to obtain the required begging permits when she moved into a new town (79–81).

It is well to recall that Jeanne Jugan was traveling from town to town begging in behalf of old people in the midst of the "starving forties," a time of crop failures and suffering all over Europe. The Irish Potato Famine was but the most notorious of the rural collapses of this decade. In the face of such need, the success of Jeanne's revival of the Catholic mendicant tradition is indeed impressive. By 1852 the Little Sisters of the Poor had been established as a regular congregation within the Church, and so compelling had been Jeanne Jugan's mission that she had succeeded in founding fifteen houses with 300 sisters and 1,500 residents under their care (138–140).

When Jeanne was sixty and there were already houses in Paris and London as well as provincial France, the Abbé ordered Jeanne Jugan to return to the mother house (137). There she remained, living among and helping the novices until her death in 1879. Her one administrative act during those years proved essential to the survival of the congregation. She advised the society's council that no endowments should be accepted. It was fitting, she said, for the Little Sisters of the Poor to own the houses and land they used for their homes, but their income ought to come from begging and therefore represent continuing support from those living around them. This rule against endowment has been one of the secrets to the success of the Little Sisters of the Poor. It keeps them in touch with their surroundings and has helped them to make successful transitions in the ever-changing circumstances of the modern world (169–172).

Why did Jeanne Jugan retire in 1852, at the moment when her fame had reached its peak? She may have felt that her straightforward message of charity and worship was being drowned in the political whirlpools around the Second Republic and Napoleon III's imperial coup. Her links to the Falloux family, whose politically inclined scion Vicomte Frédéric de Falloux led the Catholic Legitimist faction, must have been a distraction as well as a source of aid. It is also likely that Jeanne Jugan was exhausted, worn down by thirteen years of begging, and that now, at the age of sixty, she welcomed the possibility of retiring into a quiet life where she might focus on her own spiritual quest.

However it was, by 1852 the Little Sisters of the Poor were fairly launched as a world movement. Much of their progress outside France was facilitated by one of the helping men, Abbé Ernest Lelièvre (1826–1889). Lelièvre was in every way the model of a nineteenth-century Catholic humanitarian. He came from a wealthy family of industrialists, owners of textile mills and iron works in northern France. His mother died when he was eleven, but his father married the mother's sister and raised his family on an estate near Lille. One imagines a pious and paternalistic industrial family whose women actively managed the local Catholic charities, much in the manner the historian Bonnie Smith has described.[7] As a teen-age boy Lelièvre considered joining the Jesuits, but his father persuaded him to continue his secular education. He did, however, carry on an active membership in that very influential new charity founded by Frédéric Ozanam (1813–1853), the Society of Saint Vincent de Paul. In 1845 Lelièvre sent his son to Paris to study law. There Ernest applied himself, eventually taking up study for the doctorate. His progress was arrested, however, in 1849. That year his younger brother, Albert, died of tuberculosis and a distant cousin turned down the twenty-three-year-old Ernest's proposal of marriage.

In Paris, perhaps because of his membership in the Society of Saint Vincent de Paul, or perhaps owing to the encouragement of an uncle, he became involved in helping the Little Sisters of the Poor at their home in the city. Soon after he completed his doctorate in law, he went in 1852 to Rome to study for the priesthood. After his ordination, with the encouragement of his confessor in Rome, Ernest Lelièvre attached himself to the Little Sisters of the Poor as an auxiliary priest. In that role, he commenced his service as the advance man for the founding of new homes.[8] In 1856 he and another wealthy auxiliary priest, Abbé Paul Gontard, sold some of their personal property to fund the purchase of a new mother house, Le Tour, at Saint-Pern, near the village of Becherville, north of Rennes.[9]

In 1861 Abbé Lelièvre traveled to London to assist in the enlargement of the sisters' London home in Southwark and to set up homes throughout England, Scotland, and Ireland.[10] By November he was in Manchester, where, like Friedrich Engels before him, he was shocked by conditions. "There is nothing, absolutely nothing for the aged, because the 'workhouse' is a prison," he wrote.[11]

During these years of work in the United Kingdom, a Sarah Porter of Cincinnati, Ohio, began her campaign to bring the sisters to the United States. The congregation refused her initial request because they were busy with new establishments in England and in Spain. Later, during the Civil War, the bishop of New Orleans visited the mother house in Saint-Pern to make a similar request.

In 1868 Abbé Lelièvre finally made his founding tour to the United States, traveling from New York to New Orleans, St. Louis, Chicago, Cincinnati, Detroit, and Baltimore. In New York Isaac Thomas Heckler (1819–1888), an influential priest, Catholic journalist, and founder in 1858 of the Paulist Fathers, assisted the abbé. In September 1868 eight sisters arrived in New York City to set up the first American home in Brooklyn. It was the predecessor of the current Queen of Peace Residence in Queens Village.[12] Abbé Lelièvre had rented three empty wooden houses at the poor edge of Brooklyn at 606–610 DeKalb Avenue. On September 20, 1868, the sisters took in their first resident, an eighty-two-year-old Irish immigrant. The next day they went begging for food and furniture. That same year and the next, houses were established in Cincinnati, New Orleans, and Baltimore.[13]

Soon the Brooklyn sisters found themselves busy enough. The next year they purchased a large old Italianate mansion on Bushwick and DeKalb Avenues and eleven adjoining lots. Three years later they completed a new building, but in 1876 a terrible fire destroyed it and took eighteen lives. Thereafter, the old building was enlarged with new wings. In 1897 this facility was designated the provincial residence for the eastern province of the Little Sisters of the Poor. At that time the house was home to seventeen sisters, who tended to 260 residents.[14]

Wherever possible, the Little Sisters of the Poor attempted to re-create something of the quiet setting of a monastic establishment. The mother house at Saint-Pern had extensive gardens and fields around the old estate. Here in Brooklyn a wall was built surrounding the property, and within, a series of tree-lined walks and small lawns and gardens had been set out for the separate women's and men's residences and for the sisters.

In 1900, in search of a quieter place for their novitiate, the sisters purchased eleven acres of the Brown farm at Springfield Boulevard and 111th Street in Queens Village. Two years later the first sisters moved in, and in 1913 the present circumferential wall was begun by the New York City contractor Charles W. Murphy.[15]

Local priests and Little Sisters of the Poor attending a Mass in September 1968 in the Bushwick Avenue Chapel in Brooklyn, marking the centennial of the Little Sisters' arrival in America. *(Photo courtesy of the Little Sisters of the Poor, Queens Village, New York)*

After many years of service in locations throughout the United States, the Little Sisters were forced by rapid social change during the 1960s and 1970s to adapt their mission to thoroughly altered circumstances. In Brooklyn in the 1960s the sisters had focused their attention on the infirm aged poor, a group of citizens that had been excluded from American postwar prosperity.[16] In 1960 Congress passed its first legislation for federal assistance to states, granting funds for the medical care of the aged, and in 1965 it initiated its Medicare program for hospitals and medical insurance for the aged. During the 1970s

Social Security payments were substantially improved. Both medical programs offered funds to caregivers, but neither sent sufficient money to pay the full costs. As a result, the Little Sisters of the Poor needed to continue their tradition of begging for supplies, equipment, food, and money from the city and nearby parishes. Such begging and fund-raising remains as much a necessity today as in the past.

The new federal and state funds carried with them new standards for building safety, standards that the old home in Brooklyn could not meet. Accordingly, in 1967 the sisters started construction of a new

The first phases of construction of the Queen of Peace Residence, Queens Village, New York, 1967. *(Photo courtesy of the Little Sisters of the Poor, Queens Village, New York)*

home on the back fields of the Brown farm, behind their novitiate. The new facility, the present Queen of Peace Residence, opened in February 1970. It is a modern, five-story, red-brick hospital-like structure, laid out in three wings that converge on the chapel, where balcony and first-floor entrances make it easy for residents to come to the service from their rooms. Outside, lawns and gardens surround the building. The sisters make a special effort to see that residents get to enjoy these pleasant places throughout the good-weather months. It was gardens like these that Oliver Sacks recalled as restorative places in his narra-

tive of his own hospitalization, *A Leg to Stand On.*[17]

The Queen of Peace Residence was built to continue what was then the specialty of the sisters, nursing care for the infirm aged poor. The 209 beds were arranged in three-bed rooms, each bed curtained off from its neighbor. Downstairs were doctors' offices and examining rooms, and one of the wings served as the sisters' residence.

The 1970s and 1980s brought with them decades of changes even deeper than new government programs and regulations. The whole nineteenth- and early twentieth-century relationship between the Catholic

Church and its American and European women members came unstuck, setting in train a process of realignment that has not yet been completed. Young women stopped coming forward in large numbers to acknowledge vocations as nuns, and as a consequence the existing congregations began to age and shrink. Parishes lacked priests, and laypersons had to assume some of the roles formerly performed by priests. On the left wing of the Church, some women demanded that they be eligible for ordination as priests.

In these unsettled social and religious times, the Little Sisters of the Poor suffered attrition, as did many orders. A few of their homes had to be closed; now only thirty-two are operating within the United States.[18] Few novices are coming along. With regard to recruitment of new sisters and construction of new homes, the Little Sisters of the Poor now find that their most promising field of service is the Third World, where conditions for religious young women and for the elderly resemble those of Jeanne Jugan's France.

At the Queen of Peace Residence the Little Sisters of the Poor have been very alert and flexible in adapting their tradition to the altered circumstances. They have changed both residential conditions and staff work. As most of the aged population of New York City grew more affluent and better cared for medically, the sisters focused on admitting the aged poor before they fell very ill. They allowed the three-bed units to empty out on the deaths of their residents and then converted those rooms into single-bed sitting rooms or into nursing bedrooms. Today there are a hundred elderly men and women at the Queen of Peace, most in single rooms, where they receive either residential or nursing care.[19]

The extraordinary quality of the residence, what sets it apart from an ordinary good nursing home, rests on the continued vitality of the tradition of the Little Sisters of the Poor. That tradition can be described in both secular and religious terms. The sisters have been at pains to make their message clear to modern Americans within both contexts.

The secular interpretation can best be understood in the light of Dr. Richard Kaufman's observation when he visited the residence, "Here there is a moral commitment to meticulous patient care." In their literature and conversation the sisters describe their *moral* commitment in many ways. The usual language of service is transformed into a statement of human reciprocity when they write of their care as being "offered in an atmosphere of compassion and love where the elderly are able to feel esteemed and respected for their experience and contributions they have made to society."[20] Or they translate their vows of poverty and hospitality into a statement of thanks: "Blessed be God for the Elderly . . . who teach us that a person's worth is not measured in production and consumption but in Hospitality of the Heart."[21]

Their basic method for caring for the elderly poor is the same as it was in Jeanne Jugan's time. The sisters live among their residents to share their daily lives with them. They serve the meals to the residents, they work as nurses, and they participate in all the daily programs. Often they speak of creating a family out of the community of sisters and residents.[22] The goal of family, in turn, calls forth some of the deepest elements in Christian faith. It draws upon Christ's statements about the obligation to charity and the tradition of the Last Judgment: "For I was hungry and you gave me food; I was thirsty and you gave me drink; I was a stranger and you made me welcome; naked and you clothed me, sick and you visited me, in prison and you came to see me. . . . I tell you solemnly, in so far as you did this to one of the least brothers of mine, you did it to me" (Matt. 26). To which Jeanne Jugan added, "Take good care of the aged, for in them you are caring for Jesus himself."[23]

The Gardens

Americans are not settled in their ideas for the care of their old people. Currently, we debate whether they should be separated from the rest of society or be everywhere among us. It is clear that many elderly people have needs that may not be met in the society at large. Many require physical facilities that accommodate infirmities, all require safety and security, and many need special medical services. In the midst of this debate, communities designed for the aging are flourishing as alternatives to home care and nursing homes. And in these separate places the gardens often serve as the outdoor meeting spot for the old and members of the community at large.

The Queen of Peace Residence of the Little Sisters of the Poor is one of the nation's special communities for the elderly. It is not, however, a novelty of current finance and insurance but the fruit of a dominant tradition in Western history—a charitable foundation for the aged and an institution for the delivery of health care as a charity. Here gathered together are the elderly poor, many in good health, some requiring full-time nursing care, some dying. They come to live in a walled community that prizes calm and dignity, where the surrounding gardens embody the tradition of nature as a link to God. This is a place of order and routine where a tradition of worship and a commitment to a godly way of life are manifest. Although a contemporary American landscape designer would probably not find the gardens exemplary, here landscape is made rational and symbolically rich; it is designed for clear purpose.

SENSE OF PLACE

The Queen of Peace Residence is first and foremost a religious place. Reminiscent of a medieval monastery, Queen of Peace is a complex community surrounded by stout walls where both religious and laypeople live, work, visit, study, and pray. Although food is not produced here and livestock is not kept, many of the traditional monastic functions are still carried out. Laundry is done on site, food is prepared and served, nursing care is rendered to those who need it. Mass is celebrated and attended. Although the gardens are not geometric plots that produce medicinal herbs, they encircle the buildings and are an important part of the religious life. Like the monks who walked the

perimeter of the medieval cloisters while they prayed and chanted, the sisters, residents, staff, visitors, and volunteers use the garden for strolling, contemplation, and prayer. The pace of religious life seems particularly well suited to an elderly population and offers them respite and refuge at a time when poverty and waning physical strength make autonomous living difficult or impossible.

At the turn of the century the Little Sisters decided to establish a training center separate from their Brooklyn home. They sought a more pastoral setting in the New York area. "Several pieces of land were under consideration, but each had some drawback or other. Mother Provincial from Chicago had come to help decide, and after several weeks no decision had been made, but one had to be."[24] Finally, in the rain, and without knowing exactly where they were going, the two nuns and a local priest made their way to Queens Village where they were shown land they knew immediately would suit their needs. In addition to its pastoral character, it could offer a parish church nearby and rail, streetcar, water, and electric services on the street. Although the surrounding land was as yet undeveloped, a thick masonry wall was soon erected, defining this property as different and separate from its surroundings.

Decades later, when the sisters were confronted with the need to meet new building standards for their residences, they decided to close the Brooklyn home. With more land in Queens Village than was needed for a training center, the property became the logical choice for a new residence. Today, because of its proximity to Saint Ann's Novitiate, the residence differs from all the other Little Sisters' nursing homes. As the only North American house of formation, or training center, for Little Sisters, the novitiate houses approximately twenty postulants, novices, and instructors. It is home to several elderly nuns and priests as well. In addition, the novitiate serves as the location for retreats and meetings for the order as a whole. It is a busy place with close ties to the residence. This mix of functions adds a complexity that

The small Rose Garden at the Queen of Peace Residence with its Christ statue at the center is enclosed by tall hedges (*Euonymus alata*). The Saint Ann's Noviate property is seen in the background. (*Photo: Nancy Gerlach-Spriggs*)

further makes the home more like a monastery than simply a place for the elderly.

Since 1970 the elderly poor have been cared for in a large five-story building that, with its gardens and parking, occupies more than half of the eleven-acre site. This parcel is separated from the novitiate parcel by a chain-link fence, and sisters pass back and forth between the two properties numerous times a day. The character of the nursing home property was undoubtedly transformed by the construction of the monolithic building, larger than any in the neighborhood. Grass, trees, and walking paths belonging to the convent were destroyed by the construction, and in their place more formal gardens with religious themes were built.

The architectural forms of religious properties are, in the end, distillations of religious ideals. Although it is possible to discern certain specifically Roman Catholic forms of architecture, decoration, and even land use, a considerable variety prevails within the Church, depending on the particular ideology of the order. Some of the properties are splendid—grand displays of the highest quality and standards. Some of the world's greatest cathedrals were built by wealthy, highly educated monastic orders to reflect the wealth and power of the Church and to glorify God by building fine edifices in his honor. Other orders define service to God by worship, denial of earthly pleasures, or social service, and their architecture and land use express these values.

The Little Sisters of the Poor is an order whose clarity of purpose is reflected in the life of the residence. It is an order that supports its work through a combination of government insurance payments for nursing services and soliciting donations (begging) from businesses, individuals, and local parishes. The residences are quite modest. The sisters' nursing homes must satisfy modern government regulations and the contemporary community standard of comfort and dignity as well as reflect the character of the religious order.

The poverty, humility, and well-defined social service of the Little Sisters of the Poor are expressed repeatedly at Queen of Peace. The brick and tile facade of the residence is plain except for the chapel, which is differentiated from the rest by its oval form, stained glass windows, and statue of Mary. Garden materials are serviceable, not elegant. The walks and terraces are of poured concrete, not brick, bluestone, or some other fine material. Chairs and benches are wood or plastic. The land, a former farm, supports plant life easily, and the plantings are generally lush. But because they are usually acquired by donation, the choices of plant combinations can be unusual. The gardening itself is done by a few untrained volunteers who have little supervision and whose efforts are sporadic because of other demands on their time. There is a spare quality to both the building and the gardens, yet they are ample, comfortable.

The sisters live on the site, but there is no garden reserved for their exclusive use. They take little for themselves and put no priority on gardens that they use more than the residents do. One such garden, Convent Garden, serves primarily as a passageway between the residence and the novitiate. Specimen plants were taken from it, transplanted elsewhere on the property, and not replaced. Another garden, the Stations of the Cross, requires walking up stairs or up a ramp and is little used by the residents. Here the ground shows more exposed and compacted soil than plants. The sisters have no plans to improve it; other gardens take priority.

Domestic patterns and routines have always been intertwined with religious traditions and form in the monastic way of life, and that is the case at Queen of Peace. It is a home as well as a religious house. Outside are garden benches and chairs, a space for outdoor eating, and lawn swings. Elements found in suburban yards are present in abundance: lawns, flowering trees, annuals, bird feeders, bird baths, and bench swings. Other bits of everyday garden design can also be found. A small leprechaun is tucked in a flower bed, and cast-iron Labrador dogs flank a barbecue. Hardly elegant garden design elements, they nonetheless personalize the area, add interest, and allow for discovery. They are the garden memorabilia the residents most likely had or wanted in their own homes. They bring comfort and joy, distraction and stimulation.

SITE HISTORY

As is often the case, setting shapes our perception. Here both the development pattern and the changing demographics of the neighborhood make Queen of Peace a pastoral oasis in the city. When the many small towns on Long Island grew and eventually merged, Queens Village, Queens Borough, New York, became a confusing mix of major roadways and grids of repetitive housing types colliding at odd angles. Because developers obliterated the local natural features, the several acres of ornamental gardens at Queen of Peace seem large and verdant by contrast to the surrounding rows of small houses on small lots. It is now almost impossible to imagine that in colonial times this was part of the glacial sandbar that is Long Island, an almost treeless prairie that extended from Queens east to Wantagh. The area was a vast, grassy plain, broken by ponds and brooks bordered by aspen, alder, fern, and swamp cabbage. Here the Jameco Indians lived by growing corn and harvesting seafood.[25]

When the first white settlers arrived from Connecticut, the area was Dutch, and Peter Stuyvesant was governor. Farming persisted as the way of life until the twentieth century. The first significant sub-

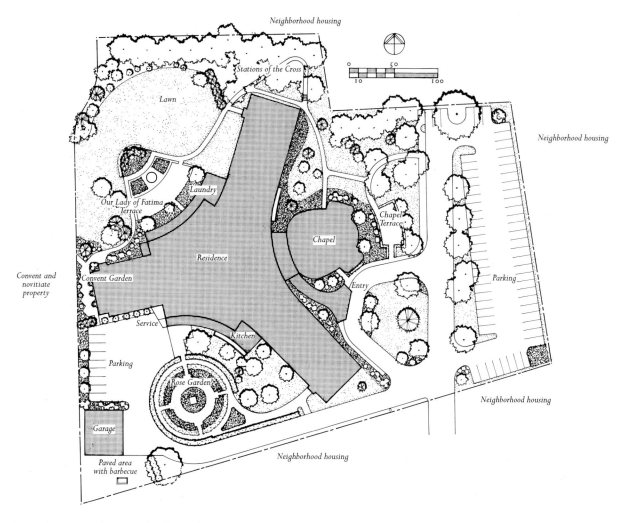

Neighborhood housing

Stations of the Cross

Lawn

Our Lady of Fatima Terrace

Laundry

Chapel Terrace

Chapel

Residence

Convent and novitiate property

Convent Garden

Entry

Parking

Service

Kitchen

Parking

Rose Garden

Garage

Paved area with barbecue

Neighborhood housing

Neighborhood housing

Neighborhood housing

Queen of Peace Residence site plan *(by David Kamp).*

urban development occurred in 1871, when Alfred Wood, a former mayor of Brooklyn, subdivided some farms and sold lots with great fanfare and promotion, but the Depression of 1873 ended his short-lived real estate boom.[26] In 1898, on the eve of the Little Sisters' land purchase, Queens Village was a "typical suburban village with a cluster of stores around the railroad station, and here and there small groups of houses on tree-lined streets, widely separated from each other by open fields."[27] The population was nine hundred.

By 1900, when the Little Sisters of the Poor purchased their eleven acres, Queens Village had been consolidated as part of New York City. As a result, it had acquired the city water, electricity, and telephone services that helped attract the sisters to the property. The Long Island Railroad had been operating for more than half a century, and streetcar lines connected the village to the city. Just after World War I, real estate activity burgeoned. Farms were sold and subdivided into lots of 25 x 100 feet, or occasionally 40 x 100 feet. New streets were laid out and the suburban

Residents and visitors gather at the front entry of the Queen of Peace Residence. With its generous canopy and garden setting, it is the most frequently used outdoor space. *(Photo: © 1996, Karen S. R. Balogh)*

produce farms disappeared. In 1923 alone, builders erected 1,033 homes and 79 stores in the Queens Village area. The newcomers were families of the "Old Immigration," Irish, Germans, and Yankees moving out from Manhattan and Brooklyn neighborhoods.[28] The Little Sisters' property today is an anchor in a dynamic community and a reminder of another time.

The residence is essentially hidden from public view, and many are probably unaware of its existence. In contrast to the pastoral scene at the time of purchase or the new developments of the 1920s, blighted neighborhoods now greet the visitor traveling from the train station along arterial roads to reach this hidden home with its well-tended secret gardens. Going through the entrance gate is a transforming experience. The prospect is immediately appealing because it contrasts so dramatically with its neighborhood.

A relatively small but adequate parking lot sits to the right of the driveway, but upon entering the compound, one is drawn to the chapel and the front entrance. The building itself is a flat-roofed, five-story, monolithic structure with three large wings and a chapel. It is a clearly institutional building, which visually dominates the land when one enters but recedes when one is immersed in the gardens themselves. The 1970s-style brick and ceramic tile facade has a heavy presence. Despite its simple hospital-like form, the Queen of Peace Residence serves highly complex functions, and hundreds of people are involved in the life there. It is home to about a hundred elderly residents, and day services are provided for elderly people who live nearby. The staff numbers about a hundred, and approximately eighty people regularly volunteer their services. Various celebrations and fund-raisers draw hundreds of visitors, in addition to the priests, doctors, family members, and friends. Hotel-like rooms have been set aside for those who need them.

Because the residence is essentially removed from the world, it draws upon its own complexity and richness. These riches, however, are not to be found in the architecture but are created by the programs, space allocation, interior decorations, and especially the gardens. As the resident population declined in number and changed in character during the 1980s, unused interior space was redecorated and allocated to new uses. There are a mini-mall with a snack bar, stores, a craft room, a library, a workshop, a gift shop, and so on. Mindful that the residents were once part of a larger world, the sisters arrange trips or, on the spur of the moment, take residents with them on errands, and, of course, encourage the use of the gardens.

Garden use is affected by many factors. Both design and programming can either encourage or discourage garden use. At the time of construction, the patient population at Queen of Peace was infirm, not independent or able to use a garden. Patient rooms, dining rooms, and social spaces were located on the upper floors, where they remain today. Such support services as doctors' offices, laundry, kitchen, and storage were placed on the ground floor, a generous gesture (they are often located in the basement). But as a result of this space allocation, patients have no direct view or access to the gardens from their rooms or social spaces. This arrangement undoubtedly works against garden use. At present, no programs have been instituted that might promote garden use. Nonetheless, a number of residents go into the gardens daily, as weather permits. They walk, sit alone or in groups, read, work on stitchery projects, and the like. On occasion, residents will assist the sisters and volunteers in planting annuals, but these are occasional events. Attachment to the gardens is strong: some residents call Queen of Peace their estate. In spring, if the lawn

furniture has not been set out, residents will sit on anything, so eager are they to be outdoors once winter is over.

The Surroundings

The outdoor area used most often is the wide sidewalk of the front entry. With its large canopy, it functions socially like a front porch. It is a fine place to "people-watch" as residents, visitors, and staff members pass by, often stopping to chat. The lightweight benches are easily moved about for better conversation or more comfortable placement. Residents can stay in the sun or the shade, and out of the wind or rain. Here at the front door, they are also near enough the front desk with its attentive receptionist to request help if necessary but still sit far enough outside to feel as if they've gone somewhere. The plantings at the edge of the walk are enough like a garden to give the space a pleasant feel. But in the end, it is probably the social activity in this area that draws residents to it. This is where they observe and participate in the life of the larger community.

The front entrance is not the only place to sit outside. Other seating is available along the paths, on terraces, or on the lawn. As sun or wind conditions change throughout the day, or as energy levels dictate, residents can vary their choice of seating. The lightweight plastic chairs with arms are comfortable and easy to move about, and they never heat up in the sun. Heavier wooden chairs with arms, though less movable, provide stability for those who need it. Cushions can be added for comfort, and some residents carry padding with them when they go out. It may be the location of the bench that makes it just right. Some furnish shade or a resting place during a long walk, others a favorite view. Chair swings on the lawn offer either sun or shade and either relative removal from others or close sharing of the same seat. They are favorites among the cigar smokers.

The paths and walks at the Queen of Peace are like a thread running through a rich fabric. There are destinations and points of interest along the way. Resting spots, small detours, and byways beckon. Neither the pace nor the course is set. The route is a natural loop that requires few decisions of strollers and provides much of interest. The walkways, wide enough for wheelchairs and people walking side by side, are concrete, smooth but not slippery. It is a surface that can accommodate a less than steady gait.

In recent years an attempt has been made to upgrade the grounds. Major tree pruning, irrigation, and planting projects have been undertaken. Leaf disposal in fall, watering during drought, hemlocks with

Garden volunteer Dan Jones was one of fifteen who planted trees and shrubs on the Queen of Peace property in the fall of 1995. Garden maintenance and improvement is primarily a volunteer effort. (*Photo courtesy of the Little Sisters of the Poor, Queens Village, New York*)

mites, and dogwoods with anthracnose are dealt with as the sisters can afford the time and assemble the resources. Lawns are fertilized and periodically herbicides and pesticides are used. Lawn mowing, pruning, and snow removal at the Queen of Peace are performed by contractors. Other gardening needs related to design, installation and maintenance are met sporadically by volunteers. It is the seasonal, weather-dependent, routine maintenance that is most difficult to accomplish without a gardener. Yet seemingly minor tasks, like watering, in the end have major impact. Absent such a staff, the basic approach in recent modifications to the garden has been to plant large areas with low-maintenance plants and to concentrate efforts on several small but frequently used or highly visible areas.

The gardens were first created on flat ground, formerly farmland with no natural water features. Only one small area on the north side has topographic variety. The mature trees add interest and character to what would otherwise be featureless land. There are terraces or gardens on both an institutional and a smaller, more domestic scale. The building can be circumnavigated by going through a series of gardens that flow from one to the next alongside the walk. In only two spots is the serenity of the gardens interrupted, by a service area and service drive that must be crossed. The loosely defined garden rooms at Queen of Peace are sufficiently distinctive to serve as orienting devices and are large enough to accommodate the needs of the institution, including a large fund-raising event and a family picnic.

Three major terraces define the garden pattern: the Chapel Terrace, Our Lady of Fatima Terrace, and the Rose Garden. These are supported by three minor gardens, or seating areas: the Stations of the Cross, the Convent Garden, and the front entrance walk and canopy.

The Chapel Terrace is located away from the building entrance, but it affords an unobstructed view of the entry gate and parking lot that makes it possible to observe the comings and goings without being

Our Lady of Fatima Garden is surrounded by a large lawn. The terrace is used for strolling, sitting, outdoor dining, and an annual family picnic and fund-raising event. *(Photo: © 1996, Karen S. R. Balogh)*

part of them. This terrace is enclosed with a yew hedge and several newly planted cherry (*Prunus kwausau*) and magnolia trees. Korean spice viburnum (*Viburnum carlesii*), which bears its fragrant blooms at Mother's Day, is planted nearby to honor the Virgin Mary, whose statue adorns the chapel facade. The furniture on the Chapel Terrace is heavy wood tables and chairs. Hardly elegant, they nonetheless provide stable seating and work surfaces and are much in demand by residents and visitors and by staff members waiting to be picked up after work.

The second terrace works in concert with a large lawn and a small garden surrounding a statue of Our Lady of Fatima. The three elements—terrace, garden, and lawn—are located behind the building and con-

stitute the largest outdoor space at Queen of Peace. The spacious concrete terrace conforms to the curve of the building's architecture and focuses outward, past a large fountain and planters, to a composition of statues: Our Lady of Fatima and the three small children with the sheep they were tending when the vision of Mary appeared. This composition is enclosed by layers of vegetation—hemlocks (*Tsuga canadensis*) a yew hedge (*Taxis media "Hicksii"*) and andromeda (*Pieris japonica*). It is a strong but static design that invites quiet contemplation. The spacious lawn is dotted with trees, several given in memory of former residents. In this verdant place there is a sense of openness not often found in a city. This area is a long way from the front door, and only the more vigorous residents come to it unescorted. The laundry looks out on this lovely spot, but because a layer of vegetation intervenes, the terrace has a private and expansive feel. Residents are sometimes served meals here, but without direct building access they are a cumbersome production. The residents must be brought downstairs and the food must be brought from another wing of the building. Although it is usually quiet, the terrace becomes a stage each September for two events: an invitational fund-raiser and a family picnic, during which the terrace and surrounding lawn are filled with tents, balloons, tables, and chairs. Hundreds of people are welcomed to these festive occasions, which feature live entertainment.

The third major terrace is a small Renaissance-inspired rose garden. A tall arborvitae (*Thuja occidentalis*) hedge defines the perimeter of the Rose Garden and screens the service area. Inner hedges of burning bush (*Euonymus alata*) and boxwood (*Buxus microphylla "compacta"*), circular paving and planting beds, and a central statue of Christ make this a strong composition. This garden is another quiet place where the flower scents and birdsongs can be experienced alone or with others. Recent work in the garden, most of it by volunteers with donated materials, has led to increased use.

These three major terraces are connected by walkways and separated by smaller gardens. The outdoor Stations of the Cross is located on the north side of the building in a small area. The shady, cool spot is welcoming on a hot day. The ground rises slightly there and is accessible by both ramp and stairs. The Stations of the Cross are in this case a sequence of plaques and reliefs depicting episodes on Christ's road to Calvary. They tell the story of his sentencing, torture, crucifixion, death, and entombment. This most private corner of the property is used primarily, but not exclusively, by the sisters, who come to the garden to pray before each station. Residents can rest on nearby benches, or continue to walk along the path.

The tiny Convent Garden with its statue of Saint Joseph is used by the sisters as a passageway between the residence and the novitiate. It is little more than a wide sidewalk, but it has an intimate quality, even though it is traversed many times a day.

When a large number of people live in a close community and when contemplation and prayer are an essential part of their day, privacy is a most important element. It can be difficult to obtain in an institution, but the Queen of Peace Residence manages, both architecturally and in its gardens, to define zones of greater or lesser privacy. The front entry sidewalk under the canopy is the most public space. The Chapel Terrace is slightly less so—still highly visible, but far enough from the main sidewalk that social engagement is not mandatory. The most private area is the Rose Garden. The high enclosing hedges and restricted points of entry set it apart from everything else.

Sometimes it is important to highlight what is missing as well as what is right about a place. And at the Queen of Peace Residence an important missing element is an outdoor room. As successfully as they meet the needs of the residents, the gardens cannot be used directly much of the year. In addition, some residents are undoubtedly too timid or infirm to use the gardens but might use a more enclosed conservatory or porch. How wonderful it would be to have a place where the sunlight poured in, or changed with the dappled shade from nearby trees, a place where plants could grow, bloom, and diffuse their fragrance and where rain could be seen and heard. In a place such as this, residents would be able to reverse for a time the pattern of being cared for and instead care for something else.

The gardens, too, could be a richer and more meaningful experience for both the residents and the sisters. They could contain more plants common to suburban gardens—lilacs, peonies, or hollyhocks. They could produce vegetables or flowers for the chapel. The gardens could shelter and feed birds, especially during the great spring and fall migratory periods. How striking it would be if vines or trees were to be coaxed to grow along an espalier in forms reminiscent of the Middle Ages. The rich, centuries-old symbolism of plants could be highlighted and reference made to the French origins of the order. To achieve such goals, however, would take time, gardening expertise, and money, all in short supply.

The significance of the Queen of Peace gardens lies within the broad tradition of religious charity. The gardens are but one aspect of the sisters' caring for the less fortunate. Revealing their historic roots, transmitting a modern version of their monastic heritage, the gardens, like the rest of life at Queen of Peace, are at a confluence of contemporary domestic need and ancient religious practice. The elderly residents take part in a Catholic community enfolded in a safe, supportive environment. The religious spirit, along with its values, memories, and symbols, permeates this place. The rhythms of daily life, religious ritual, and nature all give order to the day. Gardens' sacred forms have for centuries echoed the harmony between the religious and the natural environment; so have these gardens been designed to enhance the religious life of the community members who live and work here.

The administrative offices of the Hospice at the Texas Medical Center are in the landmark Holcombe house and overlook the formal gardens. To the right is the new inpatient facility, the Margaret Cullen Marshall Hospice Care Center, designed by Graham B. Luhn. *(Photo: Richard Payne,* FAIA*)*

The Hospice at the Texas Medical Center

Houston, Texas

The Hospice at the Texas Medical Center in Houston is an institution that early on joined the movement to reform modern-day treatment of the dying. The goals of this movement are to relieve the social and institutional isolation of the dying and the grieving, to adapt the techniques of modern science to their care, and to provide psychological and spiritual support and assistance to them.

Over the previous two hundred years, gradual developments in religious and medical practice transformed Western traditions of death and grieving. For centuries, tradition ordained that family members nurse the dying relative and gather around the deathbed to seek reconciliation. After the person's death, a church funeral, a parish burial, and a period of public mourning helped to temper the inevitable feelings of loss and grief. Hospitals and commercial undertakers, by contrast, are inventions of the nineteenth and twentieth centuries.[1]

A shift in religious outlook increasingly separated grief from public ritual and confined mourning more and more to the private realm; it became a family responsibility. Christian tradition had held that the dead await Judgment Day before being transported into Heaven. Nineteenth-century popular sentiment, however, favored the image of the dying being immediately rapt into Heaven; the belief was that as other family members died, they would join their beloved there. The family were consequently obliged to tend the memory of their dead, to erect marked graves, to visit cemeteries for moments of recollection and meditation, and to maintain the thought of a family that would be reunited in Heaven.[2]

At the same time that religious sentiment was shifting, contemporary urban and industrial society placed people in new community surroundings. People moved from nation to nation, from country to city, and from street to street within cities and suburbs. The local community lost interest in and even knowledge of the death of one of its members, except for the leaders and celebrities. The commercial undertaker rose to prominence, as a person who could manage death by offering families a menu of packaged rituals from which to choose.[3]

In the twentieth century, middle-class families began to place terminally ill patients in hospitals. This practice followed logically from the turn-of-the-century improvements in sanitation and surgery that made the hospital a better place for acute care than private home nursing. In 1949 50 percent of the deaths in the United States took place in hospitals; by 1995 the figure had risen to 80 percent.

Once in the acute-care hospital, the dying person confronts the culture of modern biotechnical medicine. That culture is oriented toward experimentation, invention, and progress in the war against disease. This culture is a sort of scientific version of the religious doctrine of perfection. In such a climate not to get better—to decline, to die—is to fail. To keep undergoing new procedures, to try once more, is to be a good patient. The very biotechnical culture that has produced the triumphs of modern medicine often extends the suffering of the dying rather than easing their path toward inevitable death.[4]

During the same decades, a much improved general standard of living seems to have fostered a culture of sanitized pleasure in which the stench of living, and the pain and grief of life, are denied and hidden behind masks of happiness. Such a popular culture inevitably isolates the sick, the dying, and the grieving.[5] At present this mix of medical and popular culture has called forth three proposals for reform. At one extreme stands the growing euthanasia movement, which advocates using modern medical knowledge to allow suffering persons to request their own death.[6] At the other extreme is the unceasing popular search for a personal attitude of fulfillment and serenity, which is imagined to ensure a comfortable death.[7]

The hospice movement stands between these two poles. It employs the techniques of modern medicine to relieve pain, help breathing, stabilize the bowels, and manage the symptoms of the dying. It uses the formidable armamentarium of modern medicine to make it possible for most patients to die as conscious as possible and without serious pain. Hospice care also ends the isolation of patients by helping them and their families and caregivers accept the idea of death as a natural process, as a stage of life itself. The considerable psychological problems, of anger, fear, and depression, are addressed by a skilled interdisciplinary team. Spiritual distress and the search for meaning or fairness or hope in the context of terminal illness are also high priorities for hospice teams in their interventions.

To seek hospice care, whether in one's own home or in an inpatient program, is to let one's secret out, to acknowledge the inevitability of death. It also guarantees that one does not move to the screened beds or isolated rooms at the end of the hospital corridor. Instead, one enters the society of friends, relatives, and professionals who can talk about death and dying, if and when one chooses. They will work to make the patient's remaining days peaceful and full. Hospice also ends the isolation of the dying by employing teams that include doctors, nurses, social workers, and clergy and by encouraging family and friends to share in the caregiving.

The American hospice services of today probably owe their existence to the practice and publications of Elisabeth Kubler-Ross and Dame Cicely Saunders. Their example and teaching encouraged many professionals and laypeople to establish modern hospice care as an alternative to contemporary medical and popular culture and the constraints they impose. There were, in earlier centuries as well, precedents for this reform, at institutions of charity and hospitals and homes for chronic diseases.

A general wave of charity and humanitarianism supported Catholic, Protestant, and Jewish social innovations. In the nineteenth and early twentieth centuries, especially, old people who were unable to work and had no families to look after them ended their days in poverty. The public workhouse, the poor farm, or a paltry public allowance was the lot of the aged infirm as well as of sufferers from cancer and tuberculosis. In France many charitable inventions grew from an informal confederacy of wealthy bourgeois women and poor working-class girls. The wealthy provided the patronage; the poor women joined the many new congregations of sisters founded to nurse the sick and care for and teach young children.[8] In Protestant countries, young women took up nursing in private homes and voluntary hospitals and staffed the new public schools.

A house for those dying of cancer was established in Lyons in the 1840s. In Germany a terminal hospital opened in the 1880s for those dying of tuberculosis. By 1900 in London several specialized hospitals for the dying existed—for example, Trinity Hospice and Saint Luke's House, whose histories have been well documented.[9]

These precedents provided the background for the reinvention of the hospice and the subsequent founding of the Hospice at the Texas Medical Center. The immediate impulse came from the friendship between a Jewish survivor of the Warsaw ghetto and an English social worker who had served as a nurse during World War II.

David Tasma was a forty-year-old Polish refugee dying of cancer in a lonely fifty-bed hospital ward in

London. During his last weeks he and Cicely Saunders, then a medical social worker, often discussed his isolation, his pain, and what decent path he might take toward death. In these conversations Saunders and Tasma imagined a house where people could find relief from pain, where they would meet with encouragement for self-awareness and sociability, and where the setting would nourish their humanity. When Tasma died, he left Saunders five hundred pounds so that one day he might be, as he said, "a window in your Home."

Subsequent to these conversations of 1948, Saunders trained to be a physician, studying and practicing in hospitals that focused on pain control. She was impressed by Saint Joseph's Hospice in East London, a nineteenth-century foundation of the Irish Sisters of Charity for the terminally ill. When she opened her own institution, Saint Christopher's Hospice, in suburban London in 1967, Dr. Saunders adopted the term used by the Irish sisters, "hospice."[10]

Dr. Saunders's work in England found reinforcement in contemporary studies by Elisabeth Kubler-Ross in the United States, and by other physicians in England and Europe. In 1974 a Yale University group began a home care hospice service in New Haven. Then, in 1976, the National Cancer Institute and the Kaiser Foundation jointly sponsored three residential hospices as demonstration projects, in Branford, Connecticut; Boonton, New Jersey; and Tucson, Arizona. Today more than 2,600 hospices are registered with the National Hospice Organization.[11]

The arrival of the AIDS epidemic in the United States around 1979 lent fresh urgency to the hospice movement. Theretofore it had been directed primarily toward old people dying of cancer; now it had to assist dying young people, especially young homosexuals. The gay communities of San Francisco, New York, and Boston took up the idea of establishing residential hospices for those who could not be cared for in their own homes and sponsored a number of exemplary hospices. AIDS has spread to people in every circumstance, infants as well as adults, thereby

giving further impetus to reforms in the care of the dying. Today, as the panic over contact with AIDS patients has subsided, HIV-positive patients being treated in hospitals and hospices are no longer routinely segregated from other patients.[12]

The Hospice at the Texas Medical Center came into being through the energy and persistence of Marion Wilson and the small group of people she gathered around herself. Marion Wilson conceived the goal of starting a hospice out of her personal experiences of loss: the death of her infant twins, the death of a beloved stepson, the death of her mother from breast cancer, and the loss of her husband through sickness and divorce. In the deep depression that ensued, she discovered the healing powers of meditation and dreams, and ever since, she has centered her life through these processes. The outcome of her recovery was a desire to serve others.

She enrolled first in a community college and then at Rice University to prepare to become a physician. While in college, however, she discovered a book on the English hospice movement and began attending meetings of a group studying the hospice idea. At that time (1978), the Southeast Texas Hospice in Orange, Texas, was the only hospice in the state, and it had opened despite heavy opposition from nursing homes and home care companies.[13] Wilson was encouraged and aided by a visit to the hospice. Soon she began visiting dying patients in hospitals and gathering a group around her who possessed the varied skills needed to open a home care hospice service. Then she left Rice University to devote herself fulltime to her hospice project. In 1979 the group decided to incorporate as the New Age Hospice, the very name suggesting their hopes to reform the surrounding culture of medicine and health care.

The first big publicity break came in the spring of 1980, when they invited Dr. Richard Lamerton to come to Houston for a public party and a seminar on hospice treatment. Lamerton was then medical director of Saint Joseph's Hospice of the Irish Sisters of Charity in London. The dinner at a fashionable restaurant proved a great success, and Wilson told Lamerton that if he were ever on sabbatical, she would like to hire him to come to direct her hospice for a time (125–127).

Encouraged by this success and a small donation, Marion Wilson and a secretary friend set up an office in a small house near the Texas Medical Center. Wilson concentrated her efforts on expanding her board to include well-known Houston figures. In 1981 she succeeded in getting a start-up grant of $12,500 from the M. D. Anderson Foundation (155). This enabled her to hire a registered nurse and to put together a team composed of the nurse, a social worker, a part-time consulting physician, and trained volunteers. In September 1981 the team began offering free home care hospice service to patients. After five months, however, the group had to stop enrolling patients because it had exhausted all its funds (234, 240).

Wilson then reversed her fund-raising strategy. Theretofore, she had always envisioned a complete hospice service, one that stressed home care but that also possessed an inpatient facility for those actively dying but unable to be maintained at home. In her presentations, however, the inpatient facility had been subordinated to the immediate task of developing the home care service. Now she realized that the construction of an inpatient facility would be an attractive and visible project for local donors, and she began to stress this need and to plan for the remodeling of some existing hospital wing for the purpose (256).

Her vision of the facility foreshadowed the one that was eventually built.

Nature had always played such an important role in my life. As a child, trees and flowers had been what had connected me to the whole of the universe and I felt that our patients would benefit physically, emotionally and spiritually if they could see and have easy access to nature. I envisioned all patient rooms to be on the ground floor. Each room would have french doors that would allow even the beds to be rolled out onto the garden paths or if the patient was unable to be moved, the doors could be opened and patients could see, hear and feel the beauty of nature. I wanted bird feeders to be placed throughout the

garden so that the sounds of their songs and their joyful chirping could be easily heard by our patients. [248–249]

Despite the shutdown, 1982 turned out to be the real founding year. Aided by her enlarged board and a connection to a local television producer, Wilson was able to enlist Barbara Bush, the vice president's wife and a well-known figure in Houston, to serve as honorary chairwoman of the hospice board. Barbara Bush, in turn, led her to important people in Houston who joined her enterprise (272–277).

Nina Wickman, a former fund-raiser for the Houston Ballet, proved to be a key recruit. She took over the fund-raising, the organization of a Friends of the Hospice group, and public relations. Wilson and Wickman became a "rain-making" team (278–280, 319). Wickson directed the major $13,000,000 capital campaign that financed the remodeling and building of the current hospice, offices, and chapel.

The M. D. Anderson Foundation now gave a second gift of $100,000. In December 1982 Wilson was able to hire Dr. Lamerton to come to Houston on his sabbatical to take over as medical director of the New Age Hospice. He proved invaluable in training the newly reassembled team and in helping with certification. In 1983 the hospice received certification from the state and the federal government. That year, the New Age Hospice cared for sixty-five patients, although with its small budget of $50,000 it was frequently unable to pay its staff. Dr. Lamerton's administrative style, however, caused conflict, and in March 1983 he left. Fortunately, the group was able to call on one of its former volunteers, Dr. Porter Storey, as medical director (299–300).

Dr. Storey had just completed his residency in internal medicine at the Baylor College of Medicine at the Texas Medical Center. As a resident he had made a special study of geriatrics and hospice care. He had taken an elective in geriatrics, and one day on a house call he was, he said, "confronted with the complex problems of a dying patient and the dire need." He then petitioned for aid to travel to Scotland and England to study geriatrics. From August to

October 1982 he visited hospices, studied home and inpatient geriatrics, and worked as a nurse's aide in a hospice while studying under some of the leading palliative medicine specialists. Dr. Storey has continued to serve as medical director of the hospice, whose staff has by now grown to more than a hundred and scores of volunteers. He publishes articles on hospice care and is the author of a guide for physicians and nurses on the care of terminally ill patients that is used by hospices all over the country, *The Primer of Palliative Care.*[14]

In 1985 the New Age Hospice moved closer to the Texas Medical Center, to a prefabricated building next to the Saint Anthony's Center of the Sisters of Charity. The sisters leased the group a wing in their building so that the hospice could set up ten beds and offer short-term inpatient care. Those beds, like the present inpatient hospice, were occupied by patients whose medications needed to be adjusted or whose families needed some respite from caring for them. The new quarters worked out well, and the New Age Hospice's client population began to grow. Most were cancer patients referred by the M. D. Anderson Cancer Center and other Texas Medical Center institutions. After three years, owing to a financial emergency, the sisters had to close their buildings, and the hospice was forced to seek another space. One of the board members put the group in contact with the Memorial Hospital Southwest, which leased them a vacant wing for a twelve-bed unit. The unit successfully cared for hundreds of inpatients. The hospital, however, was twelve miles by freeway from the home care offices.

At this point the New Age group approached the Texas Medical Center with a request for space. The Texas Medical Center is a unique American institution, a not-for-profit medical real estate organization founded in 1945 by the trustees of the M. D. Anderson Foundation. Its goal was and is to encourage the development of a concentrated multi-institutional medical center in Houston. It owns 134 acres of park land that it leases to member institutions for a ninety-nine-year term.[15] A major milestone in the growth of the hospice was its acceptance as a member organization of the Texas Medical Center, a major endorsement by the medical establishment and confirmation that hospice care was starting to move from the fringes into the mainstream of medical services. At the time it was the only hospice in the country affiliated with a major medical center.

The center was ideally located, at 1905 Holcombe Boulevard, between the Veterans Affairs Medical Center and the M. D. Anderson Cancer Center of the University of Texas. The mansion of the former mayor, Oscar Holcombe, had fallen vacant. The property had been given to the Texas Medical Center by the daughter of the late mayor, and it had been used for a time as a dormitory for medical students. It was a large Tudor-style house with a lovely two-and-a-half acre garden sheltered by live oak trees. The gardens have now been restored by the Garden Club of Houston and the Wortham Foundation. In December 1989 the Texas Medical Center granted the hospice its lease and the hospice changed its name to the Hospice at the Texas Medical Center. An intensive capital campaign was then commenced to restore the Holcombe house for offices, and to build a twenty-five-bed inpatient facility and a chapel on the grounds. On January 12, 1995, the new inpatient care center opened, the Margaret Cullen Marshall Care Center, named for a major donor. Its top floor, not yet finished, may soon serve to house the home care staff, who are now working out of temporary buildings just down the road, or it may allow for some future expansion.

The Hospice at the Texas Medical Center is a large organization, as befits its location. It serves all of Harris County (metropolitan Houston), a population of 2.8 million, and an area thirty-five miles across. The home care is given by teams of physicians, nurses, social workers, home health aides, volunteers, and clergy, either in the patient's home or in a nursing home. Service is available seven days a week, twenty-four hours a day. Most of the patients continue to be people dying of cancer, but there are also many with end-stage Alzheimer's disease, heart disease, or AIDS. Thirty percent are between the ages of forty-five and sixty-four, and nearly 60 percent are sixty-five and older (the balance consisting of children and young people). The hospice takes all comers, regardless of their ability to pay, except that it has no facilities for the homeless. Because of the shortfall in American medical insurance arrangements, the hospice must raise about $800,000 each year to cover the costs of patients who are unable to pay. A special feature of the facility and its location is its ability to offer training to medical students and physicians in hospice care.

The Hospice at the Texas Medical Center currently faces the challenges that result from success. Its professional staff members have stayed on. They enjoy the possibility of practicing the sort of inter-disciplinary medicine and care that first attracted them to the hospice movement. As a big institution, the hospice must now invent new ways to maintain the personal closeness and sensitivity that character-ized the organization when it was staffed by a small group. Marion Wilson recalled:

> We began each morning with a team meeting. Everyone formed a circle and joined hands. Sometimes someone would read a poem or we could meditate quietly together. Other times we would silently remember patients that we had cared for and about. It was not just a joining of hands, it was the joining of our hearts. That heart bonding of each of us one to the other was what enabled us to do hos-pice work with our hearts fully open with no protective barriers up to shield us from the pain and suffering. We could be fully vulnerable to the mystery of life. [300]

The Gardens

What does it mean to have a home in time of need? To be cared for when ill or dying? There is no possi-ble way to measure it. What does it mean to have a garden, to enjoy its simple pleasures, to feel the warmth of the sun or watch a butterfly, to know we are a part of everything around us, from the cosmos to the microscopic world? Again, no ready answer presents itself. Compassion and caring can be shown

in the dreariest places, in the absence of beauty and comfort. A garden is not a requisite of caregiving, then. Yet what satisfaction it can bring, both to the sick and to those who tend them. To garden—or simply to be in a garden—is to experience both the normal and the transcendent; gardens offer an oppor-tunity to reaffirm life in the midst of illness.

Today the Hospice at the Texas Medical Center stands in antithesis to the severity of the highways, steel, and glass of the surrounding medical center of which it is a part. In a fast-moving culture dominated by automobiles, life on the superhighways of Hous-ton leaves little time to pause or to contemplate the landscape. Now, with air-conditioning, people do not even feel the outside temperature. Holcombe Boule-vard, the traffic spine that links the Texas Medical Center to the hospice and to the huge Veterans Affairs Medical Center, resembles a giant strip mall of medical institutions. To experience a garden here, lush, shaded, beautiful, and full of stimulation for the senses, is a rare and wonderful thing.

Nature can be uncompromising in Texas. A state known for its size and the intensity of its climate, it is not a landscape of comfort or obvious beauty. The prairie, mountains, and coast are more appreciated for their powerful, large-scale effects than for their subtle details. Elements on the human scale, like the tree-lined, high-grass strips along the bayous, do, of course, exist and inspire those making gardens. But to plant a garden in Texas is almost an act of defiance. A garden in the hot, dry, sunny climate of Houston, even one with native or naturalized plants, usually aims to provide an antidote to the dominant surroundings. The hoped-for result is frequently a verdant place, a shaded, lush oasis, full of texture and blossoms, with water—dripping, splashing, flowing.

THE SITE

The Hospice at the Texas Medical Center was created by a careful blending of the inherited and the new. It is an unusually sensitive adaptation of a former subur-

The chapel garden and arcade are paved with bluestone and link the patient care center to the chapel and historic house. *(Photo: Richard Payne, FAIA)*

Oscar F. Holcombe (1888–1968), mayor of Houston for twenty-two years, is shown here about 1925. After his death, his only child donated the family home to the Texas Medical Center, which then leased it to the hospice. *(Photo courtesy of San Jacinto Museum, Cecil Thomson Collection, Houston Metropolitan Research Center, Houston Public Library)*

Live oak trees (*Quercus virginiana*), native to Texas, were preserved and others were newly planted in the garden restoration and construction designed by Herbert Pickworth, landscape architect. *(Photo: Richard Payne, FAIA)*

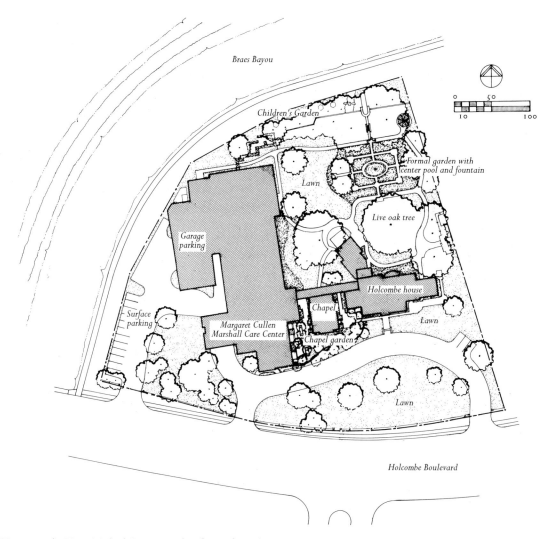

Braes Bayou

Children's Garden

Formal garden with center pool and fountain

Lawn

Live oak tree

Garage parking

Holcombe house

Chapel

Lawn

Surface parking

Margaret Cullen Marshall Care Center

Chapel garden

Lawn

Holcombe Boulevard

The Hospice at the Texas Medical Center site plan *(by David Kamp).*

ban lot and home to the goals of hospice care. When Nina Wickman was shown the Holcombe property as a possible site for the permanent location of the hospice, she realized the potential of this spot, and thanks to her Garden Club affiliation, it was eventually possible to carry out the restoration, development, and ongoing maintenance of the several small gardens that surround the hospice buildings. Without her close ties to both organizations and her extraordinary fund-raising capabilities, it its unlikely that this place would exist in the form it does. Seldom in American

medical institutions is the commitment to a garden so strong. Rarely is there money enough for its develop ment and maintenance, or sufficient expertise to achieve this level of quality. When Nina Wickman says, "We prefer it not to be an institutional environ-ment," it is an understatement.

The existing 1927 house and gardens set the tone of the hospice project, and although there was relatively little land with which to work—only two and a half acres—correct decisions, both large and small, were consistently made. Perhaps the constraints of a small site, a previously designed garden, and an established English Tudor aesthetic made the decisions easier. In any case, the use of native tree species, the live oak (*Quercus virginiana*), the willow oak (*Quercus phellos*), and the water oak (*Quercus nigra*), is an example of both sound ecological thinking and sensible cultural linkage. Continuing the planting of these tree species has ensured a shady, verdant environment hospitable to humans, one that occurs naturally in Texas only along the bayous. Because these oaks are so laden with geographical and historical associations, they immediately signal comfort, ease, and in this case, caring.

The house and gardens on Holcombe Boulevard and along Braes Bayou to the rear were the country estate of eleven-time Houston mayor Oscar Holcombe, where he and his wife, Maive Eray Miller Holcombe, a member of the River Oaks Garden Club, lived with their daughter, Elizabeth. For forty-five years it was the family home, and during this time the gardens were developed in a Gulf Coast style. Pat Flemming, a well-known Houston landscape architect, laid out the gardens.

After Mayor Holcombe's death in 1968, the house and gardens were given to the nearby Texas Medical Center. The property is at the periphery of the modern high-rise medical campus, and divided from it by Braes Bayou. For a time the house was used as a dormitory, and the buildings and gardens fell into disrepair.

The hospice took a ninety-nine-year lease on the property in 1989 and began restoring the main house, now registered as a Texas landmark. The size and distinctive Tudor style of the home and gardens were the basis for many subsequent decisions. Enough of the garden remained intact or could be described by those who knew it or studied from old photographs that designers of the hospice were able to re-create the old grounds to a large degree. A master site plan developed by the architectural firm of Graham B. Luhn ensured that the new chapel and Margaret Cullen Marshall Hospice Care Center, a building five times the size of the old family home, would coexist in unity with the gardens. Service buildings and some

portions of the old garden were removed. Yet the essence of the property, its style and ambience, as well as such original features as a garden pool and fountain, remain intact. The gardens today may offer an even richer experience than before.

THE TEAMS

The skill and energy with which the garden projects were carried out can be attributed to the mobilization of two complementary teams. The first team consisted of hands-on supporters from the Garden Club of Houston, and the second was a collaboration between the landscape architect and gardeners.

The Garden Club of Houston is one of two prominent garden clubs in the city. It is a strong women's organization with honorary male members—well organized, administered, and funded. The driving forces are generosity and service to the community. It is an important civic and financial resource, the focus of which goes beyond caring for members' homes and yards to include influencing environmental legislation and development projects throughout the city. Awards are given for preservation efforts. The Garden Club of Houston maintains the grounds at the Museum of Fine Arts and a small garden at the Texas Medical Center. It also funds garden projects. The hospice itself is in a way a women's project, in that the institution is largely staffed by women devoted to nurturing the living, growing, and dying and to teaching acceptance of the life cycle.

The Houston community, which has a strong history of private philanthropy, was urged to donate funds for the hospice gardens. Early on, the Wortham Foundation provided a grant for the infrastructure work: brickwork, drainage, and irrigation systems. The Lowe Foundation funded the new children's garden. But the Garden Club of Houston was the key to the realization of the project. It is fitting that a Garden Club member, Suzanne Nelms, also sits on the board of the hospice.

Garden Club members made important donations, for individual items in the garden, such as the fountain, the gazebo, and the terraces, and each year, provisional members of the Garden Club, usually the daughters of the current members, plant bulbs on the property. Club members donated their extra time and extra liriope from their yards and also raised money at the Bulb Mart, a joint project with the River Oaks Garden Club, for purchase of plants and trees.

Many of the plants have come from the club members' own gardens. For instance, when the bid came in for the supply of English ivy at $20,000, members donated ivy from their own gardens. Altogether the club has followed a carefully disciplined program. It did not accept all proffered donations but managed to procure material needed to carry out the restoration plans.[16]

The plans for the restoration and construction of the garden were developed by a landscape architect and gardening team. Restoration, not change, was the guiding principle. Historic photographs were studied, and advice was sought from the original designer, Pat Flemming. Flemming, a designer whose work appears in some of the important historic and public spaces of Houston, evaluated the plans to assess what should be preserved and restored and what should be sacrificed. Landscape architect Herbert Pickworth executed the final design. Meetings were held with hospice staff and Wickman to determine needs. Pickworth's intent was to create spaces that were, as he said, "easy to touch." He wanted "something that made the residents breathe easier." Knowing full well that the best designs are not just visually pleasing but experientially sumptuous, he was able to give these qualities physical form.

Early on Pickworth prepared cost estimates so that the fund-raising could begin. He was introduced to Nina Wickman by Charles Estes, a third-generation gardener, who had been working with each of them on separate projects. Estes brought an unusual commitment to the hospice. He was hired as the professional overseer of the gardens, and his salary was funded by the Garden Club of Houston. At the time of his signing on, his father was dying of cancer, and

his personal commitment far exceeded that of an employee. He crafted a birdhouse, a replica of the historic Holcombe house, that now sits atop a pole among the rhododendrons.[17] Altogether, the success of this garden project was made more likely because the team had a common purpose as well as a common aesthetic, and the personal commitment of Wickman, Pickworth, and Estes has been intense.

THE NEW BUILDINGS

The site plan located the new three-story patient care building at a right angle to the original two-and-a-half-story house. Because the taller building presents its one-story end to Holcombe Boulevard, its large mass seems minimized when the two buildings are viewed together. Other elements, such as a 1927 Tudor-style garage that screens the entry to underground parking and a generous porte-cochère for drop-off and pickup, are skillfully utilized to further diminish the perceived mass of this rather large building. An arcade connects the freestanding one-and-a-half-story chapel, the new patient care center, and the historic original house and unifies the three visually and functionally. The configuration of the three buildings encloses the garden on two sides in a protective L shape. A low brick wall defines the other garden boundaries yet permits distant views to bayou conservation land beyond. This is a private place which the majority of the patients' rooms and several offices overlook.

Good decisions about important matters—building mass and siting, configuration and size of gardens, and vehicle circulation and parking—provide context for the design. Room sizes at the new hospice building were determined not by regulation but by what was required for patient and family comfort and what was needed so that the hospital bed did not dominate the room and therefore the lives of those at the hospice. When the money raised did not suffice for the construction of large patient rooms, full-scale mockups of both a regulation room and the desired larger room were built and furnished in a nearby

The gazebo becomes a focal point of the garden as well as a destination. This seating area near the azaleas of the formal garden is one of several that can accommodate patient beds and wheelchairs or, as here, benches and chairs. (*Photo: Richard Payne,* F A I A)

parking garage. The decision was then made not to compromise room size, and fund-raising recommenced. Parking proved to be another difficult and expensive problem to solve. Surface parking on a two-and-a-half-acre parcel would have obliterated the garden's existing trees. The decision was made to separate the hospice from traffic as much as possible by parking many of the vehicles in a new underground garage and others in a purchased surface lot nearby. The valet parking necessitated by this decision added one more thing for hospice administrators to contend with, but it also meant one less concern for patients, families, and visitors in a time of stress.

But details have enormous impact in the end, too, and no detail here was too small to be considered.

Rooms have v c R s and window seats with garden views. Enough storage is available that wheelchairs and bedpans are not constantly in sight. Beds, showers, and laundry facilities have been provided for family use. The furniture is of good quality. The lighting is incandescent, rather than the usual fluorescent variety. Metal doors have been painted with faux wood panels. Great care has been taken to provide patients and visitors with support facilities, and the same sensitivity was shown in building facilities for the staff. A small "terrace" has been built on the roof of one of the chapel arcades for exclusive use by staff members. They have separate bathrooms, kitchens, lounges. The gardens are a gift to them, as well as to the patients and visitors.

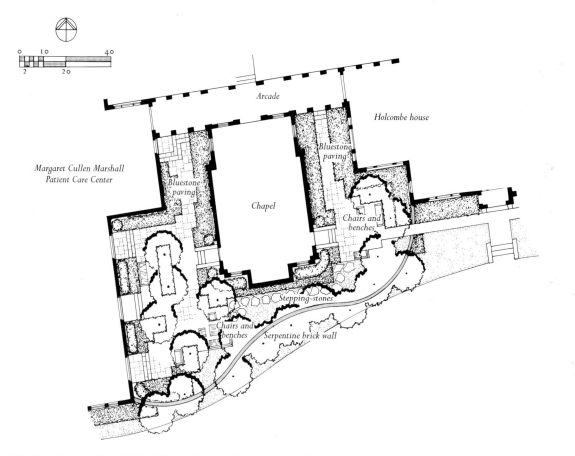

The Hospice at the Texas Medical Center chapel garden plan *(by David Kamp).*

THE GARDENS REBUILT

The hospice property is visually and experientially opulent. The architecture and gardens are in harmony, neither dominating the other, both of equal quality. The garden forms and materials are familiar to us all from the estate tradition, reflected and interpreted more modestly in our suburban yards. Even if we do not live with them, we know them. We are familiar with large trees on a lawn; at the Houston hospice the large trees are magnificent live oak. We know about hedges; in this case, they define a formal garden with a pool and a fountain. The gazebo, a favorite garden structure, in its Houston incarnation is just the right size and in just the right place, lighted for use at night and cooled by a ceiling fan. Skillful manipulation of elements makes the series of gardens familiar, yet better than what we have ourselves, and in so doing provides experiences that are part of a shared domestic culture, but also something richer than most of us experience on a daily basis.

The garden materials are of good quality but not ostentatious. The craftsmanship is superb. Bluestone paving stones are set in a random pattern with no mistakes, odd sizes, or awkward joints. The stepping-stones are large enough in size for an adult foot and spaced for natural walking, a careful but not irregular gait. The benches are classic teak, the plants those that could be found in the yards of the donors. There are no gimmicks, no new inventions. The design is tasteful, sympathetic, quiet.

Not consciously designed as garden rooms, the property is nonetheless a series of interconnected yet discrete spaces. To design garden rooms seemed to Pickworth too formal, too restrictive, yet multiple demands required some separation of spaces. Four garden areas define the hospice gardens: the lawn, the formal garden, the chapel terraces, and the children's garden.

Other areas have been designed as small gardens or to act as unifying devices for the whole. Simple things —oleander in pots at the front door, the culmination point of a path—have been given careful thought. Everything either is a garden or supports a garden.

The heart of the gardens is the lawn with its huge live oak, which is itself a symbol of life: the mass and strength of the tree remind us of forces stronger and more enduring than ourselves. The space is gracious, informal, and tranquil.

Sheltered by the buildings and sheltering the garden, the venerable live oak casts its shade on the lawn. Live oak trees are impressive sights in South Atlantic and Gulf State gardens, often twice as broad as high, rounded in form and green most winters. They are massive, dependable trees, which almost embrace a person as they provide shade and comfort in the hot Texas climate. The live oak is a well-loved native species that evokes powerful memories for many Southerners. The ancient live oak in this garden imparts a feeling of stability in a place where one of life's most difficult events is taking place.

The original Holcombe garden had ground cover under the oak, but Pickworth felt it was too "busy" and that the lawn, although more difficult to maintain, imparted more serenity. It also invites use, as ground cover does not. One can sit on the lawn or on the simple swing hanging from one of the branches of the tree. Other large live oak trees on the property give substance and structure to an otherwise new-looking garden and provide context for the most important tree. In addition, the next generation of trees has been planted to replace those lost or damaged during construction. This was done, Pickworth explains, to "touch up, blend, repair the old garden."

Near the serene oak is the formal garden, built around 1925. With its pool and fountain, it is cool, elegant, and comforting. Small, strictly geometric, defined and contained with brick paths and low hedges, it reflects a pattern repeated for centuries. Azaleas and bulbs bloom there in the spring. Spring is the most vibrant season, and the design is intended to emphasize the time of new life. In this part of Texas (Plant Hardiness Zone 10), spring blossoms are a fleeting thing: in the intense heat they will bloom only a few days. They are all the more prized for that reason.

The geometric shapes and the care with which the garden is maintained are a source of immediate intellectual and emotional satisfaction, and the experience of being in the garden affords a range of subtle, simultaneous sensory stimulations. The fountain and pool are a visual delight, constantly in flux as the water splashes and flows, catching the light. The sound of the water adds another dimension to the completeness of the experience. In Texas the change of humidity in the microclimate around the pool and fountain alone could transport a person out of the surrounding discomfort. Add to that the scents intensified by the increased moisture, the color of blossoms, varying as they mature and fade, the caress of the breeze visually reinforced by the movement of the plants, and one is immersed in a peace and well-being that resembles meditation.

The benches, chairs, and low tables that form a seating area just outside the fountain and pool square were a gift in honor of a past Garden Club president, Martha Lovett. This arrangement of furniture on paths wide enough for wheelchairs and beds was essential to adapt the old garden to the needs of today's patients. Here one can come and rest when strolling in the other areas of the garden. Even the most compromised patients are routinely wheeled out into the garden so they can relax in its sheltered spaces. Patients or family and staff members can discuss what the future may bring, either here or in the gazebo or the chapel garden.

(top) The formal garden, shown with azaleas in bloom, is like an oasis. This quality is enhanced by the sense of enclosure and removal from the surrounding neighborhood. *(Photo: Richard Payne,* F A I A *)*

(right) The children's garden, long and narrow, features a maze, a chalkboard, child-sized climbing structures, interesting plants, and a winding path with stepping-stones and a bridge over an imaginary stream. *(Photo: Richard Payne,* F A I A *)*

(left) Thanks to the skillful design, the experiences that this small property affords are many and varied. Another path separates the formal garden from the children's garden and leads to the gazebo. *(Photo: Richard Payne,* F A I A *)*

The children's garden is informal, relaxing, and fun, a place where children and adults can express themselves in relative privacy. It is a truly inventive space. Long and narrow, stretching most of the length of the back of the property, it is removed from yet close to the main gardens. It is as much a passage as a destination, a quality of its fine design. The experience it provides is like that of playing in the vacant lot a person played in as a child, but this is an elegant, composed vacant lot. It looks as if it had always been there, though it was created out of an unneeded storage area behind the wall of the main garden. Although it lacks tangles or brambles, it suggests mystery, complexity, discovery. In place of primary colors or climbing structures, it features a maze, a "chalkboard" wall, child-sized sculptures, and a path that meanders over a miniature bridge and traverses a rock "stream," complete with stepping-stones to test one's skill at crossing this imaginary water. The plants are many and varied and invite exploration. The garden is fenced, the maze is low enough that a child can be observed, and none of the plants are poisonous. These and other safety features were considered and incorporated, although they were not what drove this design.

The children's garden resulted from interview responses expressing the need to provide specifically for children who are patients, as well as for visiting children. And a surprising number of adults use the garden, too. Staff members take their breaks in the children's garden, interacting with the kids and leaving notes for each other on the chalkboard.

In designing the garden, Pickworth recalled his own childhood and that of his children. It was the sense of free, inventive play and the variety of experiences that he wanted to capture for his design. The garden had to be complex, but not overwhelming. It needed places to hide, places to wander, a high spot from which to survey the area, a way to express oneself, things to discover.

Precedents and Meanings

This hospice garden presents few innovations. Rather, two distinct traditions have been harmonized in it. The formal garden is a bow to the Tudor architectural style, but an equally strong modern influence is evident, that of the nineteenth-century naturalistic landscape. Although the best design transcends style and aims to meet basic human needs, it also carries cultural implications through the selection and use of forms. As in clothing styles and interior decoration, certain styles in architecture imply power, wealth, and sophistication, and others communicate comfort, domesticity, or modesty. The style may indicate that a place is a church, a store, a school, or a home. We can be confused by buildings that appear in other than the expected style.

The hospice buildings are Tudor in style. Tudor architecture, with its steeply pitched roofs, multi-paned windows, front-facing gables, and common materials of brick, half-timbering, and masonry, evokes an image of relaxed domestic elegance and comfort. The American version of Tudor architecture is loosely based on a variety of late medieval English forms, not on the true Tudor of the early sixteenth century. It incorporates elements from thatched-roof folk cottages to grand manor houses. The style was used frequently in American suburban building in the early part of this century, becoming particularly fashionable in the 1920s and 1930s, when the Holcombe house was constructed.[18] With its irregular forms, it is easily adapted to accommodate various functions, as the Hospice at the Texas Medical Center demonstrates. The Americanized domestic style provides strong support for the goal of a noninstitutional, homelike place for the hospice headquarters and its inpatient facility and chapel.

The gardens that accompany American suburban Tudor homes of the twentieth century often combine regular geometries with naturalistic plantings, both of which have been used at the hospice. The geometric patterns come to us from ancient times, while naturalistic plantings near the house are a nineteenth-century development. Tudor gardens in sixteenth- and seventeenth-century England drew on the precedent of the Middle Ages. In the Middle Ages a high wall would have enclosed the garden to protect it from enemies, beasts, and storms. Following the example of the cloister garden, Tudor gardens in the sixteenth century were symmetrical—square or rectangular in overall shape—but with more inventive cross-patterns than in the monastery's simple compass-point orientation and four-part divisions. Tudor gardeners varied their cross-paths by setting out hedge paths that cut the quadrangles to form triangles and other linear shapes, or even twisted shapes called knots. The spaces defined by the hedges were often filled with flowers, or even vegetables, herbs, fruits, or sometimes a tree.[19]

At the center of a medieval or Tudor garden was a water source, wellhead, fountain, or storage basin; the hospice garden has its decorative pool and fountain and a bronze statue of a cherub. In historic gardens the beds were raised a few inches, a horticultural practice employed by the early Romans that has continued uninterrupted ever since. Such a method of cultivation improves the soil and its drainage and lessens the physical strain on the gardener. At the hospice the planting beds are raised slightly and curbed with a brick detail of a soldier (vertical bricks, placed endwise) and a sidewalk of running bond to which has been added a flat band edge. Tudor gardeners placed pots about as accents, probably filled with plants less hardy than those in the beds, as is the practice in the hospice garden today. Other Tudor garden ornaments that have been interpreted for this garden include the elegant birdhouse, urns, and topiary.[20]

The hospice's gardens draw equally strongly on a modern influence: the naturalistic landscape familiar to the country gentleman and, later, the suburbanite. To be an American is to be deeply influenced by a nineteenth-century revolution in landscape design. As with many things American, this new approach, a

departure from rigid formality, was a foreign invention adapted to our conditions and needs. As early as the late eighteenth century the most traveled, mon-eyed, and famous Americans, people like George Washington at his Mount Vernon estate, had begun to employ the new English ideas about gardens. The new design drew its strength from the widespread Romantic movement of the late eighteenth century, but the gardening style did not catch on generally until the mid-nineteenth century, when Andrew Jackson Downing (1815–1852) published his influential and popular book *A Treatise on the Theory and Practice of Landscape Gardening* (1841).

Downing's basic principles included curved paths and planting beds and lawns with clumps of trees or trees planted singly so they might mature as specimens of their type. He preferred architectural styles that blended with the irregular forms of nature, and he advocated Tudor, Italianate, and Gothic. Downing's landscapes did not form walled and geometric garden rooms, but they were fashioned into distinct areas, nonetheless. The approach to the house, the lawn area, the service area, and the vegetable garden were delineated on his drawings, and often thickets and shrubs were recommended as divisions. The inherited character of the site was to be revealed and enhanced by the gardener. Nature itself was to be valued, not dominated or made to conform to right-angle geometries. The idea was to celebrate the essence of the place as it was tamed and improved.[21]

The Holcombe house and garden display many of the Downing principles. Curved paths and planting beds, trees in the lawn, thickets of shrubs and small trees can all be found here. Native live oak trees have been substituted for the New England species he recommended, and modern azaleas have replaced the less showy plants of Downing's time. But in general, the soft, lush, naturalistic garden is as he proposed at the hospice: nature tamed, improved, and perfected.

Long-standing traditions encourage Americans to make a beautiful home surrounded by a verdant landscape. The goal here in Texas is not the eastern pioneer's experience of carving a place out of a dense forest. Rather, the environment must be manipulated to provide for comfort and use. Where watering is frequent, plant material abounds, although some loss of variety is to be expected, given the climatic extremes. Texas homeowners and gardeners set out plants that cannot possibly be self-sustaining but which thrive most of the time. Considerable optimism and persistence enrich the local gardening tradition.

The exquisite gardens at the hospice became a reality because of the joint efforts of the hospice and the Garden Club. Wickman recognized that the goals of both would be furthered if the groups collaborated on the project. The Garden Club of Houston has helped preserve a historic property, contributed green space to the city, and funded a project of quality and significance that touches many. In addition, the club has an ongoing relationship with the hospice, one that allows its members to be involved in the garden's care and evolution. To build a garden is not an event but a way of life. It requires a continued commitment that Garden Club members understand and appreciate.

The benefits that this remarkable collaboration has brought to the hospice are many. It now has a garden designed for its needs, funded by donation, built to the highest standards, and maintained at little cost to itself—a beautiful place that enhances this society of friends, this community of support. The garden is in

constant use, a place that supports the important goals of the hospice movement. The garden helps relieve some of the isolation common to this time of great difficulty and encourages friends and families to gather round and care for the dying and for themselves as well. It helps make the remaining life of patients as rich and full as possible and provides a gracious space where normal activities can continue during a difficult time. Even at this point in life, patients can savor eating or reading outside, people-watching, playing, strolling, admiring plants, and just feeling the sun or breeze. The garden also affords privacy, a place for intimate conversations or a quiet moment alone.

It was primarily thanks to the vision, good taste, and energy of one woman, Nina Wickman, that this project was eventually realized. Wickman's extraordinary fund-raising supported the efforts of professionals in planning, architecture, landscape architecture, and horticulture to give the garden physical form. As with all fine gardens, this one resonates with local tradition and offers a rich and varied experience. Welcoming and truly accessible, the hospice garden is beautiful, sensually stimulating, and emotionally and intellectually moving. Although—and perhaps partly because—it unites things familiar and comforting, it has the potential, even in so poignant a time as one of serious illness, to help people endure and grow spiritually.

Lawn games are played in front of the Scattergood Building, the original patient care building of Friends Asylum, around the 1880s. *(Photo courtesy of Friends Hospital Archives)*

Friends Hospital

Philadelphia, Pennsylvania

Because people suffering from mental illnesses often do not behave in expected or proper ways, they have long been the targets of discrimination, frustration, and anger. People project their fears onto the mentally ill. Even today, despite our large cabinet of mood-altering drugs and the insights of two centuries of psychiatry, mental patients are stigmatized as different from the rest of us. Medical insurance offers little money for treatment. Mental hospitals and research into mental illness are not high on foundation lists, and psychiatry itself is regarded by many physicians as one of their lesser arts. In the past the intractable behavior of the mentally ill often drove family and neighbors to treat the insane like criminals—to confine them in wretched public institutions where they were put in cells, restrained with straps and chains, and often neglected or starved.[1]

Friends Hospital in Philadelphia was first organized in 1813, in such a climate of anger, frustration, and fear. The Quakers brought their religious radicalism to their understanding of mental illnesses. Because the Quaker founders of the institution believed that every person embodied the "divine principle," it was their hope that if a sympathetic, familylike setting of quiet and order were provided, the divine principle might manifest itself in "inward enlightenment" and a return to more rational behavior. The early superintendents spoke of their successful patients as being "restored." By that they meant that a patient's behavior had been sufficiently rational and orderly for some weeks or months that the patient could be returned to ordinary living arrangements. In their emphasis on "mild" as opposed to

"terrific" methods of treatment, they were following the innovations of Philippe Pinel in France, and especially William Tuke of York, England.

Tuke (1732–1822) was a Quaker tea and coffee merchant. He was moved by the institutional killing of a Quaker woman who had been confined in 1791 to the nearby public workhouse. Local Friends asked to visit her, since her family lived far away. The visits were refused "on the grounds that the patient [was not] in a suitable state to be seen by strangers, and, in a few weeks after her admission, death put a period to her sufferings."[2]

Tuke convinced the York Quarterly Meeting that it would be well, given the religious prejudice of the day, to establish a separate institution for afflicted Quakers so that they might find the comfort of being Friends among Friends. A committee subsequently purchased an eleven-acre tract and erected a building for twenty patients, where in 1796 Tuke opened his York Retreat. He called his methods the benevolent mode of treatment. He offered warm baths to the melancholic, and food and porter to the maniacal. He, like Pinel, very much opposed contemporary medical methods of quieting patients through depletion by bleeding, cupping, and blistering. The only restraints allowed were the locked room and the straitjacket, both used only when all else failed. The account by his grandson (Samuel Tuke, 1784–1857) of the York Retreat, published in 1813, was a landmark text in the worldwide campaign to reform the treatment of the insane, and one of the classics in the history of psychiatry.[3]

The Tukes' influence on Philadelphia Friends was immediate and direct. The city's Quakers had been instrumental in founding the Pennsylvania Hospital in 1751. It had one ward for the insane, but no mental hospital existed anywhere nearby. An itinerant preacher from Burlington, New Jersey, Thomas Scattergood (1748–1814), a man who himself suffered from depression, spent some years traveling in England, where he visited the retreat and met with William Tuke on several occasions. In 1800 he returned to the United States. Several years later he persuaded an influential group of Quakers to raise funds to establish an asylum like Tuke's in Philadelphia.[4]

The initial report of these Philadelphia founders set forth the community's needs and goals, their sense that mental illness was a partial and intermittent interruption of the rational process, and their hopes that patient recovery might follow from removal to a quiet place. "It appears very desirable that an institution should be formed, in a retired situation, with the necessary medical assistance, and wholly under the care and notice of Friends, for the relief and accommodation of persons then afflicted, including members and professors with us, of every description, with respect to property. This would serve to alleviate the anxiety of their relatives, to tranquilize the minds of the afflicted in their lucid intervals, and would, moreover, tend to facilitate their recovery."[5]

The means of governance that the sponsors established is interesting. Interesting because of the long life and success of the institution they initiated, and interesting today in contrast to the money-making structures currently being imposed on American medicine. The asylum was to be a community institution in which any person who pledged ten dollars per year or any monthly meeting that pledged two hundred dollars per year would be a member entitled to vote to elect the twenty-person board of managers.

The environmentalism that lay at the core of the Moral Treatment also informed this early prospectus. The founders believed that outbreaks of mental illness derived from the stresses of private living situations. They sought relief for the patients by placing them in quiet areas, far from the bustle of everyday life. Accordingly, the committee had purchased fifty-two acres of farm- and woodland five miles north of the city, and a mile from the village of Frankford.

The provision of abundant air and sunlight was a specification that has guided all the hospital's architects and builders since its founding, and it remains today one of the most delightful aspects of the building. Perhaps this fine practice had its origin in the best of late eighteenth-century thinking about how to ensure proper hygiene. However it came about, in 1814 the founders apologized for the grand look of their new building, owing to the central section that stood between the men's and women's wings. "The unavoidable extension of the front, arises from the necessity of affording comfort and convenience to the patients, by procuring a free admission of light and air. This important consideration will lead, in the first instance, to more expense, but we do not doubt will be fully counterbalanced by the advantages resulting from it."[6]

The Friends Asylum (now called Friends Hospital) opened in 1817 under the direction of Isaac Bonsall, a farmer, and his wife, who, with their assistants, lived among the patients. Until 1834 only Quakers were admitted. The very poor who could not afford to pay any fees and the criminally insane were excluded. Like all private hospitals, Friends has cared for middle-class and wealthy patients. The average length of stay in these early years was twenty-three weeks.[7]

Classification of patients according to their symptoms was a core procedure in both Pinel's and Tuke's methods, but in the small groups of twelve to twenty patients of these first years, little more could be done than separate the men from the women and the quiet from the boisterous. The medical director did employ contemporary methods of bloodletting and so forth to quiet the obstreperous and to stimulate the lethargic. Bonsall recorded in his diary: "John H. is excessively lazy. He pleads weakness. We propose trying the effects of medicine."[8] When patients became violent, Bonsall used a darkened room and the straitjacket.

This etching from the 1880s shows side wings added to the Scattergood Building in 1827 to provide rooms for the most disturbed patients. A mansard roof, added in 1871, made room for an additional floor. The Scattergood Building was used for inpatient care from 1817 to 1976 and now houses Friends Hospital administrative offices and outpatient care. *(Photo courtesy of Friends Hospital Archives)*

In the early decades of the nineteenth century the superintendents and staff at the asylum offered their patients a degree of trust that has been withheld since the late nineteenth century, when safe custody became the highest institutional value. In our own time the readiness of lawyers to attack any custodial errors and their failure to reward successes has perpetuated the same stultifying outlook. In early times the patients were treated as worthy of trust, even though they often failed to live up to it. They ate with knives and forks that were not chained to the table, used common farm, shop, and home tools, worked on the farm, and walked freely in the fields and woods; some were also allowed to go to Frankford on errands and to meeting. Many ran away for a spell, some several times. The runaways were not punished for such behavior because the asylum staff regarded their flight as a manifestation of the disease, not an act of rational will. Instead, special privileges like the Thursday tea or visits in the superintendent's family rooms were withheld for a time. In 1838 the staff even encouraged the patients to form a "restorative society" to schedule their work and to arrange other outdoor activities such as fishing, ball playing, kite flying, and walking. These measures suggest that the Moral Treatment in fact functioned a good deal like what we would now call behavioral modification.[9]

Aside from the quiet, orderly family setting, work constituted the chief therapeutic agent. Samuel Tuke was quoted in the 1814 prospectus:

Of all the modes by which patients may be induced to restrain themselves, regular employment is perhaps the most generally efficacious; and those kinds of employment are doubtless to be preferred, both on a moral and physical account, which are accompanied by considerable bodily action; that are the most agreeable to the patient, and which are most opposite to the illusions of his disease. . . . The female patients in the Retreat are employed, as much as possible, in sewing, knitting, or domestic affairs; and several convalescents assist the attendants.

As indolence has a natural tendency to weaken the mind, and to induce ennui and discontent, every kind of rational and innocent employment is encouraged.[10]

The farm, the gardens, and the house were the original resources for such occupational therapy. Growing hay and grain, cutting and carrying wood, tending the large kitchen garden, pumping water, washing, sewing, cooking, and cleaning were all tasks that lay at hand. As such they suggested to the patients the social meanings that such tasks carried in contemporary households. These tasks conveyed the idea that the asylum was a family and a community. Yet few of the patients had been farmers, and farmwork summoned up lower-class connotations for well-to-do city dwellers. Such patients often balked at farming, and some remained idle despite the institution's commitment to work as therapy.[11]

Finding ways to get patients to work proved a recurring difficulty. The minutes of the board of managers are full of site visits, consultations, worries, and experiments with work. The women seemed willing to engage in familiar household and garden activities, but the men, especially the rich men, often refused to work. Gardening captured the interest of only a few men. In 1821 the board proposed hiring a "suitable person . . . of lively and inventive talents whose sole business should be to contrive such employment as the capacities of the patients would be adequate to."[12]

In 1835 the board of managers' Committee on Employment Among the Patients canvassed its fellow institutions—Pennsylvania Hospital, Hartford Retreat, Bloomingdale Asylum, Boston Asylum, Worcester State Lunatic Hospital, and the York Retreat —about work programs and patient activities. They concluded by recommending a five-point program:

(1) Hire a person to offer carriage rides mornings and afternoons. (2) Purchase magazines for the day rooms, checker boards, battle doors, and materials for drawing. (3) Place a string-and-ring game in the exercise yards, and put some poultry, rabbits, and a couple of lambs there, too. (4) Add one person for men and one for women to work with employments. (5) Seek to employ men and women at the trades and tasks they are familiar with from their outside lives.[13]

Two years later, the asylum began admitting non-Quakers as a way to bring its patient numbers up to capacity—thirty men and thirty women.[14] By 1840 the board took pleasure in noting from its visiting committee's report "that increased attention has been given to the employment of patients, a large proportion of the men being employed part of each day either in the workshop or on the grounds of the Institution."[15]

Charles Evans, an attending physician who wrote a description of the asylum, advocated an alternative orientation: the passive use of the grounds for entertainment.

In the house, there are provided, games of different kinds; reading, writing, drawing, etc. The females sew, knit, quilt etc. The library is furnished with books, periodicals, drawings etc. . . . Exercise in the open air is always permitted, and the patients encouraged, whenever the weather will permit, to engage in walking and riding. A carriage and horses are always in readiness, morning and evening, for their accommodation. In the lawn fronting the house, is located a circular rail-road with a pleasure-car on it, large enough to accommodate two, which is moved by hand. Riding upon this road is a very favorite amusement, and is attended with considerable exercise, and is found highly advantageous. Every exertion is made to interest male patients in gardening, and in the various employments afforded in the cultivation of the farm.[16]

Thus, even in the early years, when the institution focused on work as a means of recovery, tension surfaced over the many needs of a good patient environment: work as opposed to diversion and entertainment; active use of materials and nature as opposed to passive observation and enjoyment.

Over the years that followed, the role of community work diminished until it disappeared in the twentieth century. Teachers and therapists took its place: classes, occupational therapy, sports and games, psychotherapy, hydrotherapy, electric shock, and medications. The farm, under professional management, flourished as a source of food and income until after World War II. The grounds, little more than a farm at first, after years of cultivation reached such a level of perfection that they became the equal of a gentleman's estate or a private arboretum. As these changes went forward, the meaning of the grounds themselves shifted from farm to symbol, from work to recreation, from nature to health. They became for patients, staff, and visitors the antithesis of the enduring social and psychological stigmas borne by mental patients and their caregivers.

This progression at the asylum mirrored the changes going on in the world beyond its fences. Arts and crafts left the homes of Philadelphians to be supplanted by specialized commercial institutions of manufacture, education, and health care. Tuke and Bonsall had begun small institutions for the mentally ill which closely matched their society. The members of the retreat and the asylum shared, for better or worse, the tasks of cooking, cleaning, gardening, and farming. The behavioral approach of the superintendents led them to teach the patients the reciprocal obligations of everyday life. As the years went by, the asylum became, like society as a whole, less and less a small interdependent community and more and more a specialized institution—a hospital, where care was given to the sick and inmates were regarded as patients, not community members.

Throughout the nineteenth and twentieth centuries the environment of the Friends Asylum grew slowly along two axes, toward a different environment and toward new methods of care. The farm and garden staff extended the lawns and plantings continually. In 1862, for example, seven thousand feet of tile drain were laid beneath the front field to make the beautiful front lawn possible.[17] In 1879 the first greenhouse was erected.[18]

As the patients ceased to work side by side with the staff, the superintendent searched for ever new ways to fill the residents' time, especially during the shut-in winter days of "wearisome feelings."[19] Dr. Evans had encouraged the study of mathematics and science. In 1838–1839 the hospital built a handsome pergola in the rear gardens to serve as a library and reading room, and in it a cabinet of natural history specimens was set out.[20] Subsequently, teachers came to give instruction in school subjects, first on the women's side, then on the men's.[21] In 1854 the patients commenced publishing a newspaper, and in 1874 a new library was constructed and the old one turned into a museum of shells, stuffed animals, and rocks.[22] In 1885 regular art classes began.

That year the superintendent's report gave some measure of how the changes in social classes and industrialized work in outside society had transformed the asylum. It was no longer a family of mentally ill patients who shared the work of its little community. Now that the asylum was becoming a specialized institution for the careful confinement of the sick, the "Address to Contributors" read:

> The course of gentle and considerate treatment provided, the absence of physical restraint, the retirement and quiet, varied at suitable intervals with pleasant social gatherings and entertainments, lawn games in proper season, lectures, displays of stereopticon views etc. tend to cheer the despondent, calm the excited, and promote the mental health and vigor of all. It is a point constantly before the managers and executive officers to employ the hands and minds of the patients who are capable of being thus occupied in such a manner as will relieve the tension and monotony which is to a considerable extent inseparable from hospital life.

The superintendent closed with an appeal for the gift of a woodworking shop.[23]

In 1906 the superintendent wrote of a new and enlarged greenhouse as a place "embowered in luxuriant foliage interspersed with walks and seats, [that] make it a sort of fairy land for the patients."[24] The environment of the hospital was now strongly divided between the grounds, which were allocated for passive recreation, and the settings in which the patients were to be kept active: education, arts and crafts, and sports. Psychotherapy, hydrotherapy, and massage were the hoped-for therapeutic agencies. The superintendent in this year was both discouraged and hopeful: discouraged at the failure of many patients to improve, and hopeful that the new therapies might prove efficacious.

The criticism is sometimes made that the percentage of recoveries at the present day is not higher than it was fifty or eighty years ago. . . . A leading neurologist, a man of world-wide fame, remarked not long ago that he was tired of telling people they could not get well. . . . Perhaps many of the mental diseases which are regarded to-day as incurable may be transferred in the course of time to the list of curable diseases. . . . The particular form of treatment at the present time that is becoming more and more popular may be expressed under the term psychotherapy.[25]

A review of the experience of the first century of the asylum supported the superintendent's concerns. During its first hundred years, 4,421 men and women had been admitted to the asylum. Of these, 1,502 had been discharged as "restored," and 503 as "nearly restored." That left a formidable remainder of 2,416, or 54.6 percent, who had not been restored. In institutional terms that meant that chronically ill patients either stayed at the asylum, if their families could afford the fees, or were returned home or remanded to a state chronic hospital.[26]

During the 1920s the superintendents' reports carried news of new medical equipment, research on the nervous system, and the progress of the school of nurses. Many of these texts recast nineteenth-century themes into contemporary language. In 1924 the superintendent repeated the old belief that the best therapeutic results can be expected only if the patients are seen in the early phases of their disease. He then returned to the issue of work, drawing a new distinction between acute and chronic cases. "The Department of Occupational Therapy has probably never been the center of so much zeal and interest as at the present. In fact the value of employment with useful occupations can scarcely be over-rated as an adjunct to the measures adapted for the treatment of recoverable types of disorder, and as the means for arresting the tendency to deteriorate in the apparently nonrecoverable disorders."[27] During the 1930s the staff seems to have taken steps toward initiating milieu therapy. The physicians began in 1935 to brief the staff on their diagnoses and assessments of each patient.[28]

Two events of great significance to the later history of the hospital took place during the 1930s. First, the issue of African-American exclusion was broached at the Philadelphia yearly meetings by the Committee on Race Relations. In the spring of 1931 two women from that committee visited the board of managers to ask them to consider the admission of "Negro patients."[29] The members of the Executive Committee took up the question of a specific application presented by "a Dr. Virginia M. Alexander (colored) for admittance to the Friends Hospital of a Negro woman, formerly a Philadelphia school teacher." The minutes continued:

Much sympathy was expressed in the case, as it had been brought to individual members of the Board prior to the meeting. There was a full discussion of the matter in which Dr. Buckley [then the superintendent] joined and pointed out what he considered the serious risk that would be involved of injury to patients in the house should they realize, as would be likely, that a colored person was a patient in the same ward with them. In view of this opinion it was decided that it would not be wise for us to accept the application in question, and the clerk was directed to write a suitable letter to Dr. Alexander advising of our decision.[30]

Despite this surrender to the racial antipathies of society at large, the hospital took its first steps toward a new and closer relationship with the community outside its gates. In 1929 Henry Hall, the business manager since 1897, who had resigned from that position, took charge of the farm, greenhouse, and gardens.[31] He immediately initiated an ambitious program to plant thousands of azaleas. By 1936 the managers reported their enthusiasm for the massive plantings.[32] Two years later, the hospital took the unprecedented step of opening the grounds to the public, so that visitors could admire the display. That same year the board of managers not only commented on the "quiet relaxing atmosphere" for the patients but also referred to the grounds as "a veritable arboretum." In subsequent years this spring show came to be known as Garden Days.[33]

This cautious first attempt at opening up the hospital to the public found much more significant expression after World War II. During the war, psychiatry received a tremendous public boost because of its successes. The combined efforts of preventive planning, Freudian and other psychotherapies, milieu therapy in hospital work, and several drugs enabled psychiatry to greatly reduce the incidence of mental illness among the armed forces personnel by comparison with that of World War I. In the postwar decades, modern psychiatry expanded in many directions. One response consisted of adding psychiatric wards to established acute-care general hospitals. Mental hospitals further added special services, especially pediatric and geriatric specialties, often offered as outpatient or day services.

The third, and most ambitious, undertaking called for taking psychiatry into urban and suburban neighborhoods, so that ordinary people under stress could receive timely and appropriate treatment and chronic sufferers could continue to live and to work in their home settings. A unique feature of this program was the formation of teams to follow particular patients in their treatment into hospitals when they were hospitalized and out into the community when they came home. Unlike the Moral Treatment of the early nineteenth century, in which the familiar was regarded as the trigger for symptoms of illness, in the community mental health movement the home and the community were seen as potentially supportive set-

tings. The community, with sufficient public education and the guidance and services of a local mental health center, could therefore become its own healing agent.[34]

In 1967 the federal government began its insurance programs, Medicaid for the poor and Medicare for the elderly. As a result, the patients coming to Friends Hospital were more and more dependent on these programs and on private medical insurance policies. At the same time, improvements in treatment and alternative solutions to full hospitalization reduced the average length of stay at Friends Hospital from ninety-five days in 1967 to thirty-five days in 1975.[35]

These postwar changes forced the hospital and its supporters to re-evaluate. In 1968 the board of managers hired a consulting firm to examine the hospital's role within the Philadelphia metropolitan area. Soon their reassessment took on a special urgency because the interstate highway planners proposed building a northeast freeway either around the perimeter or through an edge of the hospital grounds.[36]

It was not clear just what course the hospital ought to take. Some felt that the original mission of the Friends Asylum had now been satisfied, and that the postwar additions of psychiatric facilities to general hospitals in the region obviated the need to preserve the Friends facility. Others favored selling the entire hundred acres and using the proceeds to relocate at a new suburban site, perhaps in Bucks County. After a real estate review, however, it was estimated that the proceeds would not be nearly sufficient to finance such a move.

In 1973 the board of managers voted to stay put and to modernize the facilities. They wished to continue the hospital's role as a "small, personalized hospital." Moreover, there was still "a great deal of feeling among the Board, the Corporation, and the staff for remaining on these beautiful grounds." In addition, the friends of the hospital had organized and gathered seven thousand signatures in a successful campaign to defeat the highway plan. Accordingly, a fund-raising campaign was initiated, a building committee formed, and the Philadelphia architectural firm of Mirik, Pearson & Bachelor hired to design what proved to be a handsome and fitting series of additions to the campus. The hospital also embarked on a series of day patient and outpatient off-campus programs in cooperation with other medical institutions.[37]

Unfortunately for the nation and Friends Hospital, the community mental health movement and the movement for adequate universal medical insurance did not prevail in the years following the 1973 decision. Americans continued to be frightened by their own mentally ill. Attempts to locate halfway houses and clinics in residential neighborhoods met with ferocious opposition. Citizens associated such places not with their own suffering relatives but with drugs, crime, violence, and loss of the property values. Few took pleasure in imagining themselves as volunteer caregivers or informal supporters of such facilities. At the same time, many physicians came to regard the new mood-altering drugs as sufficient quick fixes for mental illness, instead of understanding the new drugs to be part of a social process for healing or stabilizing mental patients.

As a consequence, the community mental health centers and halfway houses were not built in adequate numbers, and as the old giant state mental hospitals were emptied out, too few small ones replaced them to serve the numbers of people who required residential treatment. The homeless on the streets of American cities today give an awful impression that history has come full circle again: Louis XIV built the Bicêtre —the very institution Pinel later had to reform—to sweep the vagrants and beggars off the streets of Paris.

Medical insurance fared no better. Private insurance companies and corporate medical enterprises discovered that profits could be made by gathering up client pools of the well employed, the young, and the healthy, thereby shunting the poor, the ill, and the elderly into federal programs or emergency wards. The political response was not a move toward universal coverage and rationalization of care for all but rather a destructive politics of private insurance, medical profit making, and public budget cutting. At Friends Hospital, as at all medical facilities that depend on private and public insurance policies, the payments do not always meet the costs of decent care, and the hospital goes to great lengths, as part of its eleemosynary outreach, to provide treatment for the many sufferers who are uninsured.

Modern health care practitioners will readily concur with the words of Samuel Tuke, reported in the 1813 hospital prospectus:

The managers of this Institution, are far from imagining that they have arrived at a state of perfection in the moral treatment of insanity. If they have made any considerable approaches towards it, their progress has only served to convince them how much more may probably be effected; and to fill them with regret, that so little ingenuity has hitherto been exerted to increase the comforts of insane persons. There is no doubt, that if the same exertions were used for this purpose, as are frequently employed to amuse the vain, the frivolous, and the idle, many more gleams of comfort would be shed over the unhappy existence of lunatics, and the proportion of cures would be still materially increased.[38]

The Gardens

The form each place takes is the result of many forces—the physical attributes of the land in its natural state, the cultural needs that cause its alteration or adaptation, and the vision, resources, and technology available to effect change—all part of its evolution over time. No two garden spots will be the same, for the forces of change are too varied and the people effecting it choose different ways of interpreting and interacting with nature. Ultimately, it is individuals, making their own decisions and channeling their efforts toward their own goals, who largely determine the form and the use of space. A balance must be achieved between immediate needs and future concerns. Crossroads are reached, decisions are made, and the evolution continues. The wisdom of certain actions is often unknown during the lifetimes of those undertaking them.

A CULTURAL LANDSCAPE

The hundred acres of land belonging to the Friends Hospital in North Philadelphia has supported and sustained the institution for more than 175 years. It is a landscape of forest, gracious lawns, grand specimen trees, ravines, ponds, streams, and ornamental gardens. It presents rugged natural features and exquisitely tended gardens, grand gestures and quiet corners. The size and age of the plant collections rival those of estates and arboretums. The native wildlife includes great blue heron, osprey, red-tailed hawks, horned owl, deer, muskrat, and carp. Enclosed by walls, the grounds are set apart from the rest of the world—a campus for the many buildings used in the delivery of mental health services and a haven for those who work or seek treatment at Friends Hospital.

Since the original purchase of fifty-two acres in 1813, the land has been continuously interpreted, worked, and modified in support of the Friends' mission to care for the mentally ill. The vast cultural and technological changes of the past two centuries and the revolution in the treatment of the mentally ill have left their mark. The property now exhibits a layering of culture and ecology rare in American landscapes. As agrarian society was transformed into industrial society in the United States, this place changed accordingly. As treatments evolved from nineteenth-century remedies to modern medications, Friends Hospital kept pace. To visit Friends is to step back in time, move through time, and to experience the modern-day reality. Farming, lumbering, quarrying, filling, draining, gardening, and the human introduction of plant disease have all altered this property, along with its topography, vegetation, and wildlife. What has remained constant is a commitment that stems from Quaker culture—and for a time at the turn of the century, characterized American culture as a whole—that nature is essential, elemental. The Quakers believe that we are not separate from nature but a part of it, and that we should experience nature directly, intimately, and repeatedly.

As we have seen, the Friends Asylum that opened in 1817 was conceived as a version of a Quaker home, where Quaker life and beliefs would be manifest. The contributors' selection of the site was undoubtedly influenced by the presence of Friends in the vicinity, but they also thought its isolation from the city would provide an ideal retreat for those suffering from mental illness. Also, the farm would yield food for patients and staff and provide ample opportunity for work therapy, a component of the Moral Treatment.[39] As Friends' psychiatrist Dr. Edward Leonard imagined the past, "In 1817, how natural it was for a Quaker to have a purpose for each day. To go to Meeting, to weed, lets one be busy. The farm was an essential part of that" (August 11, 1995, interview).

When the property was purchased by the Friends in 1813 for an asylum for "persons deprived of the use of their reason,"[40] it was about five miles north of Philadelphia, near the small town of Frankford. It was a home in the country, a fifty-two-acre farm in an area where many Philadelphia Quakers had summer homes. By today's standards, that city of fifty-odd thousands would be considered placid and quaint, but to a resident of 1813 it seemed crowded, bustling, perhaps even overwhelming. This was the era when nine out of ten Americans farmed. To remove the mentally ill from the stress of the city was a logical remedy.

Unlike Pennsylvania Hospital in West Philadelphia, Friends Asylum was to be completely self-sufficient, and this objective necessitated the purchase of fertile land suitable for farming. The grounds of the asylum covered fifty-two acres of prime agricultural land, thirty of which were to be cultivated for hay, corn, potatoes, and wheat. Six cows would supply the asylum with plenty of milk and butter, and a separate kitchen garden would produce vegetables for the patients' meals. Even tobacco was eventually grown, but only for the "restricted consumption of the convalescent patients."[41] Medicinal plants and other "salutary" herbs were cultivated in large quantities. The "never-fail spring," near which the main building

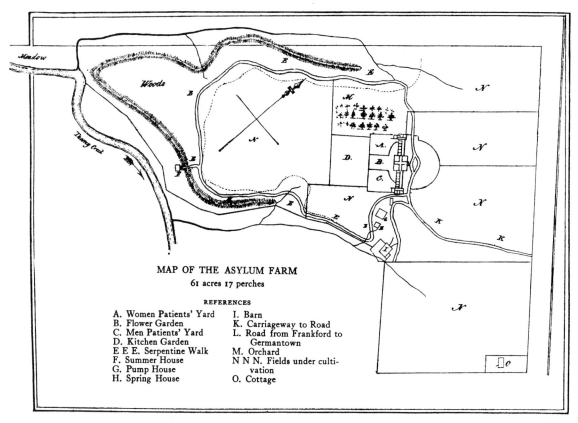

MAP OF THE ASYLUM FARM
61 acres 17 perches

REFERENCES

A. Women Patients' Yard
B. Flower Garden
C. Men Patients' Yard
D. Kitchen Garden
E E E. Serpentine Walk
F. Summer House
G. Pump House
H. Spring House
I. Barn
K. Carriageway to Road
L. Road from Frankford to
   Germantown
M. Orchard
N N N. Fields under culti-
   vation
O. Cottage

This 1832 map shows the first land purchased by the Friends for their asylum. The Scattergood Building is set back from the main road to ensure privacy for patients. The map delineates the areas of the farm used for cultivation, orchards, and gardens. The serpentine walk (E. E. E.) provided a path for less-strenuous exercise. (*Courtesy of Friends Hospital Archives*)

was located, was a crucial feature for an institution built to accommodate fifty patients. The spring furnished drinking water, and enough extra remained to feed a quiet, shaded duck pond. The woods supplied firewood, and a quarry provided the stone for the main building, which was then plastered over with stucco.[42]

This property was purchased and developed at a time when most people were directly dependent on the land for their sustenance. People still knew how to "read' the land, its soil, and its topography; they knew how many acres were needed for pasture, cultivation, and wood supply. Spring water was a kind of wealth, and to have a property with a never-fail spring was to be assured of prosperity. An early nineteenth-

century map of the Friends property shows the ravine, stream, forest, and other salient features that afforded building material, food, and heat.[43] In the presence of such bounty, some elements were reserved more for pleasure than production.

The first patients were greeted by a broad tree-lined avenue stretching from the public road to the front doors of the institution. Shaded walks, quiet forest paths, and large fields of soft grass were set aside for recreational use. One of the walks, stretching over a mile, wound through the grounds and led to a small summer house built on a hill of considerable height, three sides of which were almost perpendicular. This "house of pleasure" was shaded by oak, beech, chestnut and towering tulip trees. A rapid stream rippled over rocks nearby, producing the "melancholy" sounds of a distant waterfall. The grounds of the new asylum were carefully planned and were intended to evoke a feeling of quiet serenity, to make the institution a true "retreat". The inherent confusion of life in a large city was to be left outside the gates of the Friends Asylum. Once inside these gates the patients would be safe.[44]

Over the years, additional land was purchased and farmed. The other properties, 104 acres near Fox Chase and 326 acres at Trevose, also served as sites for "intermediate houses," or convalescent homes for patients. Later they were sold. Today, Friends Hospital sits on a parcel of approximately 100 acres, half of which was the initial purchase, the site where patient care has always been delivered. Several changes were brought about by farming. Fields were mapped out, cows put out to graze,[45] water redirected, orchards planted, logs cut. But another transformation was to come.

Landowners and successful farmers, the Quakers were intimately connected with the land. The application of new farming techniques, the collection and classification of plants, and the pleasure derived from these activities are all one with their religious beliefs. Horticulture is a longstanding tradition among Friends, and the Quaker contributions to horticulture in the United States have been numerous from early on and remain decisive and widespread. The largest plant collection effort in the then British colonies was carried out by an American-born colonist, John Bartram (1699–1777). He and his cousin Humphrey Marshall (1722–1801), both Quakers, became expert botanists, studying and collecting specimens along the East Coast and especially in Appalachia. In 1729 Bartram opened the first botanical garden in the American colonies at Kingsessing, a few miles from Friends Hospital. His nursery supplied many plants to George Washington for his Mount Vernon home. Carolus Linnaeus, the Swedish botanist and inventor of the binomial method of classifying living things, called Bartram "the world's greatest natural botanist."[46] For his part, Marshall published the first American book on botany in 1785. In the surrounding area are some of the nation's most distinguished gardens: Morris Arboretum, Awbry Arboretum, Longwood

Gardens, and the Haverford and Swarthmore Colleges gardens. All are or once were Quaker properties, and they are visited by thousands each year.[47] The Pennsylvania Horticultural Society is the oldest such society in the nation. The annual Philadelphia Flower Show is also the oldest in the nation, and the most highly esteemed.

It is in this sphere of excellence and influence that Friends Hospital is situated. Today, the grounds are a veritable arboretum, whose plant collections were actively undertaken about a century ago and now contain hundreds of trees, shrubs, and herbaceous plants. It was Henry Hall, manager of farm and grounds from 1897 to 1941, who is credited with the transformation of the hospital's landscape from that of a farm to that of a park and botanical garden designed to serve patients, family, and staff. Hall probably began planting ornamental specimen trees before the turn of the century, and he continued until his retirement. Now mature species include: ginkgo (*Ginkgo biloba*), elm (*Ulmus americana*), cucumber magnolia (*Magnolia acuminata*), bald cypress (*Taxodium distichum*), paperbark maple (*Acer griseum*), Japanese maple (*Acer palmatum*), and hundreds more.

In the 1920s Hall began the renowned azalea collection, which now covers thirty acres. In late April and early May, 150 varieties of azaleas bloom alongside rhododendrons and laurels, to the delight of Garden Days visitors. For these few days, the hospital expands its role and opens its gates, as a public arboretum would. Visitors number in the thousands, some driving through, others walking. The greenhouses are open, and staff members answer questions about plants as well as about the hospital itself. Many former employees come to Garden Days, bringing their families and sometimes plants for donation. Once Hall's basic vegetation was in place, subsequent grounds managers have added to and refined the collection, which now includes some 260 varieties of trees and many more of shrubs and herbaceous plants.

As the use of the land gradually changed from farming to ornamental horticulture, expanses that

In the early spring, geraniums wait in one of the greenhouses until they can be planted outdoors by grounds staff or used by patients in horticultural therapy. *(Photo: © 1996, Karen S. R. Balogh)*

were cultivated or "open" generally remained so. Thus, what can be seen today probably follows the same basic pattern that existed in the beginning, except for the construction of buildings. The changes, however, are many. The woodland ground plane was once open, probably grazed by cows. Now, by contrast, it is dense with understory azaleas, the result of decades of collection, propagation, and cultivation of hundreds of individual plants. Pastures, fields, and the kitchen garden are now lawn, ornamental gardens, parking lots, or building sites. Ball fields and tennis courts were added and later removed. Where an orchard once stood is now a power plant.[48] The transformation of farmland to more romantic landscape

at Friends Hospital was part of a stylistic and philosophical evolution mirrored in urban America as a whole. There is no evidence that professional design was undertaken at Friends, but all across the country, cities and institutions were designing and sculpting large-scale landscapes.

For a period in our history an attempt was made to mitigate broad social and environmental problems—unsanitary water, the assimilation of immigrants, the stress of urban life—through the design of major public works that shaped nature. At this time, in the late nineteenth century, Frederick Law Olmsted (1822–1903) defined the profession of landscape architecture as it is practiced today. In the course of his career, he designed the most noted parks in American cities, as well as college campuses and private properties. He was also instrumental in the preservation of wilderness in our National Park system. Among his commissions were designs for several mental health facilities. Olmsted designed or consulted on the design and purchase of asylums in Buffalo and White Plains, New York, and Belmont, Massachusetts. The characteristics that he sought for the location of the McLean Hospital in Belmont were similar to those which existed at Friends Hospital. Olmsted believed that the land should suit the purpose for which it was intended. He looked for physical qualities such as good drainage and adequate distance from topsoil to bedrock that would allow easy construction. He assessed the topographic relief, looking for building sites that faced southward and were protected from winter winds. He also took into account "moral" considerations, or the "natural scenery and the capabilities of the ground in this respect." He looked for a site whose qualities would "favor an inclination to moderate exercise and tranquil occupation of the mind; the least desirable those which include exertion, heat, excitement, or bewilderment."[49]

The design of the Friends Hospital property differed from Olmsted's ideal in several ways. Olmsted's "first [design] concern was to achieve visual unity: he thought in terms of organization of space, perspective, and vista." Since his greatest concern was a unified composition, details that stood out as separate effects could only dilute his larger scheme. He used "predominantly native plant materials, both because he was generally 'imitating' nature and because he did not want the enjoyer of rural scenery to be distracted by conspicuously unusual plants."[50] The Friends Hospital property was still being farmed in Olmsted's day; it developed into a botanical garden gradually, in response to its own particular needs and culture. Its beauty today derives from the combination of its romantic composition and the richness of its collections.

As the farm, the natural landscape, and the plant collections evolved, so too did the recreational facili-

ties. The farm had long had a recreational component — patients enjoyed watching lambs, poultry, English rabbits, and pigeons. They also played cricket, croquet, and tennis on the lawns. And part of the woods was given over to a deer park.[51] The first greenhouse was built in 1879.[52] In Quaker culture, then, as in late nineteenth-century society in general, nature and recreation were inseparable.

Other changes, such as the development of a railroad corridor along what is now the northwest property boundary, were the result of larger forces that lay beyond the Friends' control. At times these larger forces had positive effects. When the railroad excavated its right of way, the detritus was used to build the front lawn, a greensward now dotted with magnificent specimen trees and considered one of the most important features of the property.[53] At other times, the outside forces had destructive effects. The chestnut blight took a terrible toll. The fungus, *Endothia parasitica*, knocked down all the beautiful chestnuts at Friends, as it did elsewhere in the United States (interview with Edward C. Leonard, Jr., August 11, 1995). Yet the northern deciduous forest regenerated itself, and today it is an enchanting place dominated by beech trees, with their pale gray bark and that particular shade of green their leaves seem to emit in the sunlight. The path cut through the forest opens up soaring, cathedral-like spaces, where the wind can be heard high overhead but not felt at ground level.

The recurring theme, however, is one of adaptation and change. Excavation was undertaken in 1996 to transplant a tree from an area where a parking lot was being expanded. Pipes were uncovered that had once fed a fountain on a plot that earlier still had been part of a four-acre kitchen garden. The continually evolving design and use of the garden have been guided by Quaker beliefs for almost two centuries. During that period, the city of Philadelphia grew up around the hospital, engulfing the small town of Frankford. The area became increasingly suburban in the late nineteenth and early twentieth centuries, as new transportation systems like the Frankford

Branch of the Philadelphia & Reading Railroad and Roosevelt Boulevard were constructed. Now the area surrounding the hospital property is a densely constructed agglomeration of housing, major arterial roads, and shopping malls. It is also now on the edge of North Philadelphia, where minority populations live in devastating poverty. Finding ways to serve this population and yet remain financially viable constitutes a major challenge to the institution. The landscape is likely to feel the impact.

Like the landscape, the architecture reveals both change and continuity. The main building is now a National Historic Landmark and serves as the administration building. For a century previously, its center section housed the administrative units of the hospital and the superintendent's family quarters. Day rooms for patients and the superintendent's family rooms shared space on two floors, an indication of just how much the family ideal was part of life at Friends. Identical wings on two sides, one for men and one for women, housed the patients. Other buildings reflect the hospital's past as well. A carriage house and barn are a reminder of the preautomobile and farming cultures. The old hydrotherapy building now houses a treatment program. Other buildings—the gymnasium and the original greenhouse and conservatory—have been torn down. New greenhouses were constructed in a different location. The new dining facility stands on one former greenhouse site; there the long tradition of staff members' sharing meals with patients continues. The dining room's architecture—the high ceiling and clerestory windows—recalls the conservatory and allows a glimpse of the tall canopy of trees outside. The homes that dotted the property are now used for residential treatment programs, but they are a reminder that the staff families once lived on the grounds.

GARDENS AND PLANT COLLECTIONS

The luxuriance of the landscape at Friends Hospital is the result of the sheer size of the property, the varied topography and microclimates, and the long horticultural tradition. Large-scale features—forest, ravine, pond, and botanical garden—provide context for the buildings and their more domestic ornamental gardens and plant collections.

A spot where gardening has gone on continuously for almost two centuries is unusual in this country, and a privately owned property (as opposed, say, to a public garden) where ornamental horticulture has been practiced professionally on this scale for such a length of time is even more unusual. Rarely do individuals or institutions show a commitment strong enough to sustain an extensive gardening and collecting enterprise generation after generation.

These grounds with their mature and many unusual plants, their new acquisitions and recent pruning, would not exist without persistent effort, whose results may not be fully realized for decades. To achieve the dense understory in the woodlands alone has required sustained attention for seven decades. The thirty acres of azaleas, when in bloom, make for a grand spectacle, and the azalea collection has become an important part of the culture as well as the landscape at Friends Hospital. New plant collections are being developed, too. On the front lawn a small, variegated pink-leaved variety of beech, *Fagus sylvatica "tricolor"* (which is lacking a full complement of chlorophyll), has been added to the massive beeches already there. The newcomer, approximately six feet tall, is a slow-growing cultivar whose magnificence will be manifest only decades from now. Other collections developed or extended in recent years include viburnum (fifty varieties), witch hazel (fifteen varieties), and hosta (a hundred varieties). Perennials number between three and four thousand varieties.

Collections such as these are not like art, antique, or baseball card collections, in that they are living, growing, changing things that belong to the place itself and the culture at large. Although it is rarely the motivation for planting, these collections become a kind of investment, valuable not because of their initial cost but because plants grown in the same settings for decades are often irreplaceable. Trees of a certain size can be transplanted only at enormous expense, and some varieties are rare and difficult to locate. Intertwined shrubs cannot be separated and replanted with the same effect. Such venerable plantings are not transferable assets, but ones that define a culture and a locale.

The collections at Friends Hospital were assembled on the basis of taxonomy, the study of the principles of classification. Taxonomy collectors often choose to focus their passion on one family or genus. The du Pont family was one example. Their former estate, Winterthur, has a huge, nationally recognized collection of azaleas and plants that share their habitat, which may, in fact, have been the inspiration for the azalea collection begun at Friends in the twenties.

Taxonomy collections reflect knowledge and professionalism rarely found in gardens in medical settings. The expertise that has gone into the lovely gardens at Friends may not be apparent to most visitors, but to the well-trained eye the deliberately cultivated complexity and layering are of immeasurable value. In truth, the beautiful garden that may seem simple or natural to the casual observer often depends on this complexity of plants to sustain its beauty through the seasons. People see and comment on color, but structure, form, and texture may be even more important. One may notice a plant with an unusual form, but its setting can either enhance or detract from the effect. We may not perceive how a space is defined by magnificent trees or lush shrubbery, but it is, in the end, what we experience, what we feel. It is what makes us feel free or enclosed, exposed or protected. Landscaping may reveal the night sky or hide an urban scene to create the illusion of countryside.

At Friends, smaller-scale domestic and ornamental gardens are located near the buildings. A hospital brochure notes the presence of "numerous gardens especially created for the hospital's patients—several enabling gardens with wide paths and raised beds where those in wheelchairs or with limited movement can enjoy horticulture, an enclosed, safe garden for persons with Alzheimer's disease and other dementias,

and colorful gardens tended by some of the hospital's adolescent patients. Herb, annual, perennial, and vegetable gardens provide many materials for the hospital's horticultural therapy program."

Designing gardens for specific patient populations is a relatively new endeavor, paralleling the increasingly specific categorization and separation of patient populations. Patients hospitalized for substance abuse are grouped together, as are adolescents, the elderly, and patients with eating disorders. Designers can now take into consideration differences in patients' energy levels, interests, sun tolerance, coordination, perception, and reaction to drugs used in therapy. Design has thus become increasingly refined with regard to such issues as the intensity of color or the kind of shade or paving provided. Alzheimer's disease patients, for example, may become confused or agitated if confronted by too intense stimuli or too many choices. Designers can respond with relatively simple path configurations and planting schemes.

This approach suffers the weakness of all fine-tuning. Spaces can be rendered obsolete in today's rapidly changing health care system, in which patient units are moved, expanded, or shrunk according to market forces. A balance must be reached between the universal themes and experiences of the garden and those specific to particular patient groups. As gardens are designed to respond to the needs of the special groups, mistakes will be made, but experimentation is important. Gardens that offer a variety of experiences rather than attempt to provide the best single experience should always be available. The popular shaded open space between the old main building and the new buildings at Friends offers just such a varied use of space.

Several small specialty gardens have been designed and constructed at Friends Hospital. Each is the result, in part, of recent Flower Show entries that compelled the grounds and horticulture therapy staff to re-examine the role they play in health care. For more than thirty years the hospital has set out an exhibit on the main floor of the prestigious Philadel-

Horticulture has long been a part of life at Friends Hospital; the first greenhouse was built in 1879. Shown here (about 1950) are women planting seeds and arranging flowers, much as horticultural therapy patients do today. (*Photo courtesy of Friends Hospital Archives*)

phia Flower Show. It has evolved from a table with brochures to exhibitions of patient work to fully installed gardens. Hospital staff members conceive and execute the design and installation with support from corporate, business, and organizational sponsors. One exhibit featured a garden for use by the elderly; another focused on adaptive tools, and still another on sensory stimulation. That a health care institution would have a booth at the Philadelphia Flower Show is in itself an accomplishment. The entries obviously publicize horticultural therapy and Friends Hospital; but the further influence that they exert on the design and function of the hospital grounds is a testimony to the capabilities, commit-

ment, and cooperation of the horticultural therapy and grounds staff.

One specialty garden that originated in a Flower Show exhibit is Borgeest Garden, donated by Alice and Walter Borgeest. It is attached to the Hall Memorial Unit that serves elderly patients with Alzheimer's disease and other dementias. Because of cognitive losses, these patients are often unable to take part in horticultural therapy sessions, yet the staff felt that they could benefit from experiences with nature. The garden design, a cooperative undertaking by Dale Nemec, grounds coordinator, and Ron Durham, former horticulture therapist, attempts to balance patient safety with independence. A wrought-iron fence of hairpin design whose curved top eliminates sharp points helps "make the garden seem open and unconfined."[54] The plantings include lilacs, hydrangeas, lilies of the valley, day lilies, hollyhocks, delphiniums, and other flowers familiar to older generations. They are intended to evoke memories as well as to stimulate the senses. Care was taken to exclude toxic and irritant plants. The path of skid-free brick is laid out in a circle to obviate any confusion and return patients to a central point. Some of the flower beds are raised or movable to allow those with physical disabilities access. A shade structure is planned, as well. Though some shade is now provided by umbrellas attached to the tables, at present this lovely spot remains too sun-filled during the day to encourage summer use.

Another garden, a Flower Show installation designed for a geriatric population, includes a greenhouse attached to the end of a patient unit, which opens it to light and a view of the campus. The space, used for patient groups, offers readily accessible horticultural therapy.

The Greystone Program founded in 1980 provides supervised residential care for adults with long-term mental health problems. Patients live on the grounds in apartments or shared homes. The first building converted to this use was the 1911 Greystone House, not far from the entrance gates. The residents move about quite freely, riding bicycles and engaging in other activities. The residents have created their own kitchen garden with vegetables and herbs. An elaborate potting shed is the joy of one resident (correspondence with Mona Gold, March 23, 1997).

Most patients at Friends Hospital participate in some form of hands-on therapy, such as music, dance, art, or horticultural therapy. Renowned for its innovation and creativity, the horticultural therapy program is headed by Mona Gold, a registered horticultural therapist and longtime staff member of Friends Hospital. Patients are evaluated and usually assigned to the program, but some request involvement as a way to relax and feel productive after intense psy-

chotherapy. Few individual sessions are held; horticultural therapy is essentially group therapy in a simple medium that is not taxing. Socialization is one of the important goals, and as many as fifteen people make up the groups. The projects are tailored to patient needs: the difficulty of tasks is increased or decreased, depending on the capabilities of the gardeners. A patient who has difficulty concentrating may be assigned to strip leaves from a stem. The adolescents grow vegetables to display at the Pennsylvania Horticultural Society Harvest Show. Most patients wind up with a tangible end product—a dish garden, a wreath of dried flowers, a decorative arrangement, or a window box.

Process is important to Mona Gold. She sees horticulture as a continuum from seed to dry flower. Patients can become involved at different stages of the process. She, her staff, and her patients grow, cut, and dry many of the plants that they later use in therapy sessions. Each fall, the patients pick apples to make into cider. At Christmastime, they cut evergreens from the property and arrange them for decoration. "Horticultural therapy and use of plant mate-

Masses of mature azaleas bloom in the spring along the edges of the lawn and in the woods. It is said that Henry Hall, farm and grounds manager from 1897 to 1941, began the renowned azalea collection in the 1920s from a patient's discarded plant. Hall is credited with transforming the hospital's landscape from that of a farm to that of an arboretum. (*Photo: © 1996, Karen S. R. Balogh*)

rials is part of the moral treatment of patients," says Gold. They are respected both as individuals and as part of society and of nature. Several of the programs are designed to cultivate skills and interests that patients can pursue in the outside community after their discharge.

Horticultural therapy has long been a component of the care offered at Friends Hospital, and although it branched off from nature study and the plant collections at some unrecorded point in the past, the strong commitment to healing through garden work has remained unchanged. When the old greenhouses were torn down, new ones were built. The current production greenhouses have shed roofs, unified by a domestic-scale stucco building. In this spartan but spacious, heated and air-conditioned building, most of the horticultural therapy sessions are conducted. Patients and staff propagate azalea cuttings for Garden Days. In the spring, annuals are stored and readied for planting. The routines continue to follow the seasons.

The defining threads at Friends Hospital are so interwoven that they cannot be easily separated. Culture cannot be separated from the physical form, medical treatment from religious belief, horticulture as therapy from horticulture as a religious, intellectual, technical, or pleasurable pursuit. After more than 180 years of cultivation and care of the same piece of land, the very identity of the place is bound up in them. Again and again, hospital brochures feature the landscape and the gardens. To protect privacy, photographs never depict patients gardening, but the brochures picture distant groups of people enjoying the azaleas in bloom or working in the greenhouse or at a raised bed and provide close-ups of plant textures and colors.

During a recent fund-raising drive, donors' contributions were acknowledged on three-dimensional floral tiles that together formed a floral tile garden. The "Purple Hill" tile mural representing one of the azalea gardens at Friends is already filled with names. Another fund-raiser, the Azalea Ball, is sometimes hosted in early May, both to raise funds and to honor donors' service to the community and the mentally ill.[55]

As in all health care settings, much is changing at Friends Hospital. Although the identity of Friends Hospital is linked to its beautiful landscape and although the mission may be the same as it was in 1813, both the land and the services provided must be reinterpreted for the 1990s and beyond. We may still believe, as the founders did, that to live and work in a beautiful place in harmony with natural rhythms improves patients' skills and self-esteem and imparts tranquility, but that belief is no longer the cornerstone of treatment at Friends and no staff lives on the property now.

Today, most inpatients stay only a few days, heavily scheduled with treatment sessions, and the patients are often medicated, to control their behavior. Outpatients spend little time on campus, merely coming and going for their therapy sessions. The rest of the staff has been moved off site to accommodate an expansion of the Greystone Program. Friends Hospital has been forced to ask, about its hundred acres, What is their value? How do they contribute to patient care? Are they essential, are they an indication that patients are treated well, or are they an extravagance, a cost that a third-party payer will not assume?

In order to keep the facility financially viable, Dr. Gary Gottlieb, the director and CEO, has begun an effort to reorganize Friends Hospital into "a vertically integrated system of mental health care delivery." The hospital management is assessing how Friends is different from its competitors, most of which are for-profit institutions, and considering ways to continue treating the mentally ill. As Gottlieb says, "I care about the campus—it is an incredible resource to our patients and their families—but I have to balance that [with other factors]." The campus is continually adapting to patients' needs, including for new buildings and parking, which are crucial to the smooth operation of outpatient programs (interview with Gary Gottlieb, August 10, 1995). Other changes are likely to come. For now, the land continues to support Friends Hospital as it has in the past, and to respond to the values of society and the demands of the institution.

Friends Hospital is a singular place. The grounds offer tranquility, the strength of the great trees, and joy and hope each spring, when the azaleas blossom. As Leonard says, "To have respect for growing things, to put away tools, means that possibly we will have respect for ourselves and our futures" (interview with Edward C. Leonard, Jr., August 11, 1995).

The value and use of the land of Friends Hospital, as in the world around it, is different from ever before. Urban youth is afraid of nature. We all seem to own cars and want to park at the front door. We have no time to adapt to the pace of nature and less and less ability to appreciate its subtleties. Yet the landscape still gives Friends an identity and culture that distinguishes it from other places. It still, according to the staff, boosts the morale of patients, visitors, and employees. But the values of a landscape cannot be quantified on a balance sheet.

For many decades, the shift from farming to ornamental horticulture did not fundamentally change the connection to nature, the pace of life, or the experience of being out of doors at Friends. But today our most basic relationship to nature is different. The value of land is increasingly tied to the constructed environment that is the focus of modern life. The slower pace, quiet lessons, and eternal cycles of the natural world are often lost to us.

The Religious Society of Friends has never been just another business providing mental health care services but has rather reflected the shared values and religion of a group of people and their attempt to do good works. Yet Friends Hospital may find itself at the most important crossroads in its history. The value of the land today may lie in its development potential or the parking space it can provide for programs and agencies with a similar mission to Friends'. By using its land to further its mission of providing moral treatment, Friends Hospital has chosen a new interpretation of horticultural therapy.

Wausau Hospital, modern in design with its flat roof, white facade, and horizontal ribbons of dark windows, sits at the base of a small wooded hill on the outskirts of the city. (*Photo courtesy of Wausau Hospital*)

Wausau Hospital

Wausau, Wisconsin

Despite the recent rash of attempts by medical groups and corporations to squeeze profit from people's illness and injuries, most Americans and their physicians still depend on not-for-profit hospitals as health care providers. The American nonprofit hospital can take many forms: it may be a religious foundation, an ancillary to a university, or a service of a fraternal organization. But its most common and most important function is that of a community enterprise that reflects the cooperation of many groups who live in or near a city or town. Whether the community hospital is a small rural institution of twenty-five beds or a giant like New York's fifteen-hundred-bed Columbia-Presbyterian Hospital, it embodies the values of the community it serves. Instances of both excellence and carelessness demonstrate the cooperative strengths and weaknesses of the groups within the supporting community. In those cities and towns where cooperative skills abound, community hospitals thrive; in those where conflicts and oversights prevail, community hospitals may languish.

Wausau Hospital in Wausau, Wisconsin, is both a nonprofit corporation and a community hospital. Today it is an institution of 321 beds and multiple services that draws on the cooperation of many distinct groups in the surrounding area. The hospital building and grounds take the form that they do because of the hospital's rootedness in its community setting. Its unique feature, the abundant gardens for patients, staff, and visitors, also originates in community values and goals.

The institution itself was born in 1970, out of the sustained efforts of the business leaders of the town, who managed to surmount the religious prejudices and professional jealousies of former years. The hospital's historical roots, however, reach back to the town's lumber mill days.

The city of Wausau straddles the Wisconsin River at Big Bull Falls, a prime water power site. When the town was organized in 1845, it sat amid the great pine forests of northern Wisconsin. Sawmills, planing mills, and millwork companies located here to work up the timber harvest that was floated down the river each spring. At the time of the Civil War, five hundred settlers had gathered in the town; by 1900 the population had grown to nine thousand. As a mill site, a crossroads, and a county seat, Wausau attracted merchants as well as lumbermen, and lawyers and doctors as well as storekeepers. A regional center, it boasted the only concentration of physicians for miles around.

In 1892 a Dr. Douglas Sauerhering opened a small private hospital, Riverside Hospital, to accommodate twenty-five patients. Like other such facilities in the state, it was a "ticket hospital" catering to the young lumbermen who worked in the woods and on the river drives. A year's ticket cost ten dollars and was supposed to entitle the holder to free medical and surgical care and a payment of five dollars a week if he was disabled. The ticket salesmen were participants in a lumber region scheme that soon proved unable to fulfill its promises to the ten thousand men who had enrolled. A state investigation followed, and the promises had to be pared down. In 1906 the Sisters of the Divine Savior had come to Wausau and leased Riverside Hospital. These sisters were members of a new missionary order founded in 1888 in

In the nineteenth century, central Wisconsin was known as the Pinery because of the dense, mature white pine forests. In 1836, the Treaty at Cedar Point between the Menominee Indians and the federal government enabled lumbermen to buy land and cut timber. The Menominees ceded land, three miles on either side of the Wisconsin River, and the clear-cutting of virgin pine began. This photo taken around 1850 shows oxen pulling heavy loads of logs out of the forest so that they could be floated down the river to the mills. *(Photo courtesy of Marathon County Historical Museum)*

Rome. In 1895 four of the women came to Milwaukee at the invitation of the archbishop there. Their specialties were education and nursing; soon the congregation spread across the Midwest.[1]

Their service proved so popular that three supporters gave the sisters land to open Saint Mary's, a new sixty-bed hospital, in 1909.[2] The county, meanwhile, undertook to establish the sort of chronic-care facilities that were common back east. It built a county home for the sick and aged poor, an asylum for the insane, a small hospital to serve both these places, and

in 1914 a tuberculosis sanitarium. Thus by World War I, Wausau, now a city of fifteen thousand, possessed the standard U.S. health care facilities: offices for a dozen physicians in solo practice, an acute-care hospital run by the Sisters of the Divine Savior, and a full set of chronic-care hospitals managed by Marathon County. In subsequent years, Saint Mary's continued to expand, building additions in 1922, 1935, 1961, and 1968, until it reached a capacity of 250 beds. It also managed a nurses' training program from 1923 to 1967.[3]

It is not clear from the published record why this institutional arrangement did not meet the city's and the region's needs. Both Wausau and Marathon County continued to grow at modest rates: Wausau grew from twelve thousand in 1900 to twenty-four thousand in 1930 to thirty-three thousand in 1970, while Marathon County grew from forty-three thousand in 1900 to seventy-one thousand in 1930 to ninety-seven thousand in 1970. Whatever the situation, a Dr. Emile Roy founded a new general hospital in 1916. In 1923 a group of physicians and their supporters founded the Wausau Memorial Hospital Association, took over Dr. Roy's hospital, and a year later opened a new facility, Memorial Hospital. In 1948 a complete new wing gave the facility a 250-bed capacity. Religion, and perhaps certain patterns of friendship among physicians, divided Wausau's acute-care hospitals: Saint Mary's had a Catholic focus; Memorial was the center of Protestant interest.

During the same early twentieth-century years of hospital building and division, the economy and the economic leadership of Wausau underwent a complete transformation. By 1900 the pines had mostly been cut down, and the lumber business in Wisconsin was in decline. Wausau was now surrounded by farms, not forests. Fortunes had been made, however, and some of the wealthy men of the town began to band together to seek new investments. They formed syndicates to purchase timber in Arkansas, Oregon, and British Columbia. Nearer to hand, they sought to attract new kinds of business. They launched a successful paper mill that is still in operation. Then in

(above) Pioneer settlers found wild ginseng growing in the forests in Marathon County. The root was used by Native Americans for medicinal purposes. By 1900, experimentation in domesticating ginseng had begun in Hamburg, Wisconsin. Four Fromm brothers perfected the raising of ginseng under shade tents. The root was harvested after several years' growth. Shown here is the fall seed harvest by local German immigrants on a Fromm Brothers property. (*Photo courtesy of Marathon County Historical Museum*)

(*right*) In 1893, Dr. Sauerhering built the twenty-five-bed Riverside Hospital at 428 First Street in Wausau. It began as a ticket hospital—for ten dollars a year patients could have all the medical care they needed. In 1906, the Sisters of the Divine Savior arrived from Milwaukee and leased the hospital until 1908, at which time Saint Mary's Hospital was built and Riverside was remodeled into apartments. (*Photo courtesy of Marathon County Historical Museum*)

This typical Marathon County farm scene, about 1960, shows a Holstein dairy operation. The first three cows arrived in Big Bull Falls (now Wausau) in 1845, but dairying did not begin in earnest until the 1880s, after the timber had been cut down. For decades, Wisconsin has been a leading dairy producer in the United States. (*Photo courtesy of Marathon County Historical Museum*)

1911 the state of Wisconsin passed an employers' liability law making employers liable for the on-the-job injuries to their employees. In response, the Wausau millmen formed Employers Mutual Insurance Company to pool the bosses' risks. For the first years this company remained a small operation, but during the 1920s it developed an employers' safety inspection and training program that offered inexpensive insurance as a reward to careful employers. The safety program won the company many subscribers. Nowadays, Employers Insurance Company, renamed Wausau Insurance Companies, sells policies nationally and is the largest employer in Wausau.

In 1913, Chicago engineers approached Wausau investors to start up an electrical manufacturing company. The resultant Marathon Electric Company has grown to be the city's third-largest employer. The establishment of other firms followed on these early investment successes, and Wausau continued to have a pool of prosperous business leaders In addition, the old lumber families set up a number of private foundations whose endowments were to be directed toward the needs of the town. In recent years these local foundations have enabled Wausau Hospital to institute complex medical procedures that it could not otherwise have afforded. One doctor remarked that these foundations make Wausau like a university setting, where foundation grants are available for new equipment and undertakings (interview with Dr. Thomas Morehead, May 11, 1995). By the 1960s Wausau was a prosperous manufacturing center in the midst of a large dairy region.[4]

At this time the difficulties of Wausau's dual-hospital arrangement began to reveal themselves. In 1968 Saint Mary's had just completed another addition. Each hospital now had 250 beds, but both were operating at about 60 percent of their capacity. Expensive purchases—a cobalt radiation machine, for instance—had been duplicated, and the prospect of purchasing an extraordinarily expensive CAT scanner brought matters to a head. Over the years, the rivalry between the two groups had so intensified that when meetings were called to consider a merger, a great deal of patience was required to induce the committees from Saint Mary's and Memorial to discuss the issues.

The religious divisions were, however, not insuperable. Edward Drott, the chief executive of the Drott Corporation, was, though a Protestant, serving at the time on the board of Saint Mary's. William McCormick, the assistant publisher of the *Wausau Daily Herald*, had launched a series of articles on the waste and duplication that resulted from the city's having two separate hospitals. Drott, McCormick, and other town leaders began the slow process of bringing the committees of the two hospitals together. The administrator of Saint Mary's, Sister Regina, proved a stalwart supporter of the merger (conversation with Edward Drott, William McCormick, and others, Wausau Club, May 10, 1995). Success was perhaps also advanced by the changing nature of medical practice. The city's physicians no longer followed the 1920s pattern of two camps of solo practitioners. Instead, many had organized themselves into group practices that served both hospitals, thereby frag-

menting the two-hospital division of power. After two years' work, the drive by the business community succeeded, and in 1970 Saint Mary's became Wausau Hospital North, and Memorial became Wausau Hospital South. The governing board of the new corporation consisted of five members from each of the formerly separate hospitals and five members chosen by the holdover members.

Wausau's business leaders had more in mind than just cost efficiency. The cobalt machines and the CAT scanner were to them symbols of modern medical practice. Employers Insurance Company wanted a modern hospital to help it recruit out-of-town talent to its Wausau headquarters. Others thought a new consolidated hospital might attract highly trained specialists to town. Accordingly, the new board did a survey of the medical facilities in the region and decided in 1974 to build a new hospital. A detailed feasibility study subsequently determined that a 260-bed hospital would suffice to replace the old facilities.

Modernity also meant adapting to the dispersed society made possible by the automobile. Employers Insurance Company had already purchased a large tract of land near the intersection of the recently built Highway 51 and State Highway 29 and had moved its offices out of town to this suburban site. It offered to give the hospital forty acres of attractive land, subject only to the company's approval of all building exteriors and plantings. The physicians at the Wausau Medical Center, a large downtown group practice, also wished to expand, and they proposed to join the hospital building project (interviews with John S. Rutt, August 28, 1993, and May 9–11, 1995, and with Martin Cohen, October 29, 1994).

At the outset, two primary goals dominated the building committee's work. The new hospital should not be expensive either to build or to operate; and both construction and maintenance should be easy. Later, when working with the architect, the committee added two goals: the building should be able to accommodate growth, and the patients, staff, and visitors should have access to either outside views or

Designed by Skidmore, Owings & Merrill, Wausau Hospital (foreground, shown here in 1984) is architecturally compatible with the Employers Insurance Group corporate headquarters (upper left), a condition agreed on at the time the land was donated to the hospital by Employers (now Wausau Insurance Companies). Because the hospital is a regional health care provider located near major highways and serving an automobile-dependent population, parking lots cover a large proportion of the site. *(Photo courtesy of Wausau Hospital)*

interior courtyards and gardens. Credit should go entirely to the building committee and the Skidmore, Owings & Merrill architectural team for accomplishing these four goals, which have brought enduring benefits to the community.

The building committee represented a variety of Wausau constituencies: John Laverty, the hospital administrator, and John Rutt, its plant manager, represented the hospital; Edward Drott, William McCormick, and Robert Wylie (president of the Valley Improvement Company, which manages the dams on the Wisconsin River), the business community; John Hattenhauer, an ophthalmologist, the medical community; and Al Kelm the rural community.

In addition to the primary design goals, they had some other basic criteria in mind. Because they wanted to be as free from federal regulations as possible, they chose not to use Hill-Burton funds but instead to finance the construction with a bond issue, as well as from the endowments and other accumulated funds accruing to the old hospitals. The committee members liked the site, an open bowl on the side of a hill that offered nice views of the surrounding countryside and Rib Mountain. Because the gift was for forty acres, they imagined a low-rise building.

The building committee was also very concerned about patient costs. They elected for private rooms in pairs, each pair sharing an adjacent bathroom. This arrangement solved all the privacy problems inherent in caring for both men and women, not to mention the contemporary clash between smokers and non-smokers. Such an arrangement also benefited patients insured by Blue Cross–Blue Shield, for such facilities could be charged at the less expensive semiprivate rate. Finally, John Rutt, the plant manager, had completed a functional study of hospital departments, giving the building committee a good grasp of how the hospital's activities ought to be grouped. Rutt proposed four clusters: one for emergency service, surgery, intensive care, radiology, and the laboratory; a second for professional offices and outpatient clinics; a third for support services—laundry, supplies, and the like; and a fourth for patient rooms.

Armed with these ideas, the building committee went in search of an architect. Committee members flew to several cities looking at newly built hospital facilities. In Dallas they found what they thought was a promising design and a potential builder. Here in the suburbs of Dallas, an organization called Medical City had developed a medical mall of a million and a half square feet. The mall consisted of three office towers, which housed 130 offices for doctors and others, and a large building that sheltered medical clinics and twenty-three businesses, including six restaurants and a bank. This cluster of medical services and stores was built around a large, air-conditioned atrium. To residents of a northern city of long dark winters, the atrium seemed a delightful feature. Moreover, the Dallas mix of clinics and doctors' offices would accommodate the group practice that was then part of the Wausau project.[5]

Robert Wright, the developer of Medical City, Dallas, did not have sufficient architectural staff to take on a distant project by himself, but fortunately his organization was a subsidiary of a large national real estate firm, Trammel-Crow, the developers of Peachtree Center in Atlanta and a number of John Portman atrium-style hotels. The friendship between the CEO of Trammel-Crow and Nathaniel Owings of Skidmore, Owings & Merrill (SOM) brought Martin Cohen, then assigned to the Washington office of SOM, in on the Wausau job. During the summer of 1975 SOM carried out the Comprehensive Planning Feasibility Study that secured the state approval for the project. That fall, Cohen and his group sat in on the long and often inconclusive design discussions with Wright and the building committee.

In December 1975 the cooperation between Dallas and Wausau foundered, and Medical City was taken off the project. The next month SOM was appointed sole architect. The weakness in the Dallas precedent turned out to lie in the dissimilarity between the Dallas-style suburban cluster of group practices and private specialty clinics on the one hand and Wausau's full-service community hospital on the other. Wausau needed to do more than accommodate fee-paying clinic patients; within its region, it had to offer a full range of service to all comers. In addition, the atrium proposed by Trammel-Crow proved too expensive. In December too, the Wausau Medical Clinic left the project. Later this group practice built its own building near the new hospital.

In January 1976 Oscar J. Boldt, a large and experienced contracting firm, was brought on as construction manager, thus completing the final team. By February Martin Cohen of SOM had submitted the basic plans for the new building, and on July 27, 1976, the new hospital was started.

Martin Cohen's personal experience proved useful to the realization of the committee's goals. Cohen's work at SOM had included a lot of hospital planning, additions, and remodeling, especially at New York University Medical Center, Mount Sinai Hospital, and Beekman Hospital. Also, unlike many designers in those years when the tower was in fashion, Cohen had not fixed upon a form as *the* form for a hospital. He appreciated the designer's dilemma of elevators as opposed to corridors. As discussed earlier, in a tall building with elevators, everyone's time is lost in waiting for the elevator; whereas in a low-rise building with long corridors, people may make faster progress, but they may not enjoy the walk. While understanding the merits of the alternative, Cohen was sympathetic to the Wausau committee's preference for a low building.

Cohen's experience also taught him that there was no such thing as a fixed hospital plant. Indeed, a design that cannot accommodate future change and

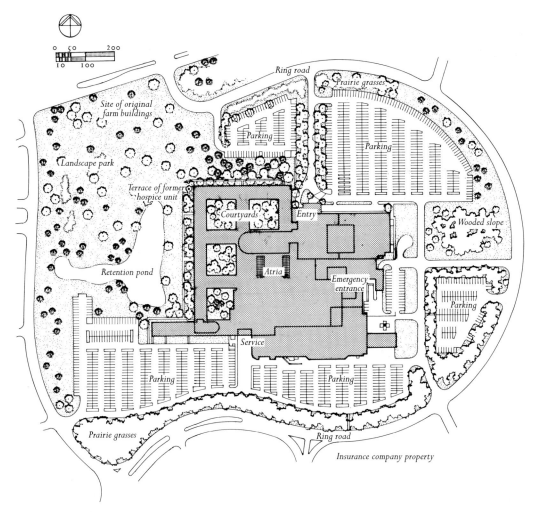

Wausau Hospital site plan *(by David Kamp).*

growth is a faulty design. Not only do hospitals grow and change, but it is impossible to know which departments and services will grow in the future: perhaps radiology, perhaps surgery, perhaps rehabilitation, or perhaps something entirely different. Therefore, he agreed with the Wausau group that their hospital must be able to accommodate an unpredictable future.

Cohen's final plan consisted of a series of large rectangular elements grouped according to John Rutt's functional analysis. The building resembled a modern shopping mall. It was a large, low white building surrounded by parking lots. The entrance opened onto a small three-story atrium to provide sunlight and a cheerful reception. The top two levels of the atrium housed physicians' offices. The first level of the atrium connected with the main two-story hospital building. Elements of the main building included an action network of emergency, surgery, laboratory, obstetrics, intensive care, radiology, and patient beds. Atop the main building, and abutting the third floor of the atrium, a steel-clad service core was built to enable easier expansion. Patient rooms were laid out along three large, square garden courtyards, each 160 feet on a side.

The patient wings and courtyards grew out of a combination of nursing goals and a community sense of what was fair and good. At Saint Mary's Hospital the staff had been experimenting with alternatives to conventional nursing layouts. There the nurses' stations and long corridors demanded a ceaseless trundling back and forth as nurses checked patients' records, fetched their medications, and replenished linens and supplies. In the new setup, supplies were located next to each patient's room, although the records and medications remained at the central nurses' stations. In the new Wausau hospital all the supplies, the patient's charts, and the necessary medications were to be located in a storage area just outside the patients' rooms. The central nurses' station was eliminated. Nurses now moved from patient to patient without having to retrace their steps.

The sides of the courtyards were arranged in double-loaded corridors, with one set of rooms facing the outside and one looking out on the interior courtyard garden. The corridors were then organized into departments—surgery, orthopedics, maternity, and the like. Since the system was continuous all round the square, a busy department could borrow rooms from a less busy service without having to scatter patients around the building in isolated quarters.

By themselves, such efficiency concerns would not have produced the courtyards and gardens. Almost any lineal plan would have met the new nursing goals. Rather, the garden courts owe their existence to an interaction between client and architect. The clients were proud of the view from the new site, and they expected that the patients would enjoy it also. It seemed to them quite unfair that some patients' rooms might face interior walls. Fairness is a deeply held value in Wisconsin, and the garden courtyards were an attempt to treat all the patients equitably.

The courtyards also drew upon other sources. As a young architect, Martin Cohen had won a Fulbright Fellowship to Italy (1954–1955), and while there he had spent time working in a office in the upper story of an old cloister in Milan. He had also worked on several Skidmore, Owings & Merrill jobs that featured gardens, two of which involved him with the outstanding landscape designer Isamu Noguchi. Last, Cohen realized that the gardens would bring welcome sunlight into the long corridors of his sprawling hospital. Taken together, these impulses of client and architect, local values, and architectural tradition combined to offer an unusual gift to the patients, staff, and visitors at Wausau.

In April 1979 patients from the two old hospitals moved into the new building. Ever since that time, the hospital has been evolving, just as Cohen predicted. Departments and facilities have moved about within the building, numerous additions have been built (and more are planned), and some services have been moved to separate buildings nearby. In 1982–1983, when hospital administrators decided that more maternity, medical, and surgical beds were needed, a fourth garden courtyard was added.

Today, like all community hospitals across the nation, Wausau is under attack from institutions that do not value the community elements in health care. Large insurance carriers are seeking to push their costly risks off on medical providers, and medical providers are being driven to imitate the ways of profit-making business to survive in the new climate. Meanwhile, the federal government continually trims its care allowances and at this writing is even contemplating pushing elderly constituents into managed-care insurance pools.

Wausau Hospital, like others, is trying to adapt. It has enlarged its outpatient services and installed a day surgery section. It has formed partnerships with far-flung clinics to reach out to future patients in north-central Wisconsin and the Northern Peninsula of Michigan. The hospital staff is seeking to adapt its services to new requirements that fit the insurance rules and payment schedules. Here, as elsewhere these days, the operative word is *management*, not *care* or *medicine*.

Currently, Wausau Hospital employs 1,570 men and women. As is common in U.S. cities under the new "service sector" economy, it is now the city's second-largest employer, after its insurance company neighbor. The excellence of the hospital derives from its roots in the community. The local businessmen on the board cooperate fully. Every day, seven hundred volunteers from the area assist the staff. The volunteers provide significant social services, but, more important, they form the primary network for feedback to the management. They register which actions are fitting and appropriate and which are not.

If ever a group had no need of being harassed into employing businesslike methods, it is Wausau Hospital. It owes its existence to a businessmen's initiative, and its habits are those of careful economy. At the time of this study, the hospital had just won a prize for efficient management.[6] What Wausau needs, and indeed what most American community hospitals need, is support for their continued cooperation and community service.

If instead of the gradual community-based processes that built this institution, greed for profits and heedless efficiency harass the hospital into becoming a health care business, then something very valuable will be lost to Wausau, Wisconsin, and to the United States.

The Gardens

Sitting on a parcel of about forty acres in an area of urban sprawl, Wausau Hospital is emblematic of modern American land use and development. It lies in an area between a viable downtown, which through great effort has managed to build a major shopping mall linked to its historic storefronts, and a large area of diffuse exurban development, now overtaking farmland.

At first glance, the hospital appears like any other, but both conceptually and practically it is uniquely suited to serving the Wausau area population. Nothing about the facade hints at the fact that the building's basic form grew out of a commitment to provide patients with views of nature. Early and unwavering decisions meant that an architectural firm known for its high-rise modern architecture would instead design a sprawling complex where views of nature dominate the patient rooms and provide vistas for all who pass down the halls. The garden plan of the facility only gradually reveals itself to those using the inpatient services. That the garden plan invites discovery rather than contemplation as an icon is typical of this modest, conservative community, where ostentatious, conspicuous, or lavish display is frowned on.

The current facility is a sprawling two- and three-story, flat-roofed structure with a white facade and ribbons of dark windows. It sits on gently sloping terrain, once the pasture of a dairy farm. It is ringed by a service road that was planned and constructed for a shopping mall that was never built (interview with Tom Mack, August 28, 1995). The hospital has several landscape features or gardens: the landscape park, in the southwestern portion of the site, which resembles the grounds of a corporate headquarters and is the dominant view from many patient rooms; two atria with subtropical plants that border the intensive care units (ICUs) and provide a conservatory view for visitors to ICU patients and for many staff members passing by or working in the area; and the four spacious courtyards with trees, shrubs, grass, and flowers, which provide views from patients' rooms that do not enjoy a view out to the landscape park.

Several factors combined to determine the form and location of the hospital, but a commitment to providing patients with a view of nature predominated. The open land with its views to Rib Mountain and nearby fields reflected the community's image of itself as a relaxed, open settlement with ties to nature (interview with John Rutt, May 10, 1995). The relationships between community, culture, and nature are the key to understanding the hospital and its gardens.

The hospital is a cross between a corporate headquarters and a shopping mall. The overall building form is that of a large square with inpatient services to the southwest of the entry and the ever-expanding outpatient services and emergency rooms to the northwest. More than thirteen hundred parking spaces ring the building on three sides, but the fourth side, the inpatient area, instead overlooks the landscape park of grass dotted with trees, and a pond.

The building plan has several unusual and well-thought-out features. The windows allow the patients to see outside when lying down—a surprisingly rare thing in hospital design. And the windows are organized so that the views are to either the landscape park, the two atria, or the interior courtyards. Theoretically, at least, the design was to afford every patient with a view of nature. Actually, the curtains of the ICU rooms toward the atria are drawn, for the privacy of the patients. The design commitment to views of nature could not, however, be fully continued in the later expansion of day surgery and outpatient services.

The gardens are a curious assembly of elements. They represent a generosity of spirit, a resolve that is heartfelt and strong, not just in their conception but in their continued development and care. In an institution with neither an articulated environmental ethic nor an artistic point of view in regard to land and design issues, and with many worthy projects vying for attention, the existence of the gardens at all is a testament to the community's ties to the land, although some of the garden elements, like the beds of annuals, are ordinary from a design standpoint. It is particularly noteworthy that all patient rooms and many staff areas have a view to nature.

Landscape Types

The postconstruction site has been described as a desert. Only a single American elm tree survived from the former farm. By the time thought was given to landscaping, all the money had been spent on the building itself, a common occurrence with construction projects. Many gardens are never fully installed for this reason, but at Wausau, a determined committee persevered in raising money for landscape installation, a project accomplished over several years, as the money came in. The plan had been sketched out conceptually by SOM but not designed in detail. Instead, a local garden center—nursery completed the designs, and the hospital staff, only one of whom was trained in horticulture, installed the plant materials. These are not gardens where lavish designs were implemented at great expense in a burst of short-lived enthusiasm. As with other hospital gardens, the relative lushness is entirely due to the commitment of the hospital administration and the continuous efforts of the groundskeeping staff. For almost fifteen years, a new project was planned and completed annually as the other areas were maintained and improved (interviews with John Rutt and Dave Zastrow, May 10–11, 1995).

Three basic types of landscapes or gardens were included in the hospital design as amenities for patients, staff, and visitors. The largest of the three types is the landscape park, with its grass, trees, and pond. At the time the design was undertaken, it was believed that this would be the best view and that patient rooms around the building's perimeter would overlook this verdant space. In order to be even-handed, the designers gave the rooms on the opposite side of the corridor views onto the open-air courtyards. Although of different character and scale, these courtyards nonetheless accomplish the same goal. The landscape park, four courtyards, and two atria that form the basic garden structure are supported by other planted areas and serve purposes beyond the purely aesthetic.

These auxiliary gardens are an assembly of fundamentally different forms serving the same purpose: this series of unrelated spaces offers splendid views of nature's vitality from patients' rooms, nurses' stations, and even the basement food-preparation area. The gardens demonstrate the capable, self-reliant, do-it-yourself nature of the community; that they were phased in over many years is typical of its frugal determination not to overreach its resources. With their plants and flowers procured from the local garden center, the gardens at Wausau provide familiarity and comfort that reflect and reinforce the community standard.

As we have seen, inpatients at Wausau Hospital

Many of the patients' rooms have views of the landscape park with its pond and spray fountain. Other patients' rooms have views of densely planted courtyards. All have large windows, lower than usual, to provide views for recumbent hospital patients. *(Photo courtesy of Wausau Hospital)*

always have a view of nature through their windows. As they walk down the halls, new views present themselves as quickly as strollers can turn their heads to look through a window. And those views, framed by a window and seen in the context of a different room each time, are exciting yet reassuring, a rare feat of design. The views also vary with the season—budding trees in spring; new leaves, deep green in summer; fall color; and finally branch structure, revealed in winter. A patient's near view may be of a carefully mowed lawn or neatly planted annuals. The distant vista, which reflects the recent growth of the community and Rib Mountain, popular with hikers and skiers, may not be "picture perfect" but is reassuring: it showcases the growing town. Adjacent rooms may

offer completely dissimilar views, depending on where the bed is placed or how near the building some tree was planted.

THE LANDSCAPE PARK

The largest garden, occupying almost a quarter of the total site, is a landscape park, whose grass and trees surround a pond and spray fountain. This expanse of ground, visible from many patient rooms, also constitutes the setting for the hospital building as seen from a nearby highway and approached from downtown. The retention pond collects storm water runoff, and the spray fountain is an aeration device. Simple in concept, the landscape park is a relatively modern form, frequently reinterpreted since it was perfected on the great estates of England in the eighteenth and nineteenth centuries. The Wausau landscape park descends from the corporate version of this historic form—the classic terrain of the English estate park. Such an estate would have featured a grand house and formal gardens, set on a slight rise overlooking the composed, contained landscape park, with its pasture land for sheep or cattle or plots under cultivation. The park was an enhancement, an attempt to perfect or idealize the natural countryside. As in other Romantic expressions, beauty consists not in order, symmetry, or geometry but in the harmony of natural forms. Trees are not planted along allées (paths or walkways bordered by trees or hedges), nor are they pruned into hedges or topiary; rather, planted in loosely scattered, informal groupings, they remain untrimmed or are pruned in natural shapes. The architecture is rectilinear, while the roads, paths, and water edges form sinuous curves. Because nature is approached comprehensively, all elements are contained in a single view. Although the elements of topography, plants, and water are those susceptible of design and modification, the sky, as in English Romantic painting, is also of great importance. Its beauty is made prominent through the containment of view and composition of landscape elements.[7]

The landscape park has been adapted to late twentieth-century needs and extensively employed in the design of modern corporate buildings in suburban and rural areas. Large structures sit on expanses of land with parking sometimes visible, other times hidden in garages. Often designed to be seen from a fast-moving automobile, the lawn, trees, and ubiquitous water features provide a setting, framing a view of the building to be glimpsed from the highway—and a view from the building back across the landscape to the highway. Despite their large scale, these modern examples are not farmland tamed or civilized but expanses already suburban in design and maintenance. At Wausau Hospital, an expanse of turf grass is merely dotted with deciduous and evergreen trees, while the land near the pond is more densely planted with pine, spruce and willow. The banks of the pond are planted with annuals to lend color to a scene that would historically have offered shades of brown and green. All is as meticulously groomed as someone's front yard. This is nature in submission, not in its wild state. Yet despite the ruling suburban aesthetic, rarely do these buildings provide domestic gardens to match those of the historic properties. Few spots here offer an opportunity to sit, garden, or just be. At Wausau, a small terrace was built at the periphery of the building, overlooking the landscape park, originally for the benefit of the hospice unit (which has since been relocated). The terrace sketches a transition between the building and the land and greatly enhances the view from the adjacent room, thus demonstrating the value of such small, personal spaces.

Like other modern examples, the landscape at Wausau Hospital stops far short of the eighteenth- and nineteenth-century Romantic expression of wilderness in the form of jagged, rough rocks, unkempt vegetation, and ruins of castles, churches, and the like, either real or re-created. The dark, isolated, forbidding statements of the Romantic movement in its pure form are not to be found on this property, for these gardens were conceived not as an outlet for emotion in all its forms but as an uplifting experience for people in difficult circumstances. Aside from maternity patients, "no one comes here for a good reason," as Dave Zastrow, former head of groundskeeping, points out (interview with Dave Zastrow, May 11, 1995). To cheer people up is as important an aspect of the charitable mission as anything else done at Wausau Hospital, and it is firmly believed that views of nature, especially of colorful flowers, are an "important factor in the psychological well-being, health, and recovery of patients" (interview with John Rutt, August 12, 1996).

COURTYARDS: HISTORICAL PRECEDENTS

The courtyard tradition is an ancient and enduring one. Evidence of it can be found in the ruins of Pompeii, ancient Greece, and medieval Europe, as well as in the present-day United States. Originally popular in hot, dry climates, where the distinction between indoors and outdoors was not so clearly marked as it is in northern climates, the courtyard was one in a series of spaces: enclosed rooms, covered walkways, and partially roofed outdoor spaces. Because the exterior of the building was almost windowless, courtyards were the outdoor aspect of an inwardly focused architecture. They served as places of safety and privacy where much of domestic life was lived. The geometry of the interior architecture defined the geometry of the courtyards (for often there was more than one per building), and the plantings were probably arranged in geometric patterns as well. Function and use were carefully worked out. Because the courtyard functioned as a kind of room, the ground plane was basically flat. It may have been tiled or paved with pebbles. Rainwater would have been collected from inwardly sloping roofs in a fountain or pool, often placed in the center. Paths were raised so that water would drain into the planting beds, small plots that evolved over centuries into what must have been an ideal form for the climate and social structure. Designed as retreats in hot, dusty places, the combination of water purling, dark green foliage, vines, and seasonal plants created oases or private gardens of paradise.

In northern Europe, monastery courtyards were a highly developed form, central to the lives of the monks. Monasteries in England were inwardly focused communities, withdrawn, protected, and basically self-sustaining. They generally included more than one courtyard, some of which were paved, others planted with medicinal or kitchen plants. The monks could walk, chant, or pray in the ambulatory, a covered arcade enclosing the square, at the center of which the wellhead was usually found. The intersect-ing pathways symbolized the four rivers of Genesis. Around the courtyard were situated the monks' cells; the space thus integrated the life of the individual with that of the monastic community.[8]

Modern architecture has made extensive use of courtyards. Such sprawling masses of buildings as corporate headquarters need egresses for fire escapes, and their interior rooms need light and ventilation. Sometimes conceived as view gardens or "art spaces," at other times modern courtyards are places to experience the outdoors, for example while dining. Unlike the historic models, these modern courtyards usually separate indoors from outdoors in a very clear fashion. Occasionally greenhouse attachments extend into the gardens, but rarely do they integrate intermediate spaces like porches or colonnades. The major differences between the modern and historic courtyards, however, derive from their use and symbolism. Contemporary business courtyards, intended for relaxation or recreation for workers who commute, are not a part of their domestic life and thus lack the richness of continuous use and individual expression. Whereas historic courtyards embodied a single religious, cultural, or moral perspective shared by the family or community enjoying them, modern courtyards generally do not. Instead, they are planned by the corporation's designers to complement the corporate image.

WAUSAU HOSPITAL COURTYARDS

The courtyards at Wausau Hospital were not built to define or enhance the image of the hospital. They do not make a corporate statement of power but provide a practical solution to a straightforward problem, adapting and reworking the courtyard concept for a cold-weather climate. They provide a close view of nature, richer, denser and more colorful than that of the park. They also afford an equally or even more important advantage that was perhaps not intended or expected. They allow the actual physical experience of being out of doors. Patients, families, and staff enjoy some of the domestic aspects of historic court-

This small terrace was built adjacent to the building at the edge of the landscape park to serve a hospice unit that has since been relocated. Its construction was inspired by the courtyards, which were originally intended to provide garden views from patients' windows but were in fact much used by staff, visitors, and patients. (*Photo courtesy of Wausau Hospital*)

yards: walking, sitting, eating, and socializing. And certain therapies are administered there, especially to adult patients on the rehabilitation unit and to children. To be out of doors in a hospital setting adds a rare dimension of normalcy and makes patients feel less vulnerable. The hospital reeks of limitation; the garden can work to ease that.

The four courtyards are typically Midwestern in several ways. Instead of being heralded, the courtyards must be discovered, and at first glance, they closely resemble one another, a true reflection of the egalitarian spirit of the culture. They are modestly identified by numbers, one through four, rather than pretentiously named. All are more or less square and dominated by the two-story windowed modern facade of the surrounding hospital. The size is adequate for a garden of significance, and the white,

essentially flat, unadorned facade contrasts well with different shades of green and most colors. Each courtyard has several large trees, shrubs, grass, annual and perennial beds, curved brick paths, and in some cases a patio. Three of the four have enclosed ramps that extend from the center of the building wall to near the center of the courtyard leading to tunnels under the hospital and out into the open landscape as means of fire egress.

On closer inspection, however, each of the courtyards has its own story. The details of the designs vary, and the annual planting that takes place changes them dramatically for a few weeks when the short growing season is at its peak. But the functions of the interior units surrounding the courtyards and the people who staff and use those areas is what determines the unique character of each of the spaces. The

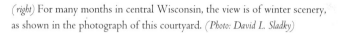

(*above*) One of four, this courtyard features raised beds densely planted with annuals and perennials; brick paths and terraces with casual seating; and a delicate copper water sculpture. Use of each courtyard varies according to the purpose of the surrounding buildings. (*Photo courtesy of Wausau Hospital*)

(*right*) For many months in central Wisconsin, the view is of winter scenery, as shown in the photograph of this courtyard. (*Photo: David L. Sladky*)

courtyards evolve and change, not just with the seasons, but in accordance with fluctuations in hospital functions and personnel, patient needs and family and visitor use, persistent or casual suggestions, and level of donations.

Courtyard 1 is essentially the domain of Sister Francine, former head of the Occupational Therapy Department—one of the staff members who came from the old Saint Mary's Hospital. Her imprint on the design of the physical and occupational therapy departments is clear and extends to the courtyard as well. Sister Francine evaluates and treats children, and it is important to her to have bird feeders outside the windows of the therapy department that she can use as a focusing device or distraction for her small patients. So despite official opposition (feeders attract muskrats and rats), she maintains bird feeders in Courtyard 1. She also has outdoor play equipment with green indoor-outdoor carpeting underneath to aid in her evaluation and therapy. Although it is a

major focal point, it is as unattractive as most play equipment, but functions basic to the care of patients take precedence over appearance in this courtyard.

Courtyard 2 is loosely designated for pediatric inpatients, although adult units surround it as well. The space is flat, because of its two concrete tunnel walls, and is more closed and rigidly geometric. The pediatric use seems confined to a corner patio; access is through a small playroom-waiting room. The most comfortable feature in this garden may be the benches, where parents sit, quietly removed from the pediatric unit yet near their children. The contrast between indoors and out is clear and refreshing, even though some users, particularly adolescents, feel they are in a fishbowl—and indeed, they are undoubtedly watched. The larger questions of what a children's garden experience should be or how to provide privacy in a courtyard have yet to be addressed.

Courtyard 3, which is adjacent to one of the cafeterias, contains a large patio furnished with picnic tables. It is frequented primarily, but not exclusively, by staff members. In good weather, cafeteria trays can easily be carried outside for a meal. Hospital functions such as the annual Employee Appreciation Day celebration are held in this courtyard, and food is cooked on grills and served by the management personnel to the other employees. This "company picnic," similar to a family reunion, is a time when such regional specialties as bratwurst are served in a jovial spirit. Yet this courtyard, too, is surrounded by patient rooms, and one wonders what it feels like to watch one's nurse or therapist having lunch; or to be the nurse or therapist watched by patients during lunch. Perhaps the staff deserves time apart from their patients and visitors. This kind of dilemma is inevitable with a design of repeating geometries, where function was not a driving force in the design.

Courtyard 4, added during an expansion of the original structure, is evidence of the hospital administration's and community's satisfaction with the courtyard concept. Lessons learned from the design of the original courtyards seem to have been applied here. No intrusive tunnels and fewer trees block views or overgrow the space. A large raised planting bed, retained by horizontal bands of limestone and similar to that used by Frank Lloyd Wright in many of his designs, provides topographic interest and embodies the ornamental gardening tradition native to the upper Midwest. This courtyard is a rich visual display, densely planted with perennials for texture and height, and with annuals, planted in rows, providing color. Spruce trees grow in tight formation, and shrubs are pruned with geometric precision. This courtyard seems to respond to the central design issue of providing views—from all angles and all sides, all the time. Although historically courtyards often had a symmetrical plan with flat, paved ground planes and relatively little vegetation, that approach would not work here. The intent was to provide views of nature. The need for cross-courtyard privacy and the stark building facade dictated that the garden designs be strong enough to define and embrace the

space. The courtyards at Wausau Hospital are most successful when the topography is "enhanced" and when paths, patios, and dense plantings dominate and define space. Not only is this garden more visually satisfying than the others, but it also expresses greater symbolism.

The hospice unit lays claim to this space and has affected its design and evolution. It seems natural, then, that it was designed for passive use and the symbolism of life, death, and memory. Here a small rose garden was planted by and later dedicated to the beloved gardener who installed most of the hospital landscape and died at an early age. Here used to stand a spruce tree, decorated each year at Christmastime by a volunteer. Known as the Tree of Love, it has recently been moved to a window near the main lobby, where lights are still hung on it in memory of those who have died. Domestic elements encourage quiet use. Patients, visitors, and staff can sit on the patio furniture or pick roses. They can admire the bright flowers and the birds that flit by, or enjoy the fountain with a multi-tiered metal sculpture, stored each winter and reinstalled each spring. It has a delightful splashing, tinkling sound and reflects the rays of the summer sun (interviews with Kathy Drengler, Linda Grilley, Ann Juliot, Sister Francine Kosednar, Kitty Switlick, and Dave Zastrow, May 10–11, 1995).

The view of the courtyards from the second-story rooms—both the near view of the treetops and the extended view of the courtyard itself—is beguiling. This microcosm is an ecosystem unto itself for patients, a natural, ordered world in which they have no responsibility. They have the opportunity to lose themselves in the view of the canopy of trees outside their windows as in another world—reminiscent of a treehouse or the way one imagines the top layer of a rain forest. The closeness to nature is sufficiently compelling and absorbing to make the larger issues of conflicting uses or quality of design and craftsmanship recede into insignificance.

The prospect of the courtyard as a whole, with its trees, paths, and lawns, is no less captivating than the

The food service is located at the basement level, as is common in medical institutions. At Wausau Hospital, food service employees, too, enjoy a view of nature, as a result of the two-story design of the atrium. *(Photo: Chris Faust, St. Paul, Minn.)*

This atrium, like its counterpart, is a surprise and a delight, especially during the long, gray, snowy winters. Tropical and subtropical plants fill the long, narrow space beneath a skylight and provide a view of nature from patients' rooms in the intensive care unit (right). Waiting rooms and a nearby chapel bring visitors and family members to this special place, where bricks scavenged from an old box factory and a small marble statue from the former nurses' quarters both found a home. *(Photo: Chris Faust, St. Paul, Minn.)*

detailed look at leaves, blossoms, and insects. These courtyards are relatively small spaces, and their ecological impact must be weighed against their cultural value. As is common, they were not designed to be self-sustaining ecosystems but to be pampered with herbicides, pesticides, irrigation, and the like. They are the most labor-intensive component of the Wausau Hospital landscape, their meticulous maintenance requiring roughly half of all the labor put in by the groundskeeping staff. The staff makes sure the walks are swept, the annuals planted and watered, and any dead flower heads removed. Roots disrupt irrigation lines and heave sidewalks. Shrubs obscure views from patient rooms and must be pruned. For several years a female mallard has built a nest and hatched ducklings in the courtyard, which has no egress. Department of Natural Resources personnel have to remove the flightless offspring to the pond (interviews with John Rutt and Dave Zastrow, May 10–11, 1995). The staff is sanguine about its ability to solve the problems in time. After all, it is not only gardens as finished products that they seek to maintain, but gardens as a process and a way of life. In a farming community this is understood in the most basic way. The act of gardening or observing gardening work, and the dialogue or experience with the garden, are as valuable as the garden's beauty.

Recent hospitalwide changes in management policy have led to the "outsourcing" of the grounds maintenance. Whether an outside contractor will tend the grounds with the same consistency and persistence as in years past remains to be seen. Because so much of gardening is anecdotal, learned by experience with a particular piece of land and its history, the current approach may not yield the same results.

ATRIA

In a place where winters are harsh, plants that flourish in warm climates provide an unexpected delight. Tropical or desert plants can transform both site and psyche. Although atria may be more fully developed elsewhere and are often rendered formulaically in shopping malls and corporate headquarters, the atria at the Wausau Hospital are an exciting and exceptional feature. They seem to have been created almost from imagination, for there is little or no reference point for these forms in the Wisconsin landscape. Long and narrow, one or two stories in height, the three gardens in two atria were conceived as a way to provide patients in the intensive care units with a diurnal rhythm. Although the requirement could have been met by providing skylights, all other inpatients had views of the outdoors, and it seemed only fair that intensive care patients have the same. It appears, however, that the windows disallow the necessary privacy from passers-by; and the sheer curtains always end up drawn.

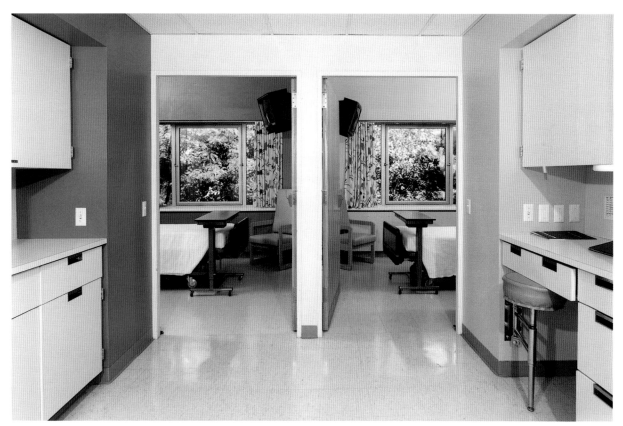

All rooms on either side of the double-loaded corridors have views of nature. The enchanting second-story view of the treetops allows an absorbing closeness to nature. (*Photo: Chris Faust, St. Paul, Minn.*)

These atrium gardens also provide a pleasant break for families occupying the waiting rooms or the nearby chapel and for staff members who work in spaces adjacent to them. At the basement level, food service employees have a wall of windows that look directly out on one of these gardens. Rarely are employees in a subterranean workspace offered such a feast for the eyes.

Neither true atria nor greenhouses, the gardens are open to the building and to light from long skylights. They are at the center of the hospital and border main hallways yet are almost private spaces that a person happens upon; they are a surprise and a delight. A small cactus garden, a tropical garden, and a garden with a subtle Victorian theme fill the spaces.

The cactus and lush tropical and subtropical plants—palms, banana, Norfolk pine, ferns, pothos—stand out in contrast against the white walls. Strong natural light pours in from a simple glass shed roof. What an escape from the gray, cold winters of Wisconsin, where snow can cover the ground from November to March! For a population that dreams of escaping on vacation to tropical islands like Hawaii, the atria offer a taste of the life of ease.

Not overtly symbolic, these spaces nonetheless contain several references to the community. The brick used for paving was scavenged from an old box factory that was being demolished at the time of the hospital's construction. And a small Italian marble muse and fountain, the focal point of one garden, were donated to the nurses' quarters of the former Memorial Hospital in the 1920s. The atria are softly lit at night and filled with lights and white poinsettias at Christmastime (interviews with Betty McEachron and Jean Morehead, May 11–12, 1995).

These oases have a distinct identity. Though not perfect displays, they are small and understandable and stand out from their surroundings as landmarks on visitors' mental image of the place. Like all the gardens in the hospital, the atria rest on a compromise between the necessity to allocate space efficiently and the desire to offer viewers the delights of a garden experience. Here the walls that separate viewers from the garden represent a compromise. If it were possible to enter that enticing world, it would seem more perfect than the real one—a garden with no dead plants, no brown leaves. Unusual species could bear informational labels. Plant shows could be organized several times a year.

Alternatively, the atria could be presented as an ecosystem rather than a show area—perhaps planted in a way evocative of the Florida wetlands, for example. Plants should be brought to the edge so that they can be examined, touched, and smelled. The best would be to open an area, perhaps nothing more than a balcony, where visitors could enter the garden and feel surrounded by it. It could contain butterflies, birds, the sound of water and wind. In emulation of those in a tropical rain forest, the plants would need to be stratified. Ten plant species composed in a more natural way would suffice, with perhaps one or two exquisite species of orchids, half hidden, to be spotted by visitors who linger. The atria should be designed as more than a visual experience, one that heightens all senses. Next to the intensive care unit would be the ideal location for the most intense garden experience. The stress of hospital life seems to call for a more beautiful, more stimulating garden than the normal circumstances of life do. The beauty, scents, and sounds should be seductive, soothing, and ultimately overpowering.

Most of all, this landscape should be a working, functioning, interdependent, vital part of the hospital. It should reflect basic human emotion, the whole range of it. The gardens cannot deny illness or death, but neither should they mirror the difficulty of the moment: they should comfort, distract, and inspire, and thus help keep life events in perspective and serve as an acknowledgment that illness and death are part of our world, and though profoundly important to the individual, are quite simply a fact of life on this earth.

One area slightly separate from the rest, no more than fifteen square feet, contains a cactus garden.

Perhaps to the surrounding community it is merely a curiosity, but in a place where patients have no personal space except a bed, it has meaning that the others lack because of its scale and clarity of design.

The desert garden at Wausau Hospital is not a representation of death and desperation but instead a representation of survival. Life may be a struggle, but living things can endure, even in a desert. This attitude is not necessarily shared by the Wausau community, but to anyone who lingers here, the cactus garden offers an available, obvious symbol.

The achievement and compromise at Wausau Hospital make it perhaps the most fully representative of mainstream American culture of all of our case studies. Inherent in the conflicts and contradictions of the gardens is the expression of the democratic ideal. Here is a place where all are welcome, which has something for everyone. No one is excluded or made to feel inferior. Wausau's providing every inpatient with a garden view is a fundamental expression of the egalitarian aspect of American culture.

The forces that came into play in the building of the hospital also reflect the course of American experience. The process at Wausau began with a piece of land that was most likely clear-cut from centuries-old forest, abandoned by the lumber company, repossessed by the county for unpaid taxes, and then sold to pioneer farmers. This land, continuously farmed for less than a hundred years, was neither encumbered by the weight of past history nor shaped in any way hostile to development. It became available for sale because of both global and personal forces. When the farmer-owner suffered a heart attack, his older son was in the military because of the Vietnam War. The younger son was not old enough to run the farm; hence the operation was scaled back and eventually abandoned. The insurance group that purchased this farm and others eventually amassed a big parcel at the outer edge of town, whose future use was not immediately clear. A long series of alternative development plans went forward in fits and starts.

The business community of Wausau led the effort to consolidate the two hospitals in town. When the decision was reached to build a facility that would express the identity of the newly merged health care system, Wausau Insurance Companies donated a portion of the land it had amassed. A sophisticated group, they wanted a building compatible with the insurance company's corporate headquarters. Moreover, the methods of the business leaders were those of small-town America. Theirs was a modest, conservative town, the heart of a rural community. They sought decision making by consensus.

The result was a serious modern hospital building compatible with the nearby corporate headquarters yet one that also manages to accommodate the community's need to be connected with nature. It is an unusual design in hospital planning today, implemented with Midwestern modesty. These gardens are quiet gifts to those unfortunate enough to be hospitalized.

The hospital is a manifestation of a land-based culture, but one that has historically used natural resources for economic gain and continues to do so. The Wausau Hospital is a community hospital in the truest sense, an institution that grew out of conflict, cooperation, and volunteerism. In the design and maintenance of its land and gardens it also demonstrates the common American devaluation of professionalism and expert knowledge. The gardens are a remarkably democratic solution to the demands of both the modern, highly technical medicine of today and the common wish for the familiar and comfortable. The gardens reflect the community values and standards, and the people of Wausau are justly proud of their accomplishment.

Community Hospital of the Monterey Peninsula. *(Photo by Dave Stock)*

Community Hospital of the Monterey Peninsula

Monterey, California

The Community Hospital of the Monterey Peninsula owes its success to its ability to balance the needs and resources of two distinct communities, a former fishing town and a resort. When the sardines had been fished out of the waters near Monterey in the 1940s, tourists and retirees replaced canneries in local importance. The Peninsula Community Hospital, however, still had to bridge the ways of separate communities, the differences between Main Street and the wealthy resorts. Fortunately, at a moment of transition for the hospital, a gifted man devoted his life to the building of a model hospital that could draw upon the goodwill and resources of both communities.

The hospital is deeply rooted in the land on which it stands, the beautiful pine and oak forest that grows on the steep hills leading down to the Pacific Ocean. This land was initially developed as a Victorian hotel resort by California's four railroad moguls. In 1878 a real estate corporation owned by Charles Crocker, Collis P. Huntington, Mark Hopkins, and Leland Stanford purchased the Del Monte forest, both hillsides and shoreline, for their Pacific Improvement Company. Two years later their Southern Pacific Railroad opened a branch to replace the then-bankrupt Monterey narrow-gauge line. The land company, in turn, built the huge, flamboyant Del Monte Hotel overlooking the sea. Alternately billed as "the largest resort hotel in the world" and "the queen of American watering places," it caught the eye of the fashionable elite. Soon two Pullman trains per day reached Monterey from San Francisco.

Charles Crocker (1822–1888) took a particular interest in the place, making it his favorite home. When the hotel burned in April 1887, he personally oversaw its rapid reconstruction. Here he spent his last days before his death in August 1888. Later, in the 1890s, the Pacific Improvement Company built a racetrack, a polo field, and the scenic carriageway, Seventeen Mile Drive, to add to the hotel's attractions.[1]

Charles Crocker, who served as the construction supervisor for the Big Four, oversaw first the transcontinental mountain line of the Central Pacific Railroad, and then the Southern Pacific extensions of the 1870s. As was the practice in those days, the Southern Pacific had been granted large tracts of public land along its right-of-way, as a construction subsidy. Crocker took over some of those railroad grants in the San Joaquin Valley and formed the Crocker and Huffman Land Company to build extensive irrigation systems at Modesto and Merced. In the hands of later generations these distant speculations led indirectly to the careful development of Pebble Beach, Pacific Grove, and Del Monte forest.

While attending Yale College, Crocker's grandson, Templeton Crocker (1884–1948), made a close friend of the football captain, Samuel F. B. Morse (1885–1969), class of 1907. On graduating, Morse went to work on a land development scheme in Hammond, California, a small town at the edge of today's Sequoia National Park. He fell seriously ill, however, and was forced to abandon the project several years later. After his recovery, Morse, through his connection to Templeton Crocker, joined the Crocker and Huffman Land and Water Company in Merced in 1910. A few years later, in 1915, the family stockholders of the Pacific Improvement Company decided to liquidate the firm's properties. They hired Morse to oversee the sales. The following year, Morse began his forty-year directorship of the Crocker First National Bank. Impressed with the Monterey resort's potential, in 1919 Morse formed a syndicate with San Francisco investors to purchase the Del Monte Hotel and peninsula land for his Del Monte Properties Company. Subsequently he managed the development of the land as a gathering of golf courses and expensive resort homes in a manner that would preserve much of the forest and keep the beach front free from all construction.[2]

At the turn of the century, Monterey fishermen mastered the work of netting and canning sardines, but their business did not expand until World War I cut off competition from Europe. For the next thirty-five years Monterey prospered, thanks to its fish harvests and canneries.

Monterey Area Population[3]

1880	1,396
1900	1,748
1920	8,453
1940	19,170
1960	66,040
1980	90,175
1990	102,540

Workers and shopkeepers attracted doctors to set up practice in Monterey, but not hospitals as we now know them. In the early decades of the twentieth century, doctors worked as solo practitioners, and the supporting "hospitals" were often located in the doctor's home or, more commonly, a house made over for the purpose and managed by a nurse. The medical history of Monterey reports many such small places. A Dr. Lilly used his home on Jackson Street as a hospital; Nurse Edith Guerin converted a downtown building and called it the Monterey Hospital; Drs. Martin and Sarah McAulay operated the El Adobe Hospital together during the 1920s; Mrs. Bertha Bowditch ran the Bayview Hospital in Pacific Grove; and Miss Edith Skeffington, R.N., set up the Carmel Hospital on Santa Fe Street in Carmel.[4]

The present Community Hospital of the Monterey Peninsula, however, grew out of the merger of two institutions—one a physician's proprietary hospital in Monterey, the other a research hospital in Carmel. The proprietary hospital developed from the busy joint practice of two brothers, Hugh and Horace Dormody. Hugh settled in Monterey in 1922, and his brother joined him there two years later, after completing his training at the Harvard Medical School and the University of California Hospital. "We used to see 125 patients a day," Horace reported. "The canneries were running full blast then and we did a lot of industrial accident work." The brothers set up the town's first x-ray machine.[5]

A few years later, in 1930, the brothers opened a modern twenty-five-bed hospital on the edge of the downtown, at 576 Hartnell Street. The impetus for the new hospital, Horace said, "was that we were asked to. There were a lot of polo games at the Del Monte Hotel, where we were the house physicians for years, and there were several accidents each season. Samuel F. B. Morse and some others were afraid they'd get disabled and have no place to go. So we borrowed money from a number of people, with non-interest notes for fifteen years." In addition to Morse, Harry C. Hunt (1884–1962), a Pebble Beach oil man, sponsored the project by serving as hospital president, and a philanthropist, Mrs. William Sage, also gave a large sum.[6]

Like their successors, the Dormodys shared the opinion that the beauty of the Monterey setting would assist their patients' recovery. Hugh dreamed of "a vast institution situated where scenery and climate could add their healing qualities to the magic of medical and surgical science; where nature would inspire the soul with the desire to live and thus make more effective the scalpel and the drug; a place, in short, where suffering humanity might enjoy the utmost opportunity for recovery."[7]

The Dormodys and their hospital struggled through the Great Depression, but World War II and the postwar boom allowed them to pay off their debts and enlarge their facility. By the time Dr. Horace Dormody sold the hospital and retired in 1975, it had grown to a hospital of eighty-six beds. By this time, though, due to the competition from the newer Community Hospital of the Monterey Peninsula, his hospital had ceased to occupy the center of the area's medical practice. On January 1, 1974, for example, only fifteen patients were being cared for there. In August 1975, Eskaton of Sacramento, a nonprofit service corporation of the Christian Church (Disciples of Christ), purchased the Dormodys' Monterey Hospital. The group modernized the facility and managed it for several years, with the assistance of a local board of trustees composed of merchants and lawyers.[8]

The resort community on the Monterey Peninsula also started a hospital during the 1920s, and it, too, struggled for survival during the Great Depression. Its difficulties, however, stemmed from the uncertain patronage of a wealthy vacation community whose families' first loyalties were to their home cities, not their vacation spot.

Mrs. Grace Deere Velie Harris of Los Angeles vacationed at Carmel-by-the-Sea. She was a childless widow, one of four heirs to the fortune of the John Deere Implement Company, manufacturers of farm machinery. Mrs. Harris, who suffered from a metabolic disease, sought the help of a specialist, Dr. Rudolph A. Kocher. Dr. Kocher, trained at Johns Hopkins, wanted to combine a clinical practice with research into the effects of diet on diabetes and cancer. Mrs. Harris, he later recalled, had often told him that she intended to leave her estate to charity. Dr. Kocher proposed that she help him establish a specialized facility in Carmel, because no such clinics existed at that time in northern California. During 1927 and 1928 Mrs. Harris's stocks had soared, so she arranged for her Los Angeles attorney to set up a foundation, the Grace Deere Velie Metabolic Clinic. The plan was for her to serve as president, the lawyer as vice president, and Dr. Kocher as secretary treasurer and medical director.

Unfortunately, Mrs. Harris died March 8, 1929. Soon afterward, the stock market crashed and her brother in Kansas City began a successful lawsuit to challenge his sister's will leaving everything to charity. These misfortunes greatly reduced the resources of the prospective clinic. Nevertheless, the building went forward, and the clinic opened in 1930, drawing its patients, primarily diabetes sufferers, from northern California. Dr. Kocher and his assistants found time for some research and published a paper on the effects of nutrition on cancer in mice.[9] The new clinic, however, lacked the funding from patients or local supporters to cover its deficits. In 1934 the outside bank directors voted to close the clinic and sell the property.

Dr. Kocher countered by appealing to eighteen local physicians to collaborate in remodeling the clinic to serve as a community hospital. The group unanimously approved his plan because at that time the Dormody brothers' Monterey Hospital was closed to other physicians. The eighteen doctors had instead to send their patients to scattered small nursing homes. Unfortunately, Dr. Kocher lacked any strong local community patrons on his board of trustees. Thus when the Los Angeles bank refused to release the remaining funds for the remodeling, the doctors had to undertake a difficult local fund-raising campaign. Nevertheless, they succeeded. In October 1934, after some alterations to the clinic, the thirty-bed Peninsula Community Hospital opened. In the process Dr. Kocher lost his special facilities and was forced to go into a joint practice of internal medicine with one of his clinic associates.[10]

As the Monterey area grew, so did its hospitals. In 1939 the Peninsula Community Hospital converted its nurses' quarters to add seven maternity beds to its capacity. Then, at the outset of World War II, it leased a small Stanford University medical annex, which it later purchased, to bring its total to fifty-seven beds. In addition, Peninsula sent its long-term patients to Nurse Skeffington's Carmel Hospital.[11]

With the Monterey Bay in the background, the building committee looks at the new hospital site—twenty-two acres donated by Samuel F. B. Morse (third from the left). Others shown are Tom Tonkin, Lewis Fenton, E. Jean Olivier, Allen Griffin, Dr. Jesse Feiring Williams, and Dr. Arnold Manor, committee chairman. *(Photo courtesy of Community Hospital of the Monterey Peninsula)*

In 1955 the Peninsula Community Hospital hired a thirty-year-old administrator, who subsequently devoted his entire professional life to the building up and management of Monterey's hospital services. Thomas E. Tonkin had graduated from the University of California, Berkeley, with degrees in public health and hospital administration. He also brought valuable experience in finance and management from his time as assistant to the director of the National Commission on Financing Hospital Care and two years as administrator at Cowell Memorial Hospital. He quickly discovered a talent for community organizing, and as a consequence his administration flourished.

At the outset he confronted the twin problems of widely dispersed buildings and out-of-date facilities of the Peninsula Community Hospital, along with the challenge of limited commitment on the part of the resort community. The best hope seemed to lie with a new building campaign that could take advantage of local population growth to attract fresh support.

Several financial alternatives presented themselves. California law allowed hospitals to form hospital districts to seek public capital, but the defeat in recent local elections of even modest school bond issues suggested that the district approach would not be a reliable one to take. Also, although federal Hill-Burton Act funding for hospital construction might have been tapped in some way, the act required both a matching grant from the community and proof that the area was in "distress." The surplus of beds at the Dormodys' Monterey Hospital foreclosed any possibility of appeal on the basis of distress, at least for some years.

Instead of these public avenues, Tonkin chose the traditional course for a community hospital: a private capital campaign. In the campaign he stressed the need for modernizing to support the "new laboratory medicine," to expand into the area's growing need for outpatient geriatric medicine, and to meet the then-popular interest in community mental health.[12] He focused on the resources of the Carmel–Pebble Beach end of the area by bringing distinguished retired military men and retired corporate executives together with loyal local supporters. So Admiral Raymond A. Spruance, hero of the Pacific Fleet in World War II, a man who with his wife had joined the Monterey Peninsula Country Club in 1948, served as the campaign finance chairman. At the same time, a leading obstetrician, Dr. Arnold Manor, took on the job as Building Committee chairman, an assignment later combined with that of Finance Committee chairman. Dr. Mast Wolfson and Dr. Jesse Feiring Williams ultimately persuaded Samuel F. B. Morse to have his Del Monte Properties Company donate twenty-two acres of forest in a prime location as a building site.

The location chosen was propitious. It was just off the main California highway, Route 1, on a side road to Pacific Grove. Also, it was next to an entrance to the Seventeen Mile Drive, and half a mile from Carmel. In short, Morse's gift was at the center of the existing and future service reach of the hospital. It was to be, and remains, a hospital in a forest. The six-year fund drive succeeded. It raised $1,750,000, or two thirds of the money required to open the new hospital in 1962.[13]

This first push marked the beginning of a well-executed continuing community campaign. The 1956 fund-raising memorandum, for example, reports forty-one members of a "women's auxiliary." In 1962 their numbers had grown to eighty-five, and they had taken their more inclusive present name, "volunteers." Today there are five hundred. Moreover, the special status of the volunteers is calculated to secure the community base of the hospital. Everyone who donates volunteer time, or at least five dollars in any given year, automatically becomes a member of the hospital corporation and entitled to vote for the board of trustees at the annual meeting. The trustees, in turn, have expanded their mix of retired military people and corporate executives to include local notables, volunteers, and hospital staff representatives. The result of this sustained outreach has been to mobilize the multiple communities of the area to support their excellent hospital.

The new 1962 hospital is quite beautiful. The designer was the famous architect Edward Durell Stone (1902–1978) of New York. The program set before Stone's firm, however, derives from Tom Tonkin's business acumen, his sense of the community, and his goals for patient environments. It was a nice combination of contemporary experiments and trends. In an interview soon after the hospital opened, Tonkin reported that he made the decision to build a hospital composed of all single rooms after reading about the success of the new Kaiser Permanente Hospital at Walnut Creek, California, and Gordon Friesen's ideas for hospital efficiency. It would be well to recall, also, that the hospital in Walnut Creek

Tom Tonkin, CEO of Community Hospital of the Monterey Peninsula, was one of forty volunteers, including doctors and other supporters, who cleared a road from the highway through the Monterey pines to the new building location on a Sunday in 1960. *(Photo courtesy of Community Hospital of the Monterey Peninsula)*

was a one- and two-story hospital surrounded by lawn and trees—as the one in Monterey would be.[14]

Friesen wanted hospitals built to reduce the number of steps that nurses had to take, put the supplies where the nurses used them, and allow unlimited visiting times for the patient's family and friends. He invented new single-room layouts, new nurses' stations, new storage and supply cabinets, and new supply carts, and he did everything he could to smooth the endlessly repeated production work of hospitals so that human caring could flourish. At the center of his practice stood the single room—an essential economy, he argued. The new chain of hospitals built for the United Mine Workers Welfare Fund gave Friesen the chance to develop his ideas.[15]

At that time, Blue Cross and other insurance programs reimbursed their patients only for semiprivate (shared double) rooms. Walnut Creek, and Friesen, however, demonstrated that the savings provided by a double room were ephemeral. Although a double necessitated less floor space and construction expense than a single, the vacancies made it more costly to operate. A hospital composed entirely of singles, like Walnut Creek, offered the advantage of flexible booking: any patient might occupy any room. Where double rooms prevailed, the sexes and the symptoms had to be matched, so that often the doubles were only half-occupied. Tonkin set up a few single test rooms in his old hospital and ran an occupancy and cost study for eighteen months to satisfy himself about the advantage that the singles represented. Ever since they were opened, the community hospitals of the Monterey Peninsula and Walnut Creek have enjoyed the highest occupancy rates in the state of California. Because hospitals must keep a large staff on duty to carry out all their many functions, they have high fixed labor costs. Thus, it costs little more to run a hospital with every bed full than it does one that is only 70 percent occupied. Through such savings Tonkin was able to meet the lower semiprivate rates of Blue Cross.[16]

The decision in favor of single rooms transcended the economics of bookings. Gordon Friesen, a former hospital director now turned consultant, preached a new message of functional design. He attacked the current inhumanity of the "unmechanized hospital with the regimented patient." By that he meant: "Hours to receive visitors are regimented, floor specialists for taking blood pressure or temperatures wake him from naps to fit him into their rounds. His meals come at outlandish hours, and so do his bedtime and his awakening, all for the convenience of the hospital which is doing its best with a design half-heartedly rationalized for supply, service, and personnel distribution."[17]

Such efficiency concerns a reflected a humane attitude about patient environments. A hospital patient necessarily loses the protective barriers of self, in giving up familiar clothes, offering the body as an object for invasive procedures by strangers, even possibly suffering loss of consciousness or loss of control of bodily functions.[18] Tonkin's response to these unfortunate losses was to call for the provision of maximum privacy and a design that fit the tastes of his community.

I think perhaps the primary consideration in the single-room plan, such as ours, is that it provides the dignity to each and every admission which our present American culture is more and more requiring. I think we are seeing an "averaging" or leveling of our population, and that extremes in hospitalization cost as to the price of a private room versus semiprivate and ward accommodations are decreasing. I think it would be well for hospitals in the future to think about the responses of the consumer, and his feelings of dignity and status and position as a human being, as well as a product requiring surgical and medical treatment. . . .

I can only say that we decided . . . to try to express the desire of our community to have a hospital that wouldn't *look like* [italics in the original] a hospital, so that people coming to it would perhaps be free of some of the fears and anxieties usually attendant on hospitalization—they would have their fears assuaged to some extent by a rather informal, beautiful, relaxing, quiet residential atmosphere.[19]

The first architect who was approached proposed the then-fashionable tower hospital, but Tonkin wanted a horizontal, less urban, less institutional building. "Walking is better than waiting for elevators, and better still if you can walk through a beautiful atmosphere," he said.[20] Besides, "to go to a drastic tower would have been a critical change in our image in the community. The former hospital was a two-story clinic in the Mission style."[21]

A few years earlier, Edward Durell Stone had completed his work at the Stanford Medical Center, a group of buildings with patterned walls around open courts. Critics have found the Stanford complex too sprawling and amorphous, but it employed many of

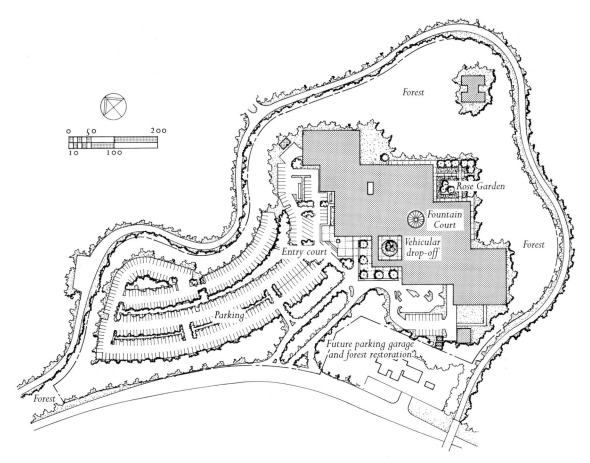

Community Hospital of the Monterey Peninsula site plan *(by David Kamp).*

the elements that later made Monterey a success. Maurine Morse (Mrs. Samuel F. B. Morse) knew Stone and got in touch with him about the project for which her husband was raising funds. Stone came to Monterey and spent some time as a guest at the Morses' home while looking over the site.

The building he conceived was an elegant low white structure that sat lightly on top of the Del Monte Forest ridge. It was of patterned concrete and laid out in two large rectangles that joined at an open-air water court. The rectangles contained private rooms clustered in groups of four around a small balcony so that each received sunlight and some view of the forest beyond. The balcony floors, in turn, were paved with glass blocks to let light penetrate to the floor below. The entrance to the hospital was an open square edged with a thin court roof, and a spreading tree was planted at its center. The hospital is situated in a coastal forest often shrouded by fogs that come in off the sea, but the patterned white walls, interior and exterior, and the courts and skylights and windows draw light inside, making the hospital a bright and cheerful place.

The new hundred-bed hospital was an instant success. Its occupancy for many years stood at 94 percent. The staff enjoyed working in such a pleasant environment, patients calls for attention fell off, and many new physicians applied to join the medical service there.

When viewed from the forest, the hospital is often mistaken for one of the large homes in the area, an error that is considered a compliment by the planners and designers. *(Photo: Chris Faust, St. Paul, Minn.)*

Tonkin had estimated that the continuing growth of the Monterey area would, in time, require a hospital of three hundred beds. According to Stone's initial plan, a space had already been set aside on the south slope to accommodate a large addition. In 1971 this new three-story wing was added. It included expanded x-ray, surgery, and emergency departments, an outpatient and inpatient mental health clinic (eighteen beds), and fifty-four new medical and surgical beds. In 1977, to respond to the needs of the older population, the hospital opened a new diagnos-

tic center for cancer, heart, and lung disease, and in 1981 construction began on a new wing in the western corner for outpatient services and a new birthing center. Occupancy remained high throughout these years, ranging from 85 percent to 95 percent, and at times there were even more patients than beds.[22]

Meanwhile, the Eskaton Monterey Hospital enjoyed only a 40 percent to 60 percent occupancy. Because both hospitals had plans for new facilities, the California medical planning office ordered them to plan jointly for future services to the area. After initial disagreements, in 1982 the Community Hospital of the Monterey Peninsula purchased the old Monterey Hospital for a mutually agreed-upon price. The next year, the Community Hospital closed the downtown hospital for medical and surgical patients. Instead it continued a successful alcohol recovery program that Eskaton Monterey had begun, and by 1985 it had enlarged the facility to make it a twenty-five-bed inpatient drug and alcohol recovery center. Two years later, the movie star Clint Eastwood, then mayor of Carmel, helped with a campaign to add twenty-five beds for a youth drug recovery program. Now the old Eskaton Monterey Hospital functions as the site for the Community Hospital's Recovery Center outpatient program as well as many other outpatient programs.[23]

During the 1980s, American medical care took a sharp turn away from hospitals and toward outpatient surgery and service oriented toward shorter hospital stays (the average stay is now 4.4 days at CHOMP). In response to that shift the Community Hospital added a new outpatient surgical center and rehabilitation wing on its northeastern corner, a site on the ridge that overlooks the bay. Currently it is building a new cancer center. All these additions and the remodeling have not added any significant number of beds to the 1972 level. The total stands at 169.[24]

In these many additions since the initial building of the hospital in 1962, the administrators have insisted on continuity of design. Each new unit is built in the patterned concrete of 1962 so that no part of the hospital appears old or out-of-date. Moreover, they have carefully limited the services offered to those a small community hospital can best provide. They send out patients who require the most elaborate procedures.

As is the case throughout the United States, occupancy rates are down because of declining hospital usage and much-increased use by both hospitals and group practices of outpatient services. Even so, the Community Hospital of the Monterey Peninsula remains at the top of the California list with a 78 per-

cent occupancy rate, the state average being 61 percent.[25] In addition, through its continuing community organizing and fund raising the hospital has managed to set aside an endowment so that it can treat indigent patients and make up the short-fall between costs and what insurance reimburses.

Altogether, the Community Hospital of the Monterey Peninsula is a wonderful demonstration of what can be done in design, management, and medical care by an American community with adequate resources and good leadership. Today it is perhaps the most beautiful hospital in the country, an outstanding community achievement.

The Gardens

When the collective culture holds itself to be a part of nature and that it can be healed by nature, then gardens are integrated into its health care settings. Such gardens may harbor plants for making medicine or tonics, they may offer a refuge in the confines of the hospital, or they may serve to foster metaphysical thought. But throughout most of human history, we were one with nature and derived our sense of being, our sustenance, and our health from it. With the rise of science, those foundations shifted, and we now set ourselves apart from the natural world. We may acknowledge that we find peace or rejuvenation in nature, but we no longer revere or worship it. Aside from an occasional medication derived from a natural source, we no longer look to nature to heal us. How rare, then, to discover a place where modern Western health care is provided consciously and deliberately in a setting where nature is acknowledged and even honored. In Monterey one finds an unusual commitment to marrying the provable and the elusive—science and technology collaborate with the most basic and yet mysterious of human experiences, immersion in the natural world.

In both practical and symbolic terms, the Community Hospital of the Monterey Peninsula offers important clues to understanding the relationship to nature and the ways it plays out in health care set-

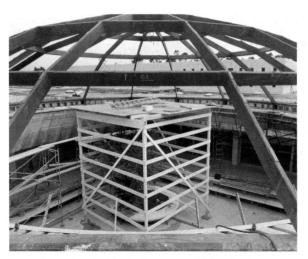

When the northern California climate proved inhospitable to use of an open-air court, a large dome was constructed over the Fountain Court. This 1971 photo shows the dome being added. (*Photo courtesy of Community Hospital of the Monterey Peninsula*)

tings. Perched on the edge of the continent where western expansion halted, the hospital seems, as if by a forced pause, to demand that we come to our senses. It is as if after destroying and remaking much of the land we crossed to get here, we finally recognized that the wilderness we have is worth preserving, worth living with, living in, caring for. Development in this area of singular beauty has been tempered by the ethic of preservation that is common among the monied, sophisticated population. Perhaps it was easy to reach such conclusions in this place, but the common wisdom exhibited here should inspire us to attempt to come to terms with ourselves, our history and culture, our place and dependence on the earth. Here modern medical science diagnoses and treats patients in a setting that allows, almost compels, the patient to connect to the natural world.

The hospital we see today is the result of an "experiment." Rather than follow the trends prevalent in health care when the hospital was built in the 1960s, the administrators made decisions based on their perception of community need and their ability to provide quality at a reasonable cost. This tradition

continues several decades later. The hospital provides a full range of both inpatient and outpatient services: medical, surgical, emergency room, critical care, rehabilitation, and the like, but it does not have programs in neonatology, open heart surgery, or burn treatment that are offered by several hospitals in the area. By defining relatively narrow objectives and delivering high-quality services at a fair price, the hospital has remained financially stable, even in time of change. This stability, in turn, has allowed the hospital to continue to develop programs to suit the needs of the community. The new wing for rehabilitation services boasts panoramic views that many health clubs cannot match. The highly trained staff and state-of-the-art equipment offer particular advantages for the rehabilitation of hand injuries. A new Cardiac Wellness Center has been built and a Family Birth Center has just opened. A comprehensive cancer center is planned for the near future.

The same philosophy has guided the design of the facilities. When the Community Hospital was planned, a homelike environment was considered more appropriate to its population than a model based on science, technology, and efficiency could be. The goal was to design a hospital that would be if not reassuring, at least nonthreatening. The first architect's proposal for a high-rise building protruding from the forest was rejected.[26] Monterey became the first hospital in the country to have all private rooms. But the homelike environment was not defined by privacy alone. The new hospital was designed not to look, smell, or feel like a hospital.

SENSE OF PLACE

The Community Hospital expresses the climate, topography, vegetation, and view of life of the Monterey Peninsula—in some sense it embodies the spirit of the region. Architecture, garden, and forest work as one, responding to both ecological and human needs. On land that once belonged to the Pebble Beach Company, the hospital is located just off Seventeen Mile Drive. The private road winds past world-class golf

Rooftop view of the 1962 dedication of the Fountain Court. The lights and fountains were turned on for the first time before a large group of supporters. The dome was added ten years later. *(Photo courtesy of Community Hospital of the Monterey Peninsula)*

courses—Pebble Beach, Spyglass, and Spanish Bay—past distinctive, expensive homes, through the forest, and along the shore of Carmel Bay and the Pacific Ocean. The area is populated by military retirees—admirals and generals—and vacationing or retired corporate executives, but the hospital's service area covers the full spectrum of classes, and includes Marina, a city with one of the most ethnically diverse populations in the state. Development has been guided by interest in the preservation of the forest ecosystem on the twenty-two-acre site, and the gardens represent a small fraction of the total acreage. Although crucial to the success of the place, their design is subordinate to both the architecture and forest.

Inspiration for site development came from a variety of sources. The nearby Pebble Beach Company proved a model: the development of Pebble Beach had been carried out with an eye to preserving the environment. The presence of a college campus, resorts, and homes also influenced the design (interview with Jay Hudson of the Community Hospital of the Monterey Peninsula, Sept. 27, 1995). In addition to first-rate medical and surgical care, the hospital was intended to provide hospitality. So successful were the efforts that a hospital brochure contains a disclaimer: although the facility looks like a luxury hotel, "it's not an accurate image, and it's not an image we try to cultivate."[27] The brochure explains that the private rooms, natural light, views to the forest, and the like, result from the attempt to create an environment to "support the healing process." It emphasizes that it cost no more to build this edifice than it would have to build one that looked like a hospital—and that the costs for treatment are actually in the lowest third of those for all hospitals in northern California.[28]

The decision to thwart convention has proved wise. In recent decades it has become common to design hospitals in a way that emphasizes the scientific, technological components of health care. Each new addition is sleeker than the last. This practice, however, leads to a jumble of styles—a new one with every season, or perhaps a new edifice for each ego. The pace of change requires constant adjustment on the part of the people using the facility. The alterations may be minor: a different mechanism for opening windows, or a different "feel" to the door handles. At other times, people must make major adjustments: to a change in floor level, an entirely different quality of light, or a confusing, disorienting floor plan. Cumulatively, the necessity to make accommodations undoubtedly adds stress to an already difficult situation. Moreover, if they are not in the newest section, patients may fear that they are receiving care of a lower quality, or employees may feel less valued.

At the Community Hospital, the original design by Edward Durell Stone set the tone for everything that followed. Delightfully Californian in style, it is a low white horizontal building set in a brown, green, vertical forest. Terraced into the hillside, it generally appears no more than two stories high. It is light-filled, elegant but relaxed. Its crisp geometries stand in dramatic contrast to the surrounding Monterey pine forest. The juxtaposition of the two strong forms, one man-made, the other natural, gives the place its distinctive character. Crucial to the success of the mix are the gardens, which bridge the extremes between wilderness and architecture, making both more approachable, more beautiful, more appreciated than they would be alone.

Several architectural features contribute to the unity and harmony of nature and buildings. The floor plan is open. Often there is no change of grade between indoors and out. The windows—at times expansive walls, at times tall and narrow to ensure privacy yet afford views—reveal nature at every turn. Interior courtyards, skylights, and lightwells become a showcase for the plants, water, and changing patterns of light. Even the wide, cantilevered capping eaves protect and shade, and extend the building into the garden. And the dominant decoration, the square-in-square-in-square pattern of the poured-in-place concrete walls, is used on both interior and exterior surfaces, further reinforcing the unity of design.

Over the years, new additions have been seamless extensions of what has already been successful. Gold carpet and rattan chairs with throw pillows have adorned the hospital since the early days. They will eventually be stylish again, but this does not really matter: they have become signature pieces, a statement that a correct decision once made need not be discarded for the sake of change. The homogeneity of the architecture, interior design, maintenance, and even housekeeping is crucial to the harmonious effect. There are no jarring transitions. At no time does one feel that one has entered another place. There is no need to adjust to a new style, scale, quality of light or life. All patients receive the same high-quality care, and energies can be focused on the task at hand, that of healing, rather than on superfluous distractions.

If something does not work, however, it is changed, seemingly without hesitation. The Fountain Court was once an underutilized exterior courtyard. In the first major expansion, about a decade after the hospital opened, the courtyard was covered with a dome, and it is now the heart of the hospital, its most public space. Building code requirements and the addition of new services and staff require constant change. New birthing rooms will allow a mother to labor, deliver, and recuperate without changing locations. A terrace was recently constructed adjacent to

(*above*) The domed Fountain Court acts much like a hotel lobby, furnishing a place to meet, receive information, find something to eat, relax, or enjoy quiet entertainment. (*Photo: © Scott Campbell*)

(*right*) Maurine Church Morse, right, discusses the model of the Fountain Court dome with trustee chair Dr. Carol McKenney (1972). Architect Edward Durell Stone is at left. Morse, a former interior designer, was the principal donor for the dome project and for the construction of the new hospital. (*Photo courtesy of Community Hospital of the Monterey Peninsula*)

Traffic flows around a circular center island in the drop-off area. The original Italian stone pine (*Pinus pinea*) has been pruned, staked, and cabled. *(Photo: Chris Faust, St. Paul, Minn.)*

the staff dining room in an attempt to relieve crowding. Nursing stations have been redesigned and are now lighter in color and more comfortably accommodate computers. Plans are under consideration to add a dome to the entry plaza. Although the front entrance is protected somewhat by the cantilevered eaves, the desirability of adding further protection from the weather is under discussion. The sense, though, is that change is a refinement to, not a rejection of, the expensive existing infrastructure.

The design seems to have sprung from the site, the climate, and the culture. The awareness of nature is everywhere. The building reveals nature, embraces it, points to it, shelters it, whether it is the forest wilderness, a garden near the building, an interior courtyard, or even just one plant under a skylight. As often happens in California, the lines between inside and out, and between indoor and outdoor life, are blurred. People who have delighted in gardens themselves want to make the experience more widely available. Similarly, the more hikes in the hills, the more walks by the oceanside, the more spectacular views a person enjoys, the more precious these experiences become. A view alone can evoke a clear and powerful memory and enhance the value that a place assumes

in the viewers' affections. Even though the cool, damp weather of northern California limits direct use of the hospital gardens for part of the year, they remain an essential, valued component of daily life.

The basic planning decision to build the hospital in the Del Monte forest ensures that the perception of the hospital is inextricably linked with nature. The building is set apart from all else, barely seen from the nearby roads. The forest may not be pristine wilderness, but it is at least a representation, an epitome of wilderness. In this forest a person can retreat, withdraw from the world that caused the illness to a haven offering the most modern medical and surgical care. It is possible to ignore everyday distractions and concentrate on healing.

At the Community Hospital of the Monterey Peninsula, gardens can be found at every turn—some large, others small; some covered, others open to the air; some filled with activity, others quiet and still. It is, in fact, an injustice to regard them as gardens in the traditional sense. Here, light-filled, plant-filled interior seating areas become gardens, as do the surrounding forest and the view of Monterey Bay. Harmonious with the site, the architecture, and the purpose of the hospital, these various pieces of nature may, in fact, be seen as a single garden of many parts. Each is unique and offers its own pleasures. Each contributes something the others do not. All are crucial components in a deceptively uncomplicated whole.

WILDERNESS PRESERVED, THE FOREST

The illusion of pristine wilderness at the Community Hospital is a consequence of the forested hilly terrain on which the hospital sits. The hospital forest is an "urban forest," the remnant of a large woodland that once covered most of the peninsula. The region has the largest remaining original stand of Monterey pine, reaching heights up to a hundred feet. It shows evidence of logging and fires from near the turn of the century on into the 1920s. The forest is now managed by the hospital and regulated by several agencies.[29]

The species found here, Monterey pine (*Pinus radiata*), coast live oak (*Quercus agrifolia*), and the native shrubs, grasses, and groundcovers that form the forest understory, although not rare or particularly valuable in themselves, constitute a plant community that is becoming scarce. As alien plant species invade the forested areas of the peninsula and as development of homes and ornamental landscapes continues, the hospital has become an ecological repository of significance.[30]

The hospital's commitment to preserving the forest mirrors that of community members, known to be extremely passionate about the natural environment (interview with Cynthia Peck, CHOMP, Aug. 7, 1996). At the hospital, the forest is not only a native ecosystem valued in its own right but a crucial part of the ambience, an element that promotes relaxation and healing. Yet the danger of having a hospital in a fire-prone urban forest is real. The first priority of management must be fire suppression. Major trees are limbed up ten feet from the forest floor, and new trees are removed every few years. During episodes of fire in the region, the hospital grounds staff stands guard in the forest with hoses at the ready. Such practices of fire suppression will ultimately transform the forest ecology so loved by the people of the community. "It

is sentimentality that leads us to build in certain ways, despite their hazards or management problems" (interview with Prof. Kristina Hill, Massachusetts Institute of Technology, Aug. 17, 1996).

At the same time, procedures for the construction of additions to hospital buildings or parking lots have become increasingly complex and expensive. Foresters and environmental landscape consultants are as involved in the process as are planners, designers, and financiers. A recent parking lot expansion project was completed with numerous conditions, large and small. The hospital agreed to set aside forested areas for preservation.[31] During construction, no unseasoned lumber could be stacked nearby, for it gives off a fragrance that attracts turpentine beetles to the area, insects that are particularly destructive to Monterey pine.[32] Certain exotic species were removed from the surrounding forest and disposed of in specified ways. Annual reports on the condition of the forest must be prepared by a registered forester and approved by the City of Monterey. And the Monterey pine planted after the construction is genetically pure stock.[33]

The genetic heritage of Monterey pine has become controversial because it is believed that crossbred varieties may not be as resistant to pine pitch canker disease as are genetically pure old-growth trees. Some experts advocate that only genetically pure Monterey pine stock be planted today. Since the 1950s, varieties crossbred with New Zealand pine have been the primary seed source for California nurseries and the State Division of Forestry. Now that some of these trees have reached maturity, the large, exotic Monterey pine varieties may no longer be distinguishable from native pine. Cross-pollination of exotic varieties and natives further complicates the picture.[34] Collecting seed from old-growth trees seems not to guarantee genetic purity; nevertheless, a botanist collected seed and planted it on the site when the hospital construction was completed.[35]

Another construction project, an underground parking ramp for approximately three hundred cars, is being planned. The result would be an actual increase in forest area. On an adjoining piece of land, a fire station was once built, on a flat site carved out of a forested slope. The fire station will be removed and a stepped, multilevel, underground parking ramp built. The newly created slope will mimic the original topography and will be forested with a mix of genetically pure Monterey pine and coast live oak.

Deterred neither by the difficulties of construction in a forest nor by the task of managing the forest, the hospital administrators seem instead to have been inspired by it. They deeply believe in its value.

The beauty and life of this place bring great pleasure to the patients. As one of the nurses describes it, the forest view "makes people feel alive. It is very uplifting" (interview with Chris Hall, R.N., manager of Oncology at CHOMP, Sept. 28, 1995). The sylvan landscape with views across wildflowers and past strong trees to Monterey Bay can take them out of the small world of their illness and connect them to

The Rose Garden is bounded by patient rooms and the Monterey pine forest. The design is based on a square pattern, resulting this time in a lush, domestic-scale garden. Soil was amended to promote drainage in planting beds. Rose pots are weighted to prevent their tipping over when deer browse. The springeri on the second-story balconies is watered from the ground through a system developed by the staff. (*Photo: © 1998, Jane Lidz*)

the greatness beyond. Viewing nature is also, always, an intimate experience: here, deer browse and quail nest and rear their young. The forest provides a touchstone for normal life.

ORNAMENTAL GARDENS

Like the hospital, the gardens have been built in phases, to complement and reaffirm the architecture. The gardens closest to the building are based on the square, circle, and rectangle, the same pure geometric forms used throughout the building. Other plantings take the surrounding forest of Monterey pine as their inspiration and backdrop. These less formal gardens make use of native species, which require little maintenance. As the building expanded into the parking lots adjacent to the original structure, new parking areas were designed and planted with species that require low maintenance and little water.

Views of the forest from patients' rooms are an almost private experience. The gardens adjacent to or inside the building itself are public, social spaces where nature has been tamed, civilized, adapted for human use. Three large gardens define nature here as a part of life, to be inhabited, not just observed. The entry plaza, or drop-off area, sets the tone for the hospital experience. It offers a point of transition between the parking lot and the building and quietly announces the ordered, welcoming atmosphere of the place. The interior Fountain Court functions much like a hotel lobby. Here one can find information, directions, something to eat, a comfortable place to sit, even quiet entertainment. The primary view from some patient rooms, the Rose Garden behind the hospital, is, like the terrace of a home, a place to sit in the sun, watch the rain, indulge in ornamental horticulture. The supporting cast of gardens thus plays a crucial role in the story.

The entry plaza, the space between the parking lot and building entrance, features a square fountain and square planters in square lawn sections. The drop-off area is a paved square defined by a concrete canopy, almost an extension of the cantilevered eave of the

The Fountain Court is both expansive and intimate, filled with the sound of water and quietly animated by the changing natural light that passes through the large dome. *(Photo: Nancy Gerlach-Spriggs)*

building. The circular center island around which traffic flows still supports the Italian stone pine (*Pinus pinea*) originally planted, now staked and cabled and cared for like an aging friend. The other plants are well cared for, pruned, healthy, and symbolic of the standard of care within the hospital. This garden is not simply a sidewalk from the parking lot to the front door but a discrete, memorable garden. It is large enough both to set the stage for the building and to enjoy an integrity of its own. Parking and entry are connected but are experienced as separate because the entry plaza is raised above the parking lot, on a different axis.

The hospital's interior Fountain Court is a distinctive point of entry. Spacious and domed, the court surrounds a forty-foot-square pool with water jets, an island of vegetation, and Koi fish. Because decoration is minimal, attention focuses on the pool. Originally an exterior courtyard with sliding glass doors, the

space was intended for patient use. But when it proved unsuitable—sunlight reflected off the glass, and the winters were too cool and damp—it was converted into an interior space. The funds were provided by Maurine Church Morse, the widow of Samuel F. B. Morse, and herself for many years an active supporter of the hospital.

Only the pool area of the Fountain Court is domed. The ceiling over the pool is low enough to provide intimacy, yet high enough to give some sense of expansiveness. The reception desk occupies one corner. A cafe serves visitors. Even local businessmen schedule lunch here. The gift shop and seating areas complete the picture. The Fountain Court becomes a familiar point, from which to explore other areas. It is possible to pass through it on the way to a patient's room or the x-ray department, or it can be a destination in itself; or it can be avoided altogether. The numerous services keep it lively,

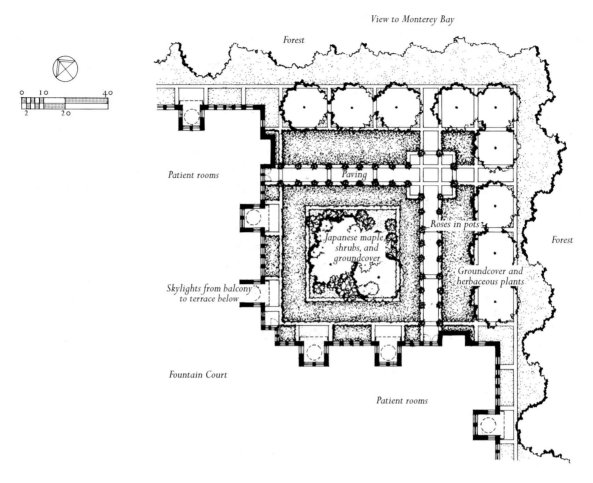

View to Monterey Bay

Forest

Patient rooms

Paving

Roses in pots

Forest

Japanese maple shrubs, and groundcover

Groundcover and herbaceous plants

Skylights from balcony to terrace below

Fountain Court

Patient rooms

Community Hospital of the Monterey Peninsula Rose Garden plan *(by David Kamp).*

but it is not overcrowded. The pure geometric forms of the architecture contrast with and complement the natural elements—plants, fish, the noise of water.

The Rose Garden is one level below the entry plaza and Fountain Court. A window of the Fountain Court overlooks this garden. A large square planter and rectangular terraces, planting beds, and walks define the site. The hospital building encloses two sides; the forest encloses the others. The geometry of the ground plane barely contains the masses of exuberant plants, but the garden is formalized by allées of potted roses on standards. Patient rooms on the ground level are partially screened by raised plantings.

The views from both levels extend past the garden to the forest.

The Rose Garden is more private, personal, and domestic than the others. Lawn furniture and sculptures of cranes and browsing deer are tastefully placed at the edge of a terrace. Visitors are tempted to imagine that the owner of this garden, who has invited them to linger here, sit in the sun, and enjoy the roses, might appear at any moment to give them a tour and tell them about the collection of roses, how the sculpture was obtained, and which plants are the favorites—so thoroughly do the elements in the garden seem to be a personal statement of an individual's interests. Japanese maple trees, rhododendron, francoa, agapanthus, and vinca are among the plants; the Rose Garden is so called because of the potted roses on standards lining the walks.

The garden is maintained in a manner befitting a fine home. The staff favors this garden for breaks and lunch, even though a terrace is now available for that purpose. Long-term patients are wheeled out to the Rose Garden in their beds. It is "beautiful, peaceful, very calming. . . . It takes you out of a pretty threatening environment," according to the manager of Pediatrics (interview with Marie Stewart-Helms, R.N., CHOMP, Sept. 28, 1995).

The grounds staff, which seems to be working together for a common goal, a larger purpose, understands these gardens. The intent, design, and horticultural requirements of the gardens are articulated clearly and without pretense. John Affinito, who for twenty years was director of the Grounds Department, retired in 1997. It is his understanding of the place and its purpose that is most clearly expressed today. Affinito articulated, for example, that the challenge with the Rose Garden was to use ornamental plants to complement the forest, to create a foreground and midground for the deep shade and strong forms of the natural landscape (interview with John Affinito, grounds manager, CHOMP, Aug. 5, 1996).

Garden work as a whole requires dealing with growth and change determined by the rhythms of nature and the needs of the plants themselves. The expertise and sophistication of the gardening staff at this institution are, however, unusual. The clay soil in the Rose Garden, for instance, required a new shale drainage system for a bed of vinca minor. Lead weights were put in the bottom of the plastic pots that support the roses. (Although plastic pots retain precious water better than clay does, they are light enough for the deer to tip over.) Fungus gnats are trapped and tracked by computer. Aphid-eating lacewings are placed on the Japanese maple trees. The Italian stone pine in the entry court is splitting and has been lightened by pruning, propped with two-by-

fours, and cabled. The lawns must be thatched, the soil sifted, the heat monitored, and the springeri on the second-story balconies watered, thanks to a system developed by a staff member.

The three large gardens are supported by a host of others. The medical-surgical nursing units surround small glassed courtyards. The first story is open to the air, and the courtyard below is lit by skylights. *Ficus nitida*, raphiolepis, and xylosma are the mainstays; other, more colorful potted plants are routinely rotated. In the areas adjacent to the courtyards, staff members can often be found doing paperwork at large tables.

Two double-height living room–like areas at the Rose Garden level, called atria, are used by patients, staff, and visitors. Simply and comfortably furnished with rattan furniture, these areas invite reading, musing, paperwork, phone calls, talks with physicians. The admitting department, essentially a long, wide corridor with a window wall, looks out on the entry court. With its rattan furniture in conversational groupings and the sound of the water from the nearby Fountain Court, it reinforces the image of the hotel lobby. The view of the comings and goings in the hospital's main entry allows for a psychological as well as an administrative transition. Several small exterior courts have been converted to delightful skylighted waiting areas.

At all the focal points of the building one encounters streams of light from above, open sculptural staircases, plants tagged with botanical names, magnificent views, places to sit. So exquisite are these elements that one is compelled on to the next. No sense of foreboding hovers over the patient rounding the corner on the way to the next diagnostic test or procedure. These memorable spaces are distinct enough to orient a person, to serve as markers on an internal map of place and meaning. There are enough of them to allow a sense of ownership. It seems fine to move a chair to just the right spot, but it is probably already *in* just the right spot. Each detail has been considered, yet nothing seems oppressive or overcontrolled. The

This atrium is one of two such double-height areas adjacent to patient care units. Furnished with gold area rugs and rattan furniture, they serve as living rooms for patients and visitors and as casual work areas for staff. *(Photo: © 1998, Dave Stock)*

patients' rooms are small, but the expansive windows and large public spaces are liberating in their variety and sweep. The nurses' stations may not have enough counter space, but charting can be done in the atrium.

Nature and architectural artifice meet one at every turn, but so do light and art, comfort and hospitality, and of course medical care. All seem equally important, nothing sacrificed for something else. The most basic notions of what a hospital should be remain intact. The white walls and the cleanliness they represent are an expected part of the hospital environment, but these walls are not cold or sterile. They are patterned, textured, lively. Everything is of good quality without being ostentatious, comfortable

without being sybaritic. It is a vital place, yet in no way demanding. Here it is easy to believe that the California awareness of and attachment to nature makes a difference in the quality of life. In this place of great natural beauty, nature is revealed as the source of life and good health.

The gardens are important to life and design here, but they are only a part of a larger whole. The concern for nature and aesthetics reflects the overall concern for the individual—for the patients, staff, and outside community that the hospital serves.

There is commitment to the idea that a well-cared-for staff is better able to provide high-quality patient care. If the staff is supported, perhaps even reinvigorated, by the workplace, it is believed, the patients, too, will reap benefits. And ultimately the community itself will be stronger. The design of the hospital is one part of the commitment to staff, but salaries and benefits are excellent, too. A staff dining room with its own terrace allows retreat from the intensities of the patient care environment, and the food is excellent. Artwork in staff offices is often selected with the individual staff member in mind. Patients, of course, are accorded the same respect and individual attention, so that they can concentrate all their energies on healing. Patients are given warm blankets and can select long or short kimono-style robes. If their doctors allow it, they can sip wine while watching the quail outside their windows. The intent is to support and heal all who come.

This special hospital exists because of a remarkable synergy between a community with high expectations, a hospital leadership capable of giving form to those expectations, and the willingness of thousands of people to sacrifice to achieve something better than the conventional standard. Community leaders donated land and made major financial contributions. Volunteers sponsored Sunday luncheons at the construction site and displayed the architectural model there and elsewhere in the community in an effort to gain support and funds. Others solicited donations over the radio. Some even sold firewood and donated the proceeds. With this support, the hospital leadership was able to hire and work with designers. The institution they created defines and translates a philosophy of life and health care into a visible, working form.

In the midst of life and growth, there is a timeless quality to this place. So stylistically clear, strong in character, predictable but not static, it must provide real comfort and a sense of connection to the people of Monterey. The institution is located on an extraordinary site. The hospital's success lies in the understanding and expression of the unique ecology and culture of the region. No other place could, or should, reproduce it exactly, for each community must build the hospital that reflects its own needs and sense of place.

Community Hospital of the Monterey Peninsula. *(Photo: © 1998, Jane Lidz)*

Recovering the Wisdom of the Garden

Coming Home

Gardens temper the terrors of patienthood. We do not suggest for an instant that gardens in any way serve as a substitute for the life-saving advances of medical technology. They are merely an adjunct, and this volume is not about faith healing or alternative medicine. On the contrary, we argue that gardens have been part of the mainstream medical environment for centuries, and for valid reasons. Precisely now, however, when medical technology has so far advanced the art of healing, it is important not to forget that the *settings* for health care also have something valuable to add. We suggest that in the extreme dislocation brought about by illness and patienthood, gardens can help to center both staff and patients. For gardens are stories. They began exclusively as places that provided sustenance, then evolved into walled-off enclaves safe from predators, and ultimately became visions of Paradise.

Each of the gardens we have looked at offers elements of sustenance, protection, and beauty, and each reflects an individual spirit and ideal. The gardens and the original garden makers at each of our chosen sites enhance the spirit of the place. Friends Hospital would remain a very good psychiatric facility even without its gardens, but with them, Friends is transformed into a halcyon emblem of respite and cure. In architecture and scale, Queen of Peace resembles any nursing home. The garden, with its profusion of religious images, renders it an embodiment of modesty, devotion, and humane care. Patients know this; and indeed, in every hospital setting that has a garden, both patients and caregivers are acutely aware of the meaning and benefit it confers. Gardens induce a sense of connectedness with the surroundings, and a sense of comfort.

Comfort may be the critical element. We have shown that in only the rarest of cases—even among the best-designed hospitals—are the entryways comforting. Perhaps that would be too much to hope for—no matter how good the signage, the directions, or the welcome, patients will feel lost. Hospitals, clinics, and hospices have always—by their history, character, and, until recently, intent—been set apart from the normal cycle of events. Patients who enter a hospital, even for the briefest treatments, barely have a sense of place. For caregivers or family members, as well, the hospital stands at a remove from normal life. And illness is the most wrenching uprooting of all. In health care settings people willingly give up their freedom, mobility, and privacy; yet if illness diminishes us, patienthood most often demeans us. Good architecture and pleasant interiors may help remedy this perceived diminution, but in the sterile and threatening environs of the hospital a garden may offer the sole opportunity for recognition of the familiar.

In the stasis of patienthood, gardens alone provide for the human needs for expanse, movement, and change. A hospital garden is incomparably evocative of other times and places, real or imagined; it removes the patient psychologically from the oppressive purity of hospital life into that melange of memory which constitutes a human being. Gardens connect a person with biological memory; they energize, stimulate the senses. At its simplest, this sensory stimulation serves as a distraction. At the most profound level, the garden offers reassurance that even in time of greatest desperation, one is part of the vast biological cycle of time and change, and subject to the biological imperatives of chance and necessity.

The connection with eternal cycles inherent in the garden may be needed most by patients, but its symbols and associations extend to families and caregivers, too, and unite them in dynamic equilibrium. When patients are at peace, their families respond. When patients and families are serene, caregivers can offer more effective assistance. This is not to say that intensive care will be half-hearted or ineffectual if patients are agitated or *in extremis*. The mechanical aspect of high-tech care will still be rendered with dispatch, efficiency, and unbiased attention, but when the patient is more in harmony with the surroundings and the situation, recovery can occur more smoothly. Professional staff members, too, feel better in the presence of gardens—and they feel better when the patients feel better. The interaction of staff, visitors, and patients—and ultimately of the entire health care community and the community as a whole—is enhanced by gardens, which assist in translating psychological well-being into physical comfort.

We have suggested throughout this book that in unique ways, gardens provide patients with a center, a sense of rootedness. They accomplish this through their historical persistence in myth and history, through their resonance with milieu and local tradition, and perhaps through their connection with deeply ingrained biological needs that link us with nature. These bonds transcend all backgrounds and cultures. Whether in local or evolutionary time, gardens remind us of home.

For most of their history, human beings lived in nature and worked directly with, or against, natural forces. Nature defined what they were. Nowadays, contact with nature is interpreted for most by other humans—farmers, developers, politicians, park service workers. People feel no need to incorporate nature into health care settings because people are no longer aware of being dependent on it for daily survival—as a source of water, food, fuel, and transport. The scientific and technological aspirations of health care since the turn of the century have devalued nature.

Nature does appear in the health care settings reserved for the most hopeless cases. When science has given up, the ill and dying are left to focus not on cure but on improving the quality of the life that is left. Religious institutions, in both the Eastern and Western traditions, are founded on the belief that humankind is part of a larger whole, that God and nature are one, and that acts of charity and harmony with nature make better people. That belief persists when a culture, even if not currently land-based, retains a collective memory of its past as a farming or logging community and prides itself on that tie; or when a few people decide to fight back against the obliteration of nature through urban development. Or natural settings may survive merely because something has to be done with the spaces left after construction—spaces between the wings of buildings or over subterranean structures.

If human beings are really a part of this larger, living, and inert whole, the earth, they need to experience it directly and routinely, almost as a tonic or preventive, and not just when they are sick or in crisis. If we have focused on gardens as a corollary to health care, it is because when people are ill, they are open to reassesssing and refocusing their lives. Often those living with illness have a heightened sense of awareness. They begin to notice the details around them: the sky is bluer, the leaves more brilliant—and gardens may well become important.

Almost everyone will enter a health care setting at some point. Such settings are definable, controllable, fundable. All of us, all our lives, resemble patients in some ways. We are all trying to maintain an equilibrium. If we restrict ourselves to providing for those who are at a given moment the patients, we miss an extraordinary opportunity. Healing must be considered in its broadest sense, not just as recovery from illness, but as a way to live as healthfully and as well as possible, even while being buffeted by surrounding forces. Health care settings should mitigate the stresses of the difficult work being done in them. They should promote good health and serve as an example of healthful living.

How do people incorporate nature into their lives? They view it from their kitchen windows, travel great distances to view it on vacation, pass through it on their way to work or to the store. They experience sun, wind, smells, temperature, plants, birds, and water. How many of these things are patients deprived of in the hospital? To be supportive, it is not enough for a health care setting to meet medical and surgical needs; it should be a caring, welcoming place. It should respond to that most American need, the need to be an individual.

Once individuals begin to understand their place in nature, they will be more likely to incorporate that understanding into their lives in places such as health care settings. The experience of a lovely garden may also become the inspiration to move from the small scale to the large and work for a more healthful, ecologically sound world.

Human beings in modern societies may never again have a close tie to the land. Reality does, however, require us at a minimum to respect nature, for it sustains life. Appreciation of nature and the knowledge of being part of it are an essential aspect of humanity and should not be relegated to a museum or to the fringes of existence.

The physical experience of the world helps shape the sense of being. The landscape, nothing but a thin crust really, is something to be inhabited, celebrated, adapted. As hard as humans may try to narrow their existence to climate-controlled, light-moderated settings, nature intrudes and insists on being recognized.

When science fails, and it often does in health care, it is natural to retreat to the commonsense position. Nature, we find, sustains people intellectually and spiritually.

In the future, gardens will appear in health care settings and others only if the collective culture or forceful individuals demand them. Historically, the maintenance of gardens in hospitals has been alternately encouraged and discouraged. The Renaissance courtyard tradition called forth the arcades for patients' beds in Santa Maria Nuova in Florence. The military

campus seems to have fostered the improved Stonehouse Naval Hospital in eighteenth-century England. Yet always some of the best moments in the caring tradition have been brought into being through the initiative of particular individuals and particular institutions. The monks of Zaragoza adapted their monastic routine to the humane care of the mentally ill. Dr. Pinel sought gardens for his confined Parisian patients. The latest high-tech hospital at Johns Hopkins was laid out on a garden campus.

It may be that no ideal restorative garden exists. Nor do we want to promote a specific future garden architecture, a style, or even a landscape type. Instead, we argue for a commitment to experience and experimentation with nature in the health care context.

The six institutions that are the subject of the case studies in this book, regardless of how professionals might judge the quality of their designs, are gracious gestures, laudable efforts. They come from different traditions, are located in different parts of the country, provide different types of care. They must overcome varying urban conditions, changing social patterns, and different climates. All are working under great economic pressure. They are a reflection of the moment in history and the culture they serve. The gardens are mere fragments of nature, yet they somehow encapsulate or represent wildness or our cultural use of land. They are interpretations, distillations of what is culturally important as well as what is socially acceptable.

We have chosen the gardens discussed here because they represent different kinds of health care settings rather than because they exemplify great garden design. These gardens are hardly perfect, but they give us the range of possibility and the range of choice. Grand horticultural showplaces are probably no more restorative than small, well-thought-out spaces. The critical requirement for a restorative garden is that it be in synchrony with its surroundings and with needs of patients and other users. A garden is home when it offers comfort. A garden affords respite and restoration when it melds with the familiar in our lives. But a great restorative garden transcends the familiar and expands the self.

Medical culture as embodied in our hospitals fits into neither the cycle of our past nor the emotional needs of the present. To humanize technology and render institutions humane and nurturing requires continual active choices. Whether through the warm blankets at Monterey or the found green spaces at Rusk, that touch of grace goes remarkably far in restoring personhood to patienthood.

Garden spaces particularly offer a human context in time of illness. That a mere view or brief moments of respite in nature can calm the spirit is more than wishful thinking. Clear-cut physiological correlates support the contention that the sense of well-being that nature confers is no mere mystical notion or placebo, but instead a true physiological relaxation of the entire organism. We feel better in the presence of nature because our bodies are less subject to stress. In the complex web of human response to stress, the experience of nature uniquely enables the various branches of our immune, endocrine, and central nervous systems—all beyond conscious control—to find repose. It is inconceivable that this mental respite and invigoration of the organ systems would not have a beneficial effect on healing and recovery.

Our plea, then, is that garden spaces be considered as important, if not essential, components of the medical endeavor. That every stage of sentient patienthood, from acute illness to the last moments before the death of consciousness and self, can be made more tolerable to the patient by the presence of nature. As we have suggested, no grand space or extensive budget is required. To be beneficial, the garden need only hint at the cycles, the variety, of nature. We call on physicians to lobby for the inclusion of gardens in health care settings. We request architects and hospital designers to allow for oases of nature wherever possible in their designs. We ask health care administrators to declare that staff, visitors, and families will all be better for the presence of nature. It takes little to accomplish these aims, with the proper planning. Awareness of the need is the starting point; implementation is almost an easier task—nature is part of good design.

We ask all who are concerned with patients and their families, with healing, and with the act of caring, to recognize the wisdom of making a place for nature in our midst.

Notes

INTRODUCTION

1. Oliver Sacks, *A Leg to Stand On* (New York: HarperCollins, 1984), 163.

THE HISTORY

1. The best single modern work expressing the power of restorative gardens and their necessity for patients who are injured, sick, or infirm is Oliver Sacks, *A Leg to Stand On*. It should be read in conjunction with Harold F. Searles's pioneering work *The Non-Human Environment in Normal Development and Schizophrenia* (New York: International Universities Press, 1960); Roger S. Ulrich's path-breaking article, "View Through a Window May Influence Recovery from Surgery," *Science* 224 (1984), 420–421; and Roger S. Ulrich and Russ Parsons's recent review of current social science literature, "Influences of Passive Experiences with Plants on Individual Well-Being and Health," in Diane Relf, ed., *The Role of Horticulture in Human Well-Being and Social Development* (Portland, Ore.: Timber Press, 1992), 93–105; and Stephen R. Kellert and Edward O. Wilson, *The Biophilia Hypothesis* (Washington, D.C.: Island Press, 1993).

2. Willet, *Synopsis papismi* (1634), 1223 (spelling modernized), quoted in Barry G. Gale, "The Dissolution and the Revolution in London Hospital Facilities," *Medical History* 11 (1967), 91.

3. Matt. 25:35.

4. The still extant Hospices de Beaune, founded in 1443, provided refuge for orphans and the aged poor and nursed the sick of the commune. See Grace Goldin, "A Protohospice at the Turn of the Century: Saint Luke's House, London, from 1893 to 1921," *Journal of the History of Medicine and Allied Sciences* 36 (October 1981), 386–388.

5. Peregrine Horden, "A Discipline of Relevance: The Historiography of the Later Medieval Hospital," *Social History of Medicine* 1 (1988), 367, 369.

6. Horden, "A Discipline of Relevance," 363–364.

7. David Knowles and R. Neville Hadcock, *Medieval Religious Houses* (London: Longmans Green, 1953), 250. The percentages are drawn from categories P, A, C, T, S, and L.

8. A. J. Kilgor, "Colony at Gheel," *American Journal of Psychiatry* 92 (January 1936), 959–965; Grace Goldin, *Work of Mercy, a Picture History of Hospitals* (Erin, Ontario: Boston Mills Press, 1994), 26, 223–227.

9. Rotha Mary Clay, *The Medieval Hospitals of England* (London: Methuen, 1909), 107–122 and Plate 8.

10. Translation by Terry Comito, in Comito, *The Idea of the Garden in the Renaissance* (New Brunswick, N.J.: Rutgers University Press, 1978), 177; from J. P. Minge, ed., *Patrologia Latina*, vol. 281 (1855), 271, col. 569.

11. For the Persian roots of the medieval monastic garden, see Ralph Pinder-Wilson, "The Persian Garden: *Bagh* and *Chahar Bagh*," and James Dickie, "The Islamic Garden in Spain," in Elisabeth MacDougall and Richard Ettinghouse, eds., *The Islamic Garden* (Washington, D.C.: Dumbarton Oaks Research Library, 1976), 72, 93–94. On the Roman architectural and garden tradition, see Clarence Glacken, *Traces on the Rhodian Shore* (Berkeley: University of California Press, 1967), 25, 33; A. R. Littlewood, "Ancient Literary Evidence for the Pleasure Gardens of Roman Country Villas," and Nicholas Purcell, "Town in Country and Country in Town," in Elisabeth Blair MacDougall, ed., *Ancient Roman Villa Gardens* (Washington, D.C.: Dumbarton Oaks Research Library, 1987), 9–30, 187–203; Clarence Grieg, *Pliny, A Selection of His Letters* (Cambridge: Cambridge University Press, 1978), 50–53; Derek Clifford, *A History of Garden Design* (London: Faber & Faber, 1962), 18–20; Wilhelmina F. Jashemski, *The Gardens of Pompeii, Herculaneum and the Villas Destroyed by Vesuvius* (New Rochelle: Carataza, 1979), 48, 89–99; Michael Conan, "Nature into Art: The Gardens and Landscapes in the Everyday Life of Ancient Rome," *Journal of Garden History* 6 (October–December, 1986), 348–356. For the Roman-Medieval transition, see Timothy Fry et al., eds., *The Rule of St. Benedict in Latin and English with Notes* (Collegeville, Minn.: Liturgical Press, 1981); Theresa McLean, *Medieval English Gardens* (New York: Viking, 1981), 16; Fay Marie Getz, "Introduction," in Sheila Campbell, Bert Hall, and David Klausner, eds., *Health, Disease, and Healing in Medieval Culture* (New York: St. Martin's Press, 1991), xvi.

12. Paul Meyvaert, "The Medieval Monastic Garden," in Elisabeth B. MacDougall, ed., *Medieval Gardens* (Washington, D.C.: Dumbarton Oaks Research Library, 1986), 52; and McLean, *Medieval English Gardens*, 16, 20–21.

13. John D. Thompson and Grace Goldin, *The Hospital: A Social and Architectural History* (New Haven: Yale University Press, 1975), 10–14.

14. Matt. 25:35–40; Tob. 1:15–20; "The Tools of Good Works," Fry et al., eds., *Rule of St. Benedict*, chap. 4.

15. Faye Marie Getz, "To Prolong Life and Promote Health," in Sheila Campbell et al., eds., *Health, Disease and Healing in Medieval Culture*, 141–151; Harold J. Cook, "The New Philosophy and Medicine in Seventeenth-Century England," in David C. Lindberg and Robert S. Wetman, eds., *Reappraisals of the Scientific Revolution* (New York: Cambridge University Press, 1990); Meyvaert, "The Medieval Monastic Garden," 25–53.

16. Today our Rose of Sharon is a hibiscus (*Hibiscus syriacus*), and our lilies-of-the-valley (*Convallaria majalis*) are not the white Easter lilies (*Lilium candium*) of the Annunciation paintings. *Hortus Third* (New York: Macmillan, 1979); and Thomas H. Everett, *New York Botanical Garden Illustrated Encyclopedia of Horticulture* (New York: Garland, 1981). The biblical plants are now thought to have been *Anemone coronaria* as the Rose of Sharon, and the lilies either some sort of crocus or narcissus; see A. W. Anderson, *Plants of the Bible* (London: Crosby Lockwood, 1956).

17. Georges Duby, *History of Medieval Art, 980–1440* (New York: Rizzoli, 1986), Part 3, 37.

18. McLean, *Medieval English Gardens*, 122–123, 130–134; John V. Fleming, *The Roman de la Rose, a Study in Allegory and Iconography* (Princeton: Princeton University Press, 1969), 55–60.

19. Barry G. Gale, "The Dissolution and Revolution in London Hospital Facilities," *Medical History* 11 (1967), 92; Wayne A. Rebhorn, "Thomas More's Enclosed Garden: *Utopia* and Renaissance Humanism," *English Literary Renaissance* 6 (Spring 1976), 140–155; W. S. C. Copeman, "The Royal Hospitals Before 1700," in F. N. L. Poynter, ed., *The Evolution of Hospitals in Britain* (London: Pitman Medical Publishing, 1964), 24–41; Peter Gay, *The Enlightenment: An Interpretation*, vol. 2, *The Science of Freedom* (New York: Knopf, 1969), 8–9.

20. Karl F. Hellinger, "The Population of Europe from the Black Death to the Eve of the Vital Revolution," in E. E. Rich and C. H. Wilson, eds., *Cambridge Economic History of Europe*, vol. 4 (Cambridge: Cambridge University Press, 1967), 5–12, 29–30, 90–95; Paul Bairoch, *Cities and Economic Development* (Chicago: University of Chicago Press, 1988), 175–210.

21. George Rosen, "The Hospital: Historical Sociology," in *From Medical Police to Social Medicine* (New York: Science History Publications, 1974), 284–300; Ann G. Carmichael, *Plague and the Poor in Renaissance Florence* (Cambridge: Cambridge University Press, 1986), 107–126. In Paris, King Henri IV built a huge suburban pesthouse, Hôpital Saint Louis (1607–1612), with the intention of enforcing the city's quarantines; see Hilary Ballon, *The Paris of Henri IV* (Cambridge: MIT Press, 1991), 178–198.

22. Grace Goldin, "Juan de Dios and the Hospital of Christian Charity," *Journal of the History of Medicine and Allied Sciences* 33 (1978), 14–19, 32–33; Ruben D. Rumbaut, "The Hospital at Zaragoza," *Bulletin of the Menninger Clinic* 39 (1975), 268–272; Dora B. Weiner, "The Brothers of Charity and the Mentally Ill in Pre-Revolutionary France," *Social History of Medicine* 2 (December 1989), 326.

23. *Catholic Encyclopedia*; Louis S. Greenbaum, "Jacques Necker and the Reform of the Paris Hospitals on the Eve of the French Revolution," *Clio Medica* 19 (1984), 220.

24. Le Jeune de Boullecourt, *Description générale de l'Hostel Royale des Invalides* (Paris: Chez l'auteur, 1682, copy in Dumbarton Oaks Library).

25. Dora B. Weiner, "The Brothers of Charity and the Mentally Ill in Pre-Revolutionary France," 321–327; Sir Nikolaus Bernhard Pevsner, *Building Types, a History* (Princeton: Princeton University Press, 1976), 146.

26. John Howard, *An Account of the Principal Lazarettos in Europe . . . Together with Further Observations on Some Foreign Prisons and Hospitals etc.* (Warrington: William Eyres, printer, 1789), 53–69; Ronald Pickvance, *Van Gogh in Saint Rémy and Auvers* (New York: Abrams, 1986), 80–92.

27. John D. Thompson and Grace Goldin, *The Hospital: A Social and Architectural History* (New Haven: Yale University Press, 1975), 31; Adrian Forty, "The Modern Hospital in England and France," in Anthony D. King, ed., *Buildings and Society* (London: Routledge & Kegan Paul, 1980), 63–64; Pevsner, *Building Types*, 143–144.

28. Andrew Wear, "Caring for the Sick Poor in St. Bartholomew's Exchange: 1580–1676," in W. F. Bynum and Roy Porter, eds., *Medical History*, supplement 11 (London: Wellcome Institute for the History of Medicine, 1991), 41–75.

29. Forty, "The Modern Hospital," 66, 69–72; Howard, *An Account of the Principal Lazarettos*, 82, 136–137, 140–141; W. S. C. Copeman, "The Royal Hospitals Before 1700," 27–41.

30. Roy Strong, *The Renaissance Garden in*

England (London: Thames & Hudson, 1979), 9–22; David Jacques and Arend Jan van der Horst, *The Gardens of William and Mary* (London: Christopher Helm, 1988); Derek Clifford, *A History of Garden Design*, 32–47.

31. Andrew Marvell, "The Garden," in J. B. Trapp et al., eds., *The Oxford Anthology of English Literature*, vol. 1 (New York: Oxford University Press, 1973), 1155–1157; and in the same vein, Sir William Temple, *Works*, vol. 1 (London: Printed for J. Round et al., 1740), 175.

32. George Rosen, *From Medical Police to Social Medicine*, 148–158; Louis S. Greenbaum, "Jean-Sylvain Bailly, the Baron Breteuil and the 'Four New Hospitals' of Paris," *Clio Medica* 8 (1973), 265.

33. Peter Gay, *The Enlightenment*, vol. 2, 9–23; Max Neuburger, *The Doctrine of the Healing Power of Nature Throughout the Course of Time*, Linn J. Boyd, trans. (New York: Homeopathic Medical College and Fowler Hospital, 1932), 73–74; Louis S. Greenbaum, "Health-Care and Hospital-Building in 18th Century France: Reform Proposals of du Pont de Nemours and Condorcet," *Transactions of the Fourth International Congress on the Enlightenment*, Theodore Besterman, ed., vol. 2 (Oxford, England: Voltaire Foundation, 1976), 195–200.

34. Barbara Duncum, "The Development of Hospital Design and Planning," in Poynter, ed., *Evolution of Hospitals in Britain*, 208–221.

35. Hospital built 1706–1727, David Willemese, ed., *The Unknown Drawings of Nicholas Bidloo* (Voorburg, Netherlands: Willemese, 1975, copy in Dumbarton Oaks Library), 27–28.

36. Guenter B. Risse, *Hospital Life in Enlightenment Scotland* (Cambridge: Cambridge University Press, 1986), 3, 29–30.

37. Pevsner calls attention to Christopher Wren's unexecuted design (ca. 1700) for the Royal Naval Hospital at Greenwich, which called for a dozen separated pavilions (see *Building Types*, 147); Thompson and Goldin, *The Hospital*, 142–143, 389–390; P. D. G. Pugh, "The History of the Royal Naval Hospital, Plymouth," *Journal of the Royal Naval Medical Service* 58 (1972), 78–94, 207–226; C. Lloyd and J. L. S. Coulter, *Medicine and the Navy 1200–1900*, vol. 3, 1714–1815 (Edinburgh: E. and S. Livingstone, 1961); John Howard, *The State of the Prisons in England and Wales, with Preliminary Observations, and an Account of Some Foreign Prisons and Hospitals*, 3d ed. (Warrington: William Eyres, printer, 1784), 389–390; Louis S. Greenbaum, "'The Commercial Treaty of Humanity,' La tournée des hôpitaux anglais par Jacques Tenon en 1787," *Revue d'Histoire des Sciences* 24 (1971), 317–350.

38. Pevsner, *Building Types*, 154–155.

39. M. [Jacques] Tenon, *Mémoires sur les hôpitaux de Paris* (Paris: Ph.-D. Pierres, 1788), l–lvi; Louis Greenbaum, "'Measure of Civilization': The Hospital Thought of Jacques Tenon on the Eve of the French Revolution," *Bulletin of the History of Medicine* 49 (Spring 1975), 43–56; Thompson and Goldin, *The Hospital*, 132–143; Ernest Flagg, "The Planning of Hospitals," *The Brickbuilder* 12 (June 1903), 114.

40. Florence Nightingale, *Notes on Hospitals*, 3d ed. (London: n.p., 1863), 18–19. The same admonitions are repeated in her *Notes on Nursing, What It Is, and What It Is Not* (Edinburgh: Churchill Livingstone, [1859] 1980), 69–71.

41. Douglas Chambers, "'Discovering in Wide Lantskip': *Paradise Lost* and the Tradition of Landscape Description in the 17th Century," *Journal of Garden History* 5 (January-March 1985), 15–31.

42. Horace Walpole, "The History of Modern Taste in Gardening," in Isabel W. U. Chase, *Horace Walpole: Gardenist* (Princeton: Princeton University Press, 1943), 27, 36.

43. Gilbert White, *The Natural History of Selborne*, Grant Allen, ed. (London: John Lane, [1789] 1900); Jane Austen, *Mansfield Park* (New York: Penguin, [1814] 1996); Leo Marx, "Does Pastoralism Have a Future?" Symposium on the Pastoral Landscape, sponsored by the Center for the Advanced Study of the Visual Arts, National Gallery of Art, and the Center for Renaissance and Baroque Studies, University of Maryland, January 20–21, 1898; Günther Bittner, "Gardens for Children," in Günther Bittner and Paul-Ludwig Weinacht, eds., *Wieviel Garten braucht der Mensch?* (Würzburg, Germany: Ergon, 1990).

44. Jean-Jacques Rousseau, *La Nouvelle Héloïse*, Judith H. McDowell, trans. (University Park: Pennsylvania State University Press, [1761] 1968), 306–307.

45. Johann Wolfgang von Goethe, *The Sorrows of Young Werther*, Victor Lange, trans., vol. 11 in *Goethe's Collected Works* (New York: Suhrkamp, [1774] 1988), 36–37. The Boston landscape architect Charles Eliot (1859–1897) traveled to Germany as a young man and was much taken by an estate built by Ludwig Heinrich von Püchler-Muskau (1785–1871), which resembled the kinds Goethe had imagined in *Elective Affinities* (1809). See Charles William Eliot, *Charles Eliot, Landscape Architect*, vol. 2 (Boston: Houghton Mifflin, 1903), 360–361.

46. Christian Cay Lorenz Hirschfeld, *Theorie der Gartenkunst*, 5 vols. (Hildesheim: Georg Olms, [1777–1785] 1973), 115–116: the passage quoted here was translated by Jacoba von Gimborn; a recent study of Hirschfeld, Wolfgang Schepers, *Hirschfeld's Theorie der Gartenkunst, 1779–1789* (Worms,

Germany: Werner'sche Verlagsgesellschaft, 1980).

47. Christine Stevenson, "Madness and the Picturesque in the Kingdom of Denmark," in *The Anatomy of Madness*, vol. 3, W. F. Bynum and Roy Porter, eds. (London: Routledge, 1988), 13–47.

48. The two Paris institutions combined the functions of poorhouse, petty criminal prison, and insane asylum. Both were built in a clean-up of the homeless of Paris in 1656, Pevsner, *Building Types*, 145; Andrew Scull, "A Convenient Place to Get Rid of Inconvenient People: The Victorian Lunatic Asylum," in Anthony King, ed., *Buildings and Society*, 42–49.

49. Dora B. Weiner, "Philippe Pinel's 'Memoir on Madness' of December 11, 1794: A Fundamental Text of Modern Psychiatry," *American Journal of Psychiatry* 149 (June 1992), 727.

50. J. Sanborne Bockoven, *Moral Treatment and Community Mental Health* (New York: Springer, 1972), 12–13, 75; Gregory Zilboorg and George W. Henry, *A History of Medical Psychology* (New York: Norton, 1941), 315–325, 407–418; Thompson and Goldin, *The Hospital*, 53–78.

51. Weiner, "Pinel's 'Memoir on Madness,'" 728.

52. Philippe Pinel, *A Treatise on Insanity*, D. D. Davis, trans., vol. 3 in *Significant Contributions to the History of Psychology, 1750–1920*, Daniel N. Robison, ed. (Washington, D.C.: University Publications of America, [1806] 1977), 109.

53. Pinel, *Treatise on Insanity*, 68.

54. Pinel, *Treatise on Insanity*, 193–194. In this connection he mentions the precedent of the Zaragoza hospital with regard to work therapy, 195.

55. Carol B. Perloff, *The Asylum: The History of the Friends Hospital and the Quaker Contribution to Psychiatry* (Philadelphia: Friends Hospital, 1994), 6–13.

56. Perloff, *The Asylum*, 12; David J. Rothman, *The Discovery of Asylum, Social Order and Disorder in the New Republic* (Boston: Little Brown, 1971), 116–129; Pinel believed in the "character of maniacal Paroxysms not depending upon exciting causes, but upon the constitution," *Treatise on Insanity*, 14–15.

57. Thomas S. Kirkbride, *On the Construction, Organization, and General Arrangements of the Hospital for the Insane*, 2d ed. (Philadelphia: Lippincott, 1880), 39, 42–44.

58. Both the Friends Hospital in Philadelphia and the Butler Hospital (founded 1859) in Providence, Rhode Island, preserve to this day the fine landscaping of their nineteenth-century origins. William Shaler Cleveland laid out the Butler grounds, and the Olmsted Brothers later revised the design of the hospital's hundred-acre site, according to Edward F. Sanderson, Providence Historic District Commission, "National Register of Historic Places Inventory," paper accompanying nomination to the National Park Service, U.S. Department of the Interior, March 25, 1976.

59. Kirkbride, *Construction of Hospitals for the Insane*, 269–270, 275–282. Charles Dickens visited such an institution in South Boston when he came to the United States in 1841; see *American Notes* (Gloucester: Peter Smith, [1841] 1968), 61–64; Rothman, *Asylum*, 138, 145.

60. Bockoven, *Moral Treatment*, 67, 74, 83; Gerald N. Grob, *The State and the Mentally Ill: A History of Worcester State Hospital in Massachusetts, 1830–1920* (Chapel Hill: University of North Carolina Press, 1966), 254. For a very fine new illustrated history of the management of insanity in the United States from colonial times to World War 1, see Lynn Gamwell and Nancy Tomes, *Madness in America* (Ithaca: Cornell University Press, 1995).

61. Bockoven, *Moral Treatment*, 43, 83–86; Albert Deutsch, *The Mentally Ill in America*, 2d ed. (New York: Columbia University Press, 1949), 229–249.

62. Thompson and Goldin, *The Hospital*, 69; Grob, *The State and the Mentally Ill*, 329.

63. Edward D. Churchill, "The Pandemic of Wound Infection in Hospitals," *Journal of the History of Medicine and Allied Sciences* 20 (October 1965), 392, 396.

64. Florence Nightingale, *Notes on Hospitals*, 52–62.

65. John Harley Warner, *The Therapeutic Perspective, Medical Practice, Knowledge, and Identity in America, 1820–1885* (Cambridge: Harvard University Press, 1986), 85, 102; Charles E. Rosenberg, *The Care of Strangers: The Rise of America's Hospital System* (New York: Basic Books, 1987), chap. 3.

66. Churchill, "Pandemic," 390, 398, 400–401.

67. Quoted in Alan M. Chesney, *The Johns Hopkins Hospital and the Johns Hopkins School of Medicine, a Chronicle*, vol. 1 (Baltimore: Johns Hopkins Press, 1943), 14.

68. Chesney, *The Johns Hopkins Hospital*, 5, 15.

69. Chesney, *The Johns Hopkins Hospital*, 20. The Boston example was the original City Hospital designed by Gridley J. F. Bryant and built in 1861–1864; see Pevsner, *Building Types*, 156.

70. Chesney, *The Johns Hopkins Hospital*, 21.

71. Chesney, *The Johns Hopkins Hospital*, 23, 26. The experts consulted were Dr. John Shaw Billings, Dr. Norton Folsom of Massachusetts General Hospital, Boston, Dr. Joseph Jane of New Orleans, Confederate Army surgeon, Dr. Caspar

Morris of the Episcopal Hospital, Philadelphia, and Dr. Stephen Smith, sanitarian, of New York. Their replies were published in *Hospital Plans: Five Essays Relating to the Construction, Organization, and Management of Hospitals* (New York: William Ward, 1875).

72. Chesney, *The Johns Hopkins Hospital*, 28, 62.

73. Charles P. Emerson, "The American Hospital Field," in Charlotte A. Aikens, ed., *Hospital Management* (Philadelphia: Saunders, 1911), 61.

74. Emerson, in his article "The American Hospital Field," estimated that in 1910 there were 2,547 general hospitals for acute medical and surgical cases; Edward F. Stevens estimated the number to have grown to 7,000 by 1914, in *The American Hospital in the Twentieth Century* (New York: Architectural Record, 1918), 1.

75. Albert J. Ochsner and Meyer J. Sturm, *The Organization, Construction, and Management of Hospitals*, 2d ed. (Chicago: Cleveland Press, 1909), 26.

76. Rosenberg, *The Care of Strangers*, 322, 331.

77. Edward F. Stevens, *The American Hospital in the Twentieth Century* (New York: Architectural Record, 1918), 2.

78. Stevens, *American Hospital*, 7.

79. Stevens, *American Hospital*, 4–6, Figure 400.

80. Stevens, *American Hospital*, 17.

81. Stevens, *American Hospital*, 228–229, Figures 401–407a.

82. Examples of such community hospitals include Wausau Hospital in Wisconsin; the Community Hospital of the Monterey Peninsula in California; and Martha's Vineyard Hospital in Massachusetts.

83. Siegfried Giedion, *Mechanization Takes Command* (New York: Oxford University Press, 1948), 698.

84. Stevens, *American Hospital*, 17, 96, 100–108, 18, 27, 119–129, 130–134.

85. Isadore Rosenfield, *Hospital, Architecture and Beyond* (New York: Van Nostrand and Reinhold, 1969), 27–28.

86. Stevens, *The American Hospital of the Twentieth Century*, 2d rev. ed. (New York: Dodge, 1928), 59–60, 97–98, 101–103.

87. Rosenfield, *Hospital, Architecture and Beyond*, 39.

88. Charles Butler and Addison Erdman, *Hospital Planning* (New York: Dodge, 1946), 10.

89. Rosenfield, *Hospital, Architecture and Beyond*, 28.

90. Butler and Erdman, *Hospital Planning*, 10–11.

91. Sheila M. Rothman, *Living in the Shadow of Death: Tuberculosis and the Social Experience of Illness in American History* (New York: Basic Books, 1994), 183.

92. Rothman, *Shadow of Death*, 194–197.

93. Rothman, *Shadow of Death*, 197, 201–204; Robert Taylor, *Saranac, America's First Magic Mountain* (Boston: Houghton Mifflin, 1986).

94. Stevens, *American Hospital*, 132.

95. Rothman, *Shadow of Death*, 227–228.

96. Rothman, *Shadow of Death*, 207–210; in England, King Edward VII was the patron of a sanitarium in Sussex that boasted a particularly fine series of gardens for the patients, some of whom did a little light gardening. Gertrude Jekyll (1843–1932) designed the gardens. See "Wall Gardening at the King's Sanatorium," *County Life* 26 (November 20, 1909), 701–705; and on the unusual school for women gardeners that built

the gardens, Jane Brown, *Eminent Gardeners: Some People of Influence and Their Gardens* (New York: Viking, 1990), 20–39, 150.

97. Stevens, *American Hospital*, 131.

98. Thomas S. Carrington, *Tuberculosis Hospital and Sanitorium Construction* (New York: Comstock, 1911), 19.

99. Rothman, *Shadow of Death*, 218.

100. Benjamin Rush, "Medical Inquiries and Observations upon the Diseases of the Mind," in Sidney Licht, ed., *Occupational Therapy Source Book* (Baltimore: Williams & Wilkins, 1948), 37.

101. Smithsonian Institution, "The Jacksonville Bandstand" ([sheet of notes], Washington, D.C.: Smithsonian Institution, 1984); for a discussion of a Muslim mosque and hospital complex with a music room for mental patients, see A. Dunbar, *Edirne* (Cambridge: Aga Khan Program, 1983), Figure 13; on ancient Greek practice, see Robert Montraville Green, *Asclepiades, His Life and Writings* (New Haven: Elizabeth Licht, 1955), 125–126.

102. Licht, *Occupational Therapy Source Book*, 14–16.

103. Susan E. Tracy, *Studies in Invalid Occupations: A Manual for Nurses and Attendants* (Boston: Whitcomb & Barrows, 1910, New York: Arno Press reprint, 1980); William Rush Dunton, Jr., *Occupational Therapy: A Manual for Nurses* (Philadelphia: Saunders, 1918); George Edward Barton, *Teaching the Sick: A Manual of Occupational Therapy and Reeducation* (Philadelphia: Saunders, 1919, New York: Arno Press reprint, 1980).

104. Audrey B. Davis, *Triumph over Disability: The Development of Rehabilitation Medicine in the U.S.A.* (Washington, D.C.: National Museum of History and Technology, 1973), 26–28; John S. Coulter, *Physical Therapy* (New York: Paul B. Hoeber, 1932), 30–33.

105. Donald Watson and Alice W. Burlingame, *Therapy Through Horticulture* (New York: Macmillan, 1960), 11.

106. Rhea R. McCandliss, "A Career in Horticultural Therapy," *Menninger Perspective* (June–July 1972); Alice J. Punwar, *Occupational Therapy: Principles and Practice* (Baltimore: Williams & Wilkins, 1994), 24–27. Sister Kenny (1880–1952), a World War I nurse, developed her technique in Australia, where she opened her clinic in 1933, followed by a clinic in England in 1937 and one in Minneapolis in 1940 (see Davis, *Rehabilitation Medicine*, 29–31).

107. Harry Stack Sullivan, "Socio-Psychiatric Research: Its Implications for the Schizophrenia Problem and for Mental Hygiene," *American Journal of Psychiatry* 10 (May 1931), 984–985, 990.

108. John Cumming and Elaine Cumming, *Ego and Milieu* (New York: Atherton, 1969), 2–3; William C. Menninger, *The Menninger Hospital's Guide to the Order Sheet* (Topeka: Menninger Clinic, 1943), 13–19; Herbert J. Schlesinger and Philip S. Holzman, "The Therapeutic Aspects of the Hospital Milieu," *Bulletin of the Menninger Clinic* 34 (January 1970), 1–11.

109. Karl Menninger, *The Vital Balance* (New York: Viking, 1963), 335–336.

110. Emily G. Davis, *Occupational Therapy, One Means of Rehabilitation: A Selected List of Books and Magazine Articles* (New York: New York Public Library, 1945); "Garden in Capital Designed to Bring Sick Soldiers Cheer," [Walter Reed Hospital], *New York Times* (April 26, 1931); Laval S. Morris, "Hospitals and Land," *Landscape Architecture* 37 (October 1946), 6–11; Watson and Burlingame, *Therapy Through Horticulture*, 7–8, 11.

111. "Flowers for Camp Hospitals—A Great Need," *Horticulture* 20 (September 1, 1942), 321; "Gardening at a Naval Hospital," *Horticulture* 21 (September 15, 1943), 341; *Florist's Review* 95 (March 29, 1945), 15–16; 96 (June 21, 1945), 19–21; 96 (October 11, 1945), 33.

112. National Garden Therapy Committee, *Garden Therapy Manual*, 2d ed. (St. Louis, Mo.: National Council of State Garden Clubs, 1975); Rhea R. McCandliss, "Results of a Survey on Horticultural Therapy," 1968 typescript on file at the Menninger Foundation Library in Topeka, Kans., pp. 4, 5, 9, 11.

113. Watson and Burlingame, *Therapy Through Horticulture*, 110–111.

114. "First Course in Horticulture for Therapists," *HortScience* 11 (June 1976), 179.

115. William C. Menninger and J. F. Pratt, "The Therapy of Gardening," *Menninger Quarterly* (June 1958), 27–28.

116. Charles F. Menninger, "Horticulture," *Bulletin of the Menninger Clinic* 6 (May 1942), 65–67; Charles A. Lewis, "Evolution of Horticultural Therapy in the United States," National Council for Therapy and Rehabilitation Through Horticulture," *Lecture and Publication Series* 2 (October 1976), 3; Pete Goering, "A Career in Horticultural Therapy," *Menninger Perspective* 3 (June–July 1972), 20–21.

117. Watson and Burlingame, *Therapy Through Horticulture*; Alice Wessels Burlingame, *Hoe for Health: Guidelines for Successful Horticultural Therapy Programs* (Birmingham, Mich.: Alice Wessels Burlingame, 1974).

118. Howard D. Brooks and Charles J. Oppenheim, *Horticulture as a Therapeutic Aid*, research monograph 49 (New York: Institute for Rehabilitation Medicine, New York University Medical Center, 1973), 26.

119. Lewis, "Evolution of Horticultural Therapy," 4.

120. McCandliss, "Results of a Survey," 4; for a useful survey of horticultural therapy programs, see Charlotte Franes Grant, "The Healing Garden: Incorporating Garden Experience in Hospitals and Other Health Care Facilities" (MLA dissertation, Department of Landscape Architecture, University of Georgia, 1994).

121. Lewis, "Evolution of Horticultural Therapy," 5.

122. Steven Jonas, ed., *Health Care Delivery in the United States* (New York: Springer, 1977), 261–269, 439–446.

123. The giant Columbia Presbyterian Hospital tower in New York City has skirted this problem by providing many escalators, as well as full banks of elevators.

124. Rosenfield, *Hospital, Architecture and Beyond*, 37–38.

125. Rosenfield, *Hospital, Architecture and Beyond*, 41, 43–44; Sheila Clibborn and Marvin L. Sachs, "Creating Consolidated Clinical Techniques Spaces for an Expanding Role in Health Care," *Architectural Record* (February 1971), 105–112.

126. In Payette Associates designs for Salem Hospital (Mass.), 1974, Eastern Maine Medical Center (Bangor, Me.), 1980, Leonard Morse Hospital (Natick, Mass.), 1969, Holton Hospital (Me.), 1976, and Martha's Vineyard Hospital (Mass.), 1973.

127. Thomas D. Church, *Gardens Are for People* (New York: Reinhold, 1955).

128. Peter Walker, *Invisible Gardens: The Search for Modernism in the American Landscape* (Cambridge: MIT Press, 1994), 99–101.

129. Lawrence Halprin, *Cities* (New York: Reinhold, 1963), Figure 69.

130. David Charles Sloane, "In Search of a Hospitable Hospital," *Dartmouth Medicine* (Fall 1993), 23–31; C. Robert Horsburgh, "Healing by Design," *New*

England Journal of Medicine 333 (September 14, 1995), 735–740.

TOWARD A THEORY OF THE
RESTORATIVE GARDEN

1. Roger S. Ulrich, "View Through a Window May Influence Recovery from Surgery," *Science* 224 (1984), 420–421.

2. Phillip Keep, Josephine James, and Michael Inman, "Windows in Intensive Therapy Unit," *Anesthesia* 35 (1980), 257–260; Larkin M. Wilson, "Intensive Care Delirium: The Effect of Outside Deprivation in Windowless Unit," *Archives of Internal Medicine* 130 (1972), 225–226. "Windows" research has been extensively summarized in Belinda L. Collins, *Windows and People: A Literature Survey, Psychological Reaction to Environments with and Without Windows*, National Bureau of Standards Science Series 70 (Washington, D.C.: U.S. Department of Commerce, 1975).

3. Steven Verderber, "Dimensions of Person-Window Transactions in the Hospital Environment," *Environment and Behavior* 18 (1986), 450–466.

4. Donald P. Watson and Alice W. Burlingame, *Therapy Through Horticulture* (New York: Macmillan, 1960).

5. The diversity and general trends in 'horticulture—healing' research are well documented in three excellent summary volumes: Irwin Altman and Joachim E. Wohlwill, eds., *Behavior and the Natural Environment* (New York: Plenum, 1983), reviews the psychological literature on nature and human well-being up to 1980. Diane Relf, ed., in her deservedly well-known *Role of Horticulture in Human Well-Being and Social Development* (Portland, Ore.: Timber Press, 1992), updates the literature to 1990. Moreover, she includes important information on horticulture therapy. Charles A. Lewis, *Green Nature/Human Nature: The Meaning of Plants in Our Lives* (Urbana: University of Illinois

Press, 1996), updates the literature to 1996. Although Lewis's treatment is less scholarly than the other two, it draws on many of the same disciplines that inform our own view of the restorative garden.

6. Claire Powell, *The Meaning of Flowers: A Garland of Plant Lore and Symbolism from Popular Custom and Literature* (Boulder: Shambala, 1979); Peter Coats, *Flowers in History* (New York: Viking, 1970); Jules Janick, "Horticulture and Human Culture," in Relf, *Role of Horticulture*; Marie Louise Gothein, *A History of Garden Art* (New York: Dutton, 1928) —the classic work; Charles W. Moore, William J. Mitchell, and William Turnbull, Jr., also have much to say about gardens as art in *The Poetics of Gardens* (Cambridge: MIT Press, 1988). They cite the film director Sergei Eisenstein: "Every spectator, in correspondence with his individuality, and in his own way and out of his own experience— out of the wonder of his fantasy, out of the warp and weft of his associations, all conditioned by the premises of his character, habits and social appurtenances, creates an image," 81.

7. Mirabel Osler, *In the Eye of the Garden* (New York: Macmillan, 1993), 16.

8. Roger Ulrich and Russ Parsons, "Influences of Passive Experiences with Plants on Individual Well-Being and Health," in Relf, *Role of Horticulture*, 93–105.

9. This very brief overview does a disservice to the extensive and thoughtful work of the Kaplans. In numerous articles and books they have articulated cogent constructs to account for our psychological responses to nature. The book summarizing their voluminous work is Rachel Kaplan and Stephen Kaplan, *The Experience of Nature, A Psychological Perspective* (Cambridge: Cambridge University Press, 1989). Synopses are

to be found in Rachel Kaplan, "The Psychological Benefits of Nearby Nature," in Relf, *Role of Horticulture*, 134–142. Also Stephen Kaplan, "Environmental Preference in a Knowledge-Seeking, Knowledge-Using Organism," in Jerome H. Barkow, Lida Cosmides, and John Tooby, *The Adapted Mind, Evolutionary Psychology and the Generation of Culture* (New York: Oxford University Press, 1992).

10. Rachel Kaplan, "Psychological Benefits," 128–129.

11. On prisoners' response, see Ernest O. Moore, "A Prison Environment's Effect on Health Care Service Demands," *Journal of Environmental Systems* 2 (1981–1982), 17–33; on Alzheimer's patients, see Claire Cooper Marcus and Marni Barnes, *Gardens in Healthcare Facilities: Uses, Therapeutic Benefits and Design Recommendations* (Martinez, Calif.: Center for Health Design, 1995); Marta Nadel Nelson and Robert J. Paluck, "Territorial Markings, Self-Concept and Mental Status of the Institutionalized Elderly," *The Gerontologist* 20 (1980).

12. Marc Fried, "Residential Attachment: Sources of Residential and Community Satisfaction," *Journal of Social Issues* 38 (1982), 107–120; Terry M. Hartig, Gary W. Evans, and Marlis Mang, "Restorative Effects of Natural Environmental Experiences," *Environment and Behavior* 23 (1991), 3–26.

13. Kaplan and Kaplan, *The Experience of Nature*, 50–57.

14. Sylvia Crowe, *Garden Design* (New York: Hearthside Press, 1958), 12.

15. Over the past twenty years, Roger Ulrich has pioneered the psychophysiological studies on responses to nature and landscape and written extensively on the subject. His findings are summarized in Roger S. Ulrich, "Biophilia, Biophobia, and Natural Landscapes,"

in Stephen R. Kellert and Edward O. Wilson, eds., *The Biophilia Hypothesis* (Washington, D.C.: Island Press, 1993), 73–137; Roger S. Ulrich, "Natural Versus Urban Scenes: Some Psychophysiological Effects," *Environment and Behavior* (1981), 523–556; Roger S. Ulrich, Robert F. Simons, Barbara D. Losito, Evelyn Fiorito, Mark A. Miles, and Michael Zelson, "Stress Recovery During Exposure to Natural and Urban Environments," *Journal of Environmental Psychology* 11 (1991), 201–230; Roger S. Ulrich and Russ Parsons, "Influences of Passive Experiences with Plants and Individual Well-Being and Health," in Relf, *Role of Horticulture*, 93–105.

16. Hans Selye, *Stress in Health and Disease* (Woburn, Mass.: Butterworth, 1976).

17. Ulrich, "Biophilia, Biophobia," 104.

18. R. G. Coss, "Picture Perception and Patient Stress: A Study of Anxiety Reduction and Postoperative Stability," unpublished paper, Department of Psychology, University of California, Davis, cited in Ulrich, "Biophilia, Biophobia," 105.

19. Roger Ulrich and Outi Lunden, "Effects of Nature and Abstract Pictures on Patients Recovering from Open Heart Surgery," paper presented at the International Congress of Behavioral Medicine, June 27–30, Uppsala, Sweden, cited in Ulrich, "Biophilia, Biophobia," 136.

20. Ulrich, "Influences of Passive Experiences"; "Biophilia, Biophobia."

21. Hans Selye, *The Stress of Life* (New York: McGraw-Hill, 1976).

22. Edward J. Goetzl, Sunil P. Sveedharan, and W. Scott Harkonen, "Pathogenetic Roles of Neuroimmunologic Mediators," *Immunology and Allergy Clinics of North America* 8 (1988), 183–200.

23. Gerald M. Edelman, *Bright Air, Brilliant Fire: On the Matter of Mind* (New York: Basic Books, 1992).

24. Gerald M. Edelman, *Neural Darwinism: The Theory of Neuronal Group Selection* (New York: Basic Books, 1987).

25. Bryan M. Gebhart and J. Edwin Blalock, "Neuroendocrine Regulation of Immunity," in *Encyclopedia of Immunology*, Ivan M. Roitt and Peter J. Delves, eds. (London: Academic Press, 1992), 1145–1149.

26. Douglas A. Weijant, Daniel J. Carr, and J. Edwin Blalock, "Bidirectional Communication Between the Neuroendocrine and Immune Systems: Common Hormones and Hormone Receptors," *Annals of the New York Academy of Sciences* 579 (1990), 17–27.

27. Edward O. Wilson, *Biophilia* (Cambridge: Harvard University Press, 1984).

28. Edward O. Wilson, *Sociobiology: The New Synthesis* (Cambridge: Belknap Press of Harvard University Press, 1975). In this somewhat controversial book and later in *On Human Nature* (Cambridge: Harvard University Press, 1978), Wilson articulates quite cogently that human behaviors and responses to the environment have evolved in ways similar to those of other animal species. The political brouhaha this notion first caused seems to have died down, and I think we can now peacefully accept that some of our behaviors and responses may be evolutionarily and genetically encoded—though always subject to learned modification. Our response to gardens probably fits this evolutionary-genetic mold.

29. John D. Balling and John H. Falk, "Development of Visual Preference for Natural Environments," *Environment and Behavior* 14 (1982), 5–28. The savanna preference seems clearest in the young. As we mature, other forms of wilderness may entice equally, but nature continues to be the preferred visual object and environment for relaxation.

30. Jay Appleton, *The Experience of Landscape*, rev. ed. (Chichester, England: Wiley, 1996).

31. Ulrich, "Biophilia, Biophobia."

32. Gordon H. Orians and Judith H. Heerwagen, "Evolved Responses to Landscapes," in Jerome H. Barkow, Leda Cosmides, and John Tooby, eds., *The Adapted Mind, Evolutionary Psychology and the Generation of Culture* (New York: Oxford University Press, 1992).

33. Gordon H. Orians, "Habitat Selection: General Theory and Application to Human Behavior," in J. S. Lockard, ed., *The Evolution of Human Social Behavior* (New York: Elsevier, 1980). Perhaps the best detailed summary of their work is Judith H. Heerwagen and Gordon H. Orians, "Humans, Habitats, and Aesthetics," in Kellert and Wilson, *The Biophilia Hypothesis*.

34. Simon Schama, *Landscape and Memory* (New York: Knopf, 1995), gives us a history of the enormous extent to which Renaissance princes went to have water in their gardens. Water was intimately allied with myths of vitality. Sir Geoffrey Jellicoe, the great garden historian and landscape designer, refers to water in a garden as "the most versatile of all materials. It disappears and reappears, and in a moment its clamour has become the song of the garden and its waywardness the countless different forms of pattern." *The Collected Works of Geoffrey Jellicoe*, vol. 2 (Woodbridge, England: Garden Arts Press, 1995), 37–38.

35. Wilson, *Biophilia*, 111.

36. Heerwagen and Orians, "Humans, Habitats, and Aesthetics," 147–153.

37. Heerwagen and Orians, "Humans, Habitats, and Aesthetics," 156–164.

38. Ellen Dissayanake, *Homo Aestheticus: Where Art Comes From and Why* (Seattle: University of Washington Press, 1995).

39. Richard Gerber, *Vibrational Medicine: New Choices for Healing Ourselves* (Santa Fe, N.M.: Bear and Company, 1988). I have purposely avoided addressing the vast and seductive literature on alternative therapies. There is little theoretical support and little or no valid scientific proof for their efficacy. Gerber's book is representative of this genre. Nature and gardens are not medicinal, and for us, not some alternative therapeutic modality. We address this matter more fully in our conclusion.

40. Lewis, *Green Nature/Human Nature*, 54–73.

HOWARD A. RUSK INSTITUTE

1. Howard A. Rusk, *A World to Care For* (New York: Random House, 1977), 77 (hereafter cited parenthetically in the text by page number).

2. New York University Medical Center Public Relations Department, unpublished typescript of statement for the 1994 edition of *Best Hospitals in America*, 2.

3. Claude Edwin Heaton and Alan Eliot Dumont, *The First One Hundred Twenty-Five Years of the New York University School of Medicine* (New York: NYU School of Medicine, 1966), 34–35.

4. Allan Eliot Dumont and Jules Leonard Whitehill, *NYU School of Medicine, Origins and Evolution, 1841–1981* (New York: New York University, 1981), 19–20.

5. Howard A. Rusk, Foreword to Howard D. Brooks and Charles J. Oppenheim, *Horticulture as a Therapeutic Aid*, Rehabilitation Monograph 49 (New York: Institute of Rehabilitation Medicine, NYU Medical Center, 1973).

6. Brooks and Oppenheim, *Horticulture as a Therapeutic Aid*, 12.

7. Memorandum, Paul R. Clark to Howard A. Rusk, July 23, 1959 (Occupational Therapy Department files).

8. Memorandum, Paul R. Clark to Howard A. Rusk, January 14, 1960 (Occupational Therapy Department files).

9. Paul R. Clark and M. Elizabeth Hannesson, "Proposal for the Use of the Greenhouse as an Integral Part of the Occupational Therapy Program at the Institute of Physical Medicine and Rehabilitation," October 13, 1960 (Occupational Therapy Department files).

10. Date supplied by Nancy Chambers of the Rusk Institute, and corroborated by the records of Martin H. Cohen, at that time New York University Medical Center planner for Skidmore, Owings & Merrill.

11. IRM "1971 Issue" (brochure, Institute of Rehabilitation Medicine, New York University Medical Center, 1971), 11.

12. Federal Writers Project, WPA, *New York City Guide*, American Guide Series (New York: Octagon Books, [1939] 1970), 208. Cited hereafter as WPA Guide.

13. WPA Guide, 184, 208.

14. WPA Guide, 208.

15. Citizens' Association of New York, *Report of the Council of Hygiene and Public Health upon the Sanitary Condition of the City* (New York: Citizens' Association, 1865), 268.

QUEEN OF PEACE RESIDENCE

1. "Illth" is a useful term coined by John Ruskin to describe the actively destructive qualities of the actions of the wealthy upon the poor. Ruskin, *Unto This Last* (1860), reprinted in *Works*, E. T. Cook and Alexander Wedderburn, eds., vol. 17 (London: George Allen, 1905), 89. George Bernard Shaw took up the term in his essay "The

Basis of Socialism," *Fabian Essays* (London: Allen & Unwin, 1948), 21.

2. Karl Marx, "Manifesto of the Communist Party," in Robert C. Tucker, ed., *The Marx-Engels Reader* (New York: Norton, [1848] 1978), 476.

3. George Rosen, *A History of Public Health* (New York: M.D. Publications, 1958), 139.

4. Before her beatification, a French Eudist priest wrote a biography of Jeanne Jugan. The text is Paul Milcent, *Jeanne Jugan: Humble, So As to Love More* (London: Darton, Longman & Todd, 1980), hereafter cited parenthetically in the text by page number; *New Catholic Encyclopedia*, vol. 8 (New York: McGraw-Hill, 1967) lists two earlier biographies. There is also a short biography with a useful map in *Serenity* (Fall 1975). Jeanne Jugan was beatified by Pope John Paul II on October 3, 1982.

5. *Serenity* (Fall 1975), 21; Milcent, *Jeanne Jugan*, 99–101.

6. Bonnie G. Smith, *Ladies of the Leisure Class: The Bourgeoises of Northern France in the Nineteenth Century* (Princeton: Princeton University Press, 1981).

7. Smith, *Ladies of the Leisure Class*.

8. Little Sisters of the Poor, *Ernest Lelièvre, 1826–1889* (Baltimore: Little Sisters of the Poor, 1990), 9–13.

9. Milcent, *Jeanne Jugan*, 132, 162. Paul le Picard was a third industrialist friend of the Little Sisters: see "Our Beginnings in the United States," *Serenity* (Spring 1976), 12.

10. The Southwark home dated from 1851; see Catholic Truth Society, *Caroline Sheppard, Little Sister of the Poor* (London: Catholic Truth Society, 1984), 20–25.

11. Little Sisters of the Poor, *Ernest Lelièvre*, 18; Friedrich Engels, *Conditions of the Working Classes in England in 1844*

(Stanford, Calif.: Stanford University Press, [1844] 1968).

12. *Serenity* (September 1976), 4, 12.

13. *Serenity* (Spring 1976), 15, 19.

14. John Kean Sharp, *History of the Diocese of Brooklyn, 1853–1953: The Catholic Church on Long Island* (New York: Fordham University Press, 1954), vol. 1, 221–222.

15. Little Sisters of the Poor, "Silver Celebration" (Queens Village: Little Sisters of the Poor, 1995), 4.

16. Michael Harrington, *The Other America: Poverty in the United States* (New York: Macmillan, 1962), chap. 6.

17. Oliver Sacks, *A Leg to Stand On* (New York: Summit Books, 1984), 163; "25 Years" (clipping from an unidentified newspaper, n.d., ca. 1995), and letter from Pat Parks recalling her youth in Queens Village, both in Queen of Peace files.

18. Little Sisters of the Poor, "Dear Friends" (brochure sent out as a thank-you for all gifts, ca. 1995–1996), 4; the *New Catholic Encyclopedia* estimated that there were about forty houses in the United States in 1963.

19. "Dear Friends" (brochure, ca. 1995–1996), 2.

20. "Dear Friends" (brochure, ca. 1995–1996), 1.

21. "Time and Life" (newsletter), 2 (Fall 1995), 4.

22. "Time and Life," 1 (Fall 1994), 2.

23. "150 Years of Service to the Elderly" (Small two-sided single sheet, n.d., Queen of Peace files), 1.

24. Loose sheets in folder, photocopy with photographs, author and date unknown, Little Sisters of the Poor, Queen of Peace Residence file.

25. Vincent F. Seyfried, *The Story of Queens Village* (Queens Village: Centennial Association, Robert J. Cassidy, Chairman, 1974), 7–9.

26. Seyfried, *Queens Village*, 77; Federal Writers Project, WPA, *New York City Guide* (New York: Octagon Books, [1939] 1970), 585.

27. Seyfried, *Queens Village*, 93.

28. Seyfried, *Queens Village*, 93.

THE HOSPICE AT THE TEXAS
MEDICAL CENTER

1. Blanche Linden-Ward, *Silent City on a Hill* (Columbus: Ohio State University Press, 1989); David Charles Sloane, *The Last Great Necessity, Cemeteries in American History* (Baltimore: Johns Hopkins University Press, 1991).

2. Philippe Ariès, *Western Attitudes Toward Death: From the Middle Ages to the Present* (Baltimore: Johns Hopkins University Press, 1974), 63–79; Ariès, *The Hour of Our Death* (New York: Knopf, 1981), 595.

3. Ariès, *The Hour of Our Death*, 612–613.

4. Sherwin B. Nuland, *How We Die* (New York: Knopf, 1993); Abraham Verghese, *My Own Country* (New York: Simon & Schuster, 1994).

5. Ariès, *The Hour of Our Death*, 583.

6. Peter Singer, *Rethinking Life and Death: The Collapse of Our Traditional Ethics* (New York: St. Martin's Press, 1994).

7. M. Scott Peck, *The Road Less Travelled* (New York: Simon & Schuster, 1978).

8. Bonnie G. Smith, *Ladies of the Leisure Class: The Bourgeoises of Northern France in the Nineteenth Century* (Princeton: Princeton University Press, 1981), 123–149; "Sisters of Charity," *New Catholic Encyclopedia*, vol. 3 (New York: McGraw-Hill, 1967).

9. Sarah Lush, *Trinity Hospice: A History of Care, 1891–1991* (London: Trinity Hospice, 1991), 8–10; Grace Goldin, "A Protohospice at the Turn of the Century: St. Luke's House, London, from 1893–1921," *Journal of the History of Medicine and Allied Sciences* 36 (October 1981), 383–415.

10. Grace Goldin, "British Hospices," Encyclopaedia Britannica *Medical Annual*, 1983, 82–83; Robert Buckingham, *The Complete Hospice Guide* (New York: Harper & Row, 1983), 12–13; Dame Cicely Saunders, *Living with Dying: The Management of Terminal Disease* (New York: Oxford University Press, 1983); Saunders, "Patiently Speaking," *Nursing Times* (June 12, 1980), 1035–1036.

11. Robert W. Buckingham, *The Complete Hospice Guide* (New York: Harper & Row, 1983), 14; Elisabeth Kubler-Ross, *On Death and Dying* (New York: Macmillan, 1969); for her story of the local campaign that defeated her plan to open a hospice for children in Virginia, see Kubler-Ross, *AIDS, the Ultimate Challenge* (New York: Macmillan, 1987), chap. 4; the December 31, 1995, statistics of the National Hospice Organization list 2,620 hospices in operation or planned. Hospices served 15 percent of all patients who died that year (see "Fact Sheets," available from the National Health Organization, 1901 N. Moore St., Suite #901, Alexandria, Va., 22209).

12. Ron Aran and David E. Rogers, "AIDS in the United States: Patient Care and Politics," *Daedalus* 118 (Spring 1989), 41–58; Allan M. Brandt, *No Magic Bullet: A Social History of Venereal Disease in the United States Since 1880*, expanded AIDS edition (New York: Oxford University Press, 1987).

13. The narrative of the founding of the Hospice at the Texas Medical Center is largely based on a book manuscript by Marion Wilson, "The Mustard Seed," (n.d., ca. 1995), 110, hereafter cited parenthetically in the text by page number.

14. Porter Storey's *The Primer of Palliative Care* (Gainesville, Fla.: The Academy of Hospice Physicians, 1994) sold more than thirty thousand copies its first year in print.

15. *Texas Medical Center News* 17 (January 15, 1995), 1, 10.

16. Eileen A. Ellis, "Margaret Cullen Marshall Hospice Care Center Is Dedicated," *Texas Medical Center News* 17 (February 1, 1995), 1.

17. Ellis, "Margaret Cullen Marshall Hospice Care Center Is Dedicated," 20.

18. Virginia and Lee McAlester, *A Field Guide to American Houses* (New York: Knopf, 1986), 358.

19. Rudy Favretti and Joy Favretti, *For Every House a Garden* (Hanover, N.H.: University Press of New England, 1990), 15–18.

20. Favretti and Favretti, *For Every House a Garden*, 18.

21. Favretti and Favretti, *For Every House a Garden*, 41–49.

FRIENDS HOSPITAL

1. Michel Foucault, *Madness and Civilization: A History of Insanity in the Age of Reason* (New York: Random House, 1965).

2. Samuel Tuke, *Account of the Rise and Progress of the Asylum, Proposed to be Established, near Philadelphia, for the Relief of Persons Deprived of their Reason. With an Abridged Account of the Retreat, a Similar Institution near York, in England* (Philadelphia: Kimber & Conrad, 1814), 25.

3. Charles L. Cherry, *A Quiet Haven: Quakers, Moral Treatment, and Asylum Reform* (Rutherford, N.J.: Fairleigh Dickinson University Press, 1989), 94–103.

4. Cherry, *A Quiet Haven*, 135–136.

5. Tuke, *Account of the Rise of the Asylum*, 4.

6. Tuke, *Account of the Rise of the Asylum*, 10.

7. Norman Dain and Eric T. Carlson, "Milieu Therapy in the Nineteenth Century: Patient Care at the Friends Asylum, Frankford, Pennsylvania, 1817–1861," *The Journal of Nervous and Mental Disease* 131 (October 1960), 277, 280.

8. David S. Roby, *Pioneer of Moral Treatment: Isaac Bonsall and the Early Years of the Friends Asylum as Recorded in Bonsall's Diaries, 1817–1823*, booklet (Philadelphia: Friends Hospital, 1982), 14.

9. Dain and Carlson, "Milieu Therapy in the Nineteenth Century," 281–282, 287.

10. Tuke, *Account of the Rise of the Asylum*, 54, 67.

11. Dain and Carlson, "Milieu Therapy in the Nineteenth Century," 281.

12. Board of Managers, Friends Asylum, Minutes, March 12, 1821, vol. 1, Quaker Collection, Haverford College Archives, Haverford, Pa.

13. Board of Managers, Friends Asylum, Minutes, January 12, 1835.

14. Friends Hospital, *Friends Asylum for the Insane, 1813–1913* (Philadelphia: Friends Hospital, 1913), part 2, Chronology.

15. Board of Managers, Friends Asylum, Minutes, October 12, 1840.

16. Charles Evans, *Account of the Asylum, for the Relief of Persons Deprived of the Use of Their Reason, near Frankford, Pennsylvania* (Philadelphia: T. K. & P. G. Collins, 1839), 10.

17. Board of Managers, Friends Asylum, Minutes, March 10, 1862.

18. *Friends Asylum for the Insane, 1813–1913*, 50.

19. Board of Managers, Friends Asylum, Minutes, March 8, 1847.

20. Dain and Carlson, "Milieu Therapy in the Nineteenth Century," 287.

21. Board of Managers, Friends Asylum, Minutes, March 8, 1847.

22. Board of Managers, Friends Asylum, Minutes, March 13, 1876.

23. Board of Managers, Friends Asylum, Minutes, March 9, 1885. See also Friends Asylum, *66th Annual Report of the State of the Asylum, 1883*, 10–13.

24. Friends Asylum, *89th Annual Report, Friends Asylum for the Insane* (Frankford, Philadelphia, 1906), 26.

25. Friends Asylum, *89th Annual Report*, 28–29.

26. *Friends' Asylum, 1813–1913*, part 2, Chronology.

27. Friends Asylum, *107th Annual Report, 1924*, 24, 29.

28. Friends Asylum, *118th Annual Report, 1935*, 29.

29. Board of Managers, Friends Asylum, Minutes, April 13, 1931.

30. Board of Managers, Friends Asylum, Minutes, November 9, 1931, 124.

31. Board of Managers, Friends Asylum, Minutes, April 9, 1928.

32. Friends Asylum, *119th Annual Report, 1936*, 9.

33. Gary R. Clausen, "Garden Days Threatened by the Northeast Freeway," course paper in environmental issues, Temple University, April 22, 1974 (copy at Friends Hospital), 3; Friends Asylum, *121st Annual Report, 1938*, 9.

34. J. Sanborne Bockoven, *Moral Treatment in Community Mental Health* (New York: Springer, 1972), 132–147, 248–255.

35. Friends Hospital, *175th Annual Report, Friends Hospital: Transition, a Twenty-Five Year Retrospective, 1967–1992*, 8.

36. Clausen, "Garden Days Threatened," 14a–15 and map.

37. Friends Hospital, *156th Annual Report: The Future of Friends Hospital*, 1972, 2–3.

38. Tuke, *Account of the Rise of the Asylum*, 69–70.

39. Carol B. Perloff, *The Asylum: The History of Friends Hospital and the Quaker Contribution to Psychiatry* (Philadelphia: Friends Hospital, 1994), 14.

40. Kim Van Atta, *An Account of the Events Surrounding the Origin of Friends Hospital and a Brief Description of the Early Years of Friends Asylum, 1817–1820* (Philadelphia: Friends Hospital, 1980), 9.

41. Perloff, *The Asylum*, 14.

42. Van Atta, *An Account of the Events* (Philadelphia: Friends Hospital), 14–18; interview with Dale R. Nemec, May 20, 1996.

43. Perloff, *The Asylum*, 14.

44. Van Atta, *An Account of the Events*, 15–16.

45. Perloff, *The Asylum*, 24, photograph; Van Atta, *An Account of the Events*, 14–15, map; Roby, *Pioneer of Moral Treatment*, 15.

46. Ken Druse, *The Collector's Garden* (New York: Clarkson Potter, 1996), 27.

47. Perloff, *The Asylum*, 46.

48. Perloff, *The Asylum*, 24, photograph; Van Atta, *An Account of the Events*, 14–15, map; Roby, *Pioneer of Moral Treatment*, 15.

49. Correspondence between Frederick Law Olmsted and Henry B. Rogers, chairman of the Board of Trustees of Massachusetts General Hospital, December 13, 1872. Appears as Appendix E in Margie A. Lamar, "A Study of the History of Landscape Architecture: McLean Hospital, Belmont, Massachusetts," unpublished paper, Harvard University Graduate School of Design, 1975.

50. Lamar, "A Study of the History of Landscape Architecture."

51. Perloff, *The Asylum*, 27.

52. Perloff, *The Asylum*, 50.

53. Perloff, *The Asylum*, photograph, 24; Van Atta, *An Account of the Events*, 14–15, map; Roby, *Pioneer of Moral Treatment*, 15.

54. Donald Wyman, *Wyman's Gardening Encyclopedia*, 2d ed. (New York: Macmillan, 1986).

55. *Friends Hospital: An Environment for Healing*, brochure, n.d.

WAUSAU HOSPITAL

1. *New Catholic Encyclopedia* (New York: McGraw-Hill, 1967).

2. S. M. B. Smith, "Reminiscences of a Family Doctor," January 15, 1955, Wausau Hospital files; *Wausau Daily Herald*, May 20, 1970.

3. Michael Kronenwetter, *Wisconsin Heartland: The Story of Wausau and Marathon County* (Midland, Mich.: Pendell Publishing, n.d., c. 1983), 414.

4. Kronenwetter, *Wisconsin Heartland*, 135–154.

5. David Charles Sloane, "Scientific Progress to Hospital Mall: The Evolving Design of the Hospital," *Journal of Architectural Education* 48 (November 1994), 91.

6. HCIA, a health care investment firm in Baltimore, Md., and Mercer Health Care Provider Consultants ranked Wausau among the top one hundred hospitals in the United States in 1994. The combined criteria were low expenses, reduced lengths of patient stay, low mortality, and high levels of investment in equipment and capital (see letter, HCIA and Mercer, November 14, 1994, Wausau Hospital files).

7. Norman T. Newton, *Design on the Land: The Development of Landscape Architecture* (Cambridge: Belknap Press of Harvard University Press, 1971), 207–220.

8. Newton, *Design on the Land*, 23–29.

COMMUNITY HOSPITAL OF THE MONTEREY PENINSULA

1. Oscar Lewis, *The Big Four* (New York: Knopf, 1938), 120–123, 249; Augusta Fink, *Monterey: The Presence of the Past* (San Francisco: Chronicle Books, 1972), 130–132.

2. Fink, *Monterey*, 132; Templeton Crocker, *Who Was Who*, 2 (Chicago: A. N. Marquis, 1950); Yale University, *History of the Class of 1908, Yale College* (New Haven, Conn.: Yale University, 1933); Samuel F. B. Morse, Yale University, *History of the Class of 1907, Yale College* (New Haven, Conn.: Yale University, 1913); *Class of 1907, Decennial Record* (New Haven: 1921); *History of the Class of 1907, Yale College* (New Haven, 1932); *Who Was Who*, 5 (Chicago: A. N. Marquis, 1973).

3. It is difficult to estimate the changing population of the catchment area of the local hospitals because so much unincorporated county land came to be incorporated bit by bit throughout the twentieth century. Approximations for different years can be obtained from different sources, as follows: for Monterey City in 1880 and Monterey City and Pacific Grove in 1900 and 1920, see Donna Andriot, ed., *Population Abstract of the United States, 1993* (McLean, Va.: Document Index, 1993), 55; for Monterey City, Pacific Grove, Carmel-by-the-Sea in 1940, see U.S. Bureau of the Census, *Sixteenth Census of the U.S.: 1940, Population*, 1 (Washington, D.C.: Government Printing Office, 1942), 124; for Carmel-by-the-Sea, Carmel Valley, Del Rey Oaks, Monterey City, Pacific Grove, Seaside, and the unincorporated areas of Carmel, Del Monte Heights, Del Monte Park in 1960, see *Eighteenth Census of the U.S., Census of Population: 1960*, 1, *Characteristics of the Population*, Pt. 6, *California*, Table 8 (Washington, D.C.: Government

Printing Office, 1963); for Carmel-by-the-Sea, Carmel Valley, Del Rey Oaks, Monterey City, Pacific Grove City, Seaside City in 1980, see *U.S. Census of Population: 1980, General Population Characteristics, California* (PC80–1-B6) (Washington, D.C.: Government Printing Office, 1982), Table 14; for Carmel-by-the-Sea, Carmel Valley Village, Del Monte Forest, Del Rey Oaks, Monterey City, Pacific Grove, Sand City, Seaside in 1990, see *U.S. Census of Population: 1990, General Population Characteristics, California*, Section 1 (1990 CP-1–6) (Washington, D.C.: Government Printing Office, July 1992), Table 1.

4. John Welton, John Gratiot, and Paul Michael, *The Medical History of Monterey County* (Monterey: Monterey Literary Associates, 1969), 50–55.

5. Hugh Dormody, *Monterey Peninsula Herald*, December 21, 1953.

6. *Sunday Peninsula Herald*, April 13, 1980, 7; Hugh Dormody, *Monterey Peninsula Herald*, December 21, 1953; Harry C. Hunt, *Monterey Peninsula Herald*, October 23, 1962; *Who Was Who*, 7 (Chicago: A. N. Marquis, 1981).

7. *Sunday Peninsula Herald*, April 13, 1980, 7.

8. *Sunday Peninsula Herald*, April 13, 1980, 7; *Monterey Peninsula Herald*, May 28, 1982, and October 23, 1984; Community Hospital of the Monterey Peninsula, "Business Plan for the Acquisition of Monterey Hospital," May 1982; Memo, Eskaton Monterey Hospital, list of the Board of Trustees, February 1982. All unpublished materials are in the files of the Community Hospital of the Monterey Peninsula (CHOMP), September 1995.

9. Michael Lerner, *Choices in Healing* (Cambridge: MIT Press, 1994), 195–352; Andrew Weil, *Spontaneous Healing* (New York: Knopf, 1995).

10. Walton, Gratiot, and Michael, *Medical History of Monterey*, 50–51; *San Francisco Chronicle*, Rotogravure Section, March 29, 1931; *Carmel Pine Cone*, March 16, 1934; *Monterey Peninsula Herald*, May 24, 1962.

11. "History of Community Hospital," n.d., ca. 1971, 3, CHOMP files.

12. Peninsula Community Hospital, "A New Hospital for the Monterey Peninsula," August 1956, 4–5, CHOMP files.

13. Richard A. Miller, "Hospitals," *Architectural Forum* 117 (October 1962), 110; "Hospital Proves It Pays to Be Beautiful," *The Modern Hospital* (March 1966), 109.

14. "Today's Most-Talked-About-Hospital," *Architectural Forum* 101 (July 1954), 108–115.

15. Miller, "Hospitals," *Architectural Forum* 117 (October 1962), 110; Steven Jones, "Hospitals," in Steven Jones, ed., *Health Care Delivery in the United States* (New York: Springer, 1977), 174.

16. "A Hospital Plan for Easy Operation," *Architectural Forum* 104 (April 1956), 146.

17. "A Hospital Chain for the United Mine Workers," *Architectural Forum* 99 (August 1953), 132–138; (September 1953), 152–153; (November, 1953), 132–139.

18. Nancy Martin, "The Trend Toward Private Rooms Only," *Medical Economics* (June 13, 1966), 100–109.

19. Marilyn E. Ludwig, "A Study of Two Hospital Concepts," *AIA Journal* 43 (February 1965), 65.

20. John Peterson, "Hospital Proves It Pays to Be Beautiful," *The Modern Hospital* (March 1966), 110.

21. "Two Hospital Concepts," *AIA Journal* 43 (February, 1965), 65.

22. "Business Plan for the Acquisition of Monterey Hospital," May 1982, 2–3, CHOMP files.

23. "Business Plan," 3–4; Community Hospital of the Monterey Peninsula, "Information and Services," brochure, n.d., ca. 1992, 7–8.

24. Community Hospital of the Monterey Peninsula, "Fact Book: 1995," 23.

25. "Fact Book: 1995," 23.

26. Peterson, "Hospital Proves It Pays to Be Beautiful," 130.

27. Brochure explaining design intent, Community Hospital of the Monterey Peninsula, n.d.

28. Brochure explaining design, Community Hospital of the Monterey Peninsula, n.d., 44.

29. Hugh E. Smith, "Forest Management Plan for Parking Lot Extension . . . for the Community Hospital of the Monterey Peninsula," April 11, 1994, 3–9.

30. Bruce Cowan, "Attachment B" to Smith, "Forest Management," 1–7.

31. Smith, "Forest Management," Appendix, City of Monterey Planning Department, Use Permit 92–06.

32. Smith, "Forest Management," 14–15.

33. Stephen R. Staub, "Attachment A" to Smith, "Forest Management," 1, 3.

34. Smith, "Forest Management," 6–7.

35. Staub, "Attachment A" to Smith, "Forest Management," 1.

Bibliography

Ackerman, Diane. *A Natural History of the Senses* (New York: Random House, 1990).

Altman, Irwin, and Joachim E. Wohlwill, eds. *Behavior and the Natural Environment* (New York: Plenum, 1983).

Appleton, Jay. *The Experience of Landscape*, rev. ed. (Chichester, N.Y.: John Wiley & Sons, 1996).

Barkow, Jerome H., Lida Cosmides, and John Tooby. *The Adapted Mind: Evolutionary Psychology and the Generation of Culture* (New York: Oxford University Press, 1992).

Barrett, Marilyn. *Creating Eden: The Garden as a Healing Place* (San Francisco: HarperCollins, 1992).

Bockoven, J. Sanborne. *Moral Treatment and Community Mental Health* (New York: Springer, 1972).

Campbell, Sheila, et al. *Health, Disease and Healing in Medieval Culture* (New York: St. Martin's, 1991).

Cherry, Charles L. *A Quiet Haven: Quakers, Moral Treatment, and Asylum Reform* (Rutherford, N.J.: Farleigh Dickinson University Press, 1989).

Chesney, Alan M. *The Johns Hopkins Hospital and the Johns Hopkins School of Medicine: A Chronicle*, vol. 1 (Baltimore: Johns Hopkins Press, 1943).

Curtis, John T. *The Vegetation of Wisconsin: An Ordinance of Plant Communities* (Madison: University of Wisconsin Press, [1959] 1971).

Davis, Audrey B. *Triumph over Disability: The Development of Rehabilitation Medicine in the U.S.A.* (Washington, D.C.: National Museum of History and Technology, 1973).

Dissayanake, Ellen. *Homo Aestheticus: Where Art Comes from and Why* (Seattle: University of Washington Press, 1995).

Edelman, Gerald M. *Bright Air, Brilliant Fire: On the Matter of Mind* (New York: Basic Books, 1992).

Favretti, Rudy, and Joy Favretti. *For Every House a Garden: A Guide for Reproducing Period Gardens* (Hanover, N.H.: University Press of New England, 1990).

Francis, Mark, and Randolph T. Hester, Jr., eds. *The Meaning of Gardens* (Cambridge, Mass.: MIT Press, 1993).

Fries, Robert F. *Empire in Pine: The Story of Lumbering in Wisconsin* (Sister Bay, Wisc.: Caxton, [1951] 1989).

Glacken, Clarence. *Traces on the Rhodian Shore* (Berkeley: University of California Press, 1975).

Goldin, Grace. *Work of Mercy, A Picture History of Hospitals* (Erin, Ontario: Boston Mills Press, 1994).

Gothein, Mary Louise. *A History of Garden Art* (New York: E. P. Dutton, 1928).

Grant, Charlotte F. "The Healing Garden: Incorporating Garden Experience in Hospitals and Other Health Care Facilities." Unpublished masters' dissertation, Department of Landscape Architecture, University of Georgia, Athens.

Kaplan, Rachel, and Stephen Kaplan. *The Experience of Nature: A Psychological Perspective* (Cambridge: Cambridge University Press, 1989).

Kellert, Stephen R., and Edward O. Wilson, eds. *The Biophilia Hypothesis* (Washington, D.C.: Island Press, 1993), 73–137.

Kirkbride, Thomas S. *On the Construction and General Arrangements of Hospitals for the Insane* (Philadelphia: Lippincott, 1880).

Klueter, Howard R., and James J. Lorence. *Woodlot and Ballot Box: Marathon County in the Twentieth Century* (Stevens Point, Wisc.: Worzalla, 1977).

Lewis, Charles A. *Green Nature / Human Nature: The Meaning of Plants in Our Lives* (Urbana: University of Illinois Press, 1996).

Lush, Sarah. *Trinity Hospice: A Century of Care, 1989–1991* (London: Trinity Hospice, 1991).

Marcus, Claire Cooper, and Marnie Barns. *Gardens in Healthcare Facilities: Uses, Therapeutic Benefits and Design Recommendations* (Martinez, Calif.: Center for Health Design, 1995).

McLean, Theresa. *Medieval English Gardens* (New York: Viking, 1981).

Messervy, Julie Moir, and Sam Abell. *Contemplative Gardens* (Charlottesville, Va.: Howell Press, 1990).

Minter, Sue. *The Healing Garden* (Boston: Charles E. Tuttle Company, 1993).

Moore, Charles W., William J. Mitchell, and William Turnbull, Jr. *The Poetics of Gardens* (Cambridge, Mass.: MIT Press, 1988).

Newton, Norman T. *Design on the Land: The Development of Landscape Architecture* (Cambridge: Belknap Press of Harvard University, 1971).

Nightingale, Florence. *Notes on Nursing*, 3rd ed. (London: 1863).

Osler, Mirabel. *In the Eye of the Garden* (New York: Macmillan, 1993), 16.

Perloff, Carol B. *The Asylum: The History of the Friends Hospital and the Quaker Contribution to Psychiatry* (Philadelphia: Friends Hospital, 1994).

Poynter, F. N. L., et al. *The Evolution of Hospitals in Britain* (London: Pitman Medical Publishing, 1964).

"A Protohospice at the Turn of the Century: St. Luke's House, London from 1893–1921," *Journal of the History of Medicine and Allied Sciences* 36 (Oct. 1981), 383–415.

Relf, Diane, ed. *The Role of Horticulture in Human Well-Being and Social Development* (Portland, Ore.: Timber Press, 1992).

Risse, Guenter B. *Hospital Life in Enlightenment Scotland* (Cambridge: Cambridge University Press, 1986).

Rosen, George. *From Medical Police to Social Medicine* (New York: Science History Publications, 1974).

Rosenberg, Charles E. *The Care of Strangers: The Rise of America's Hospital System* (New York: Basic Books, 1987).

Rosenfield, Isadore. *Hospital Architecture and Beyond* (New York: Van Nostrand & Reinhold, 1969).

Rothert, Gene. *The Enabling Garden* (Dallas: Taylor Press, 1994).

Rothman, Sheila M. *Living in the Shadow of Death: Tuberculosis and the Social Experience of Illness in American History* (New York: Basic Books, 1994).

Rusk, Howard A. *A World to Care For* (New York: Random House, 1977).

Sacks, Oliver. *A Leg to Stand On* (New York: Harper, 1993).

————. *The Island of the Colorblind* (New York: Knopf, 1997).

Sanders, Scott Russell. *Staying Put* (Boston: Beacon, 1993).

Saunders, Dame Cicely. *Living with Dying: The Management of Terminal Disease* (New York: Oxford University Press, 1983).

Schama, Simon. *Landscape and Memory* (New York: Knopf, 1995).

Searles, Harold F. *The Non-Human Environment in Normal Development and Schizophrenia* (New York: International Universities Press, 1960).

Silko, Leslie Marmon. *Ceremony* (New York: Penguin, 1977).

Snyder, Gary. *The Practice of the Wild* (New York: North Point, 1990).

Stevens, Edward F. *The American Hospital in the Twentieth Century* (New York: Architectural Record Publishing, 1918).

Strong, Roy. *The Renaissance Garden in England* (London: Thames & Hudson, 1979).

Swan, James A. *The Power of Place* (Wheaton, Ill.: Quest, 1991).

Thompson, John D., and Grace Goldin. *The Hospital: A Social and Architectural History* (New Haven: Yale University Press, 1975).

Tuan, Yi-Fu. *Space and Place* (Minneapolis: University of Minnesota Press, 1977).

Walker, Peter. *Invisible Gardens: The Search for Modernism in the American Landscape* (Cambridge: MIT Press, 1994).

Watson, Donald, and Alice W. Burlingame. *Therapy Through Horticulture* (New York: Macmillan, 1960).

Wilson, Edward O. *Biophilia* (Cambridge: Harvard University Press, 1984).

————. *The Diversity of Life* (Cambridge: Harvard University Press, 1992).

————. *In Search of Nature* (Washington, D.C.: Shearwater, 1996).

————. *Sociobiology: The New Synthesis* (Cambridge: Harvard University Press, 1975)

Yeoman, Kathleen. *The Able Gardner* (Pownal, Vt.: Garden Way, 1992).

Index